Neil was born in North Nottinghamshire in 1965 and started helping out in pubs as a glass collector. It wasn't long before the pub life became his career goal and with the help from a couple of mentors who worked for Whitbread at the time, the life of a publican had begun. Neil embarked on a crazy journey that saw him move home more times than he can remember, each time taking on a new challenge in another broken down pub, or managing the opening of a shiny new pub in a city centre. Sometimes the job was to open a whole new brand of pub or bar, most of the time role was very exciting, but also very much blood, sweat and tears hard graft. As Neil approachers the final few years serving beer and food to what feels like millions of people, he has a story to tell, secrets to spill, so has has written it all down.

I owe a huge amount to John Utley, the licensee who smoked like a chimney, drank coffee by the gallon, and taught me how it should be done. Glenn Coburn was a constant support for well over a decade, the best boss anyone could ever have, and I am happy to say, a friend. Becci, Tracy, Lesley, Kelly & Annie, all special friends who shared my workplace and kept me on the straight and narrow. Far too many special friends to name, even more enemies to forgive, and so many amazing team members I was so proud to work with and support. And finally, my better half, Dammy, the reason I grew up at 45 and stopped drinking Jager-Bombs… with Scott, Fordy, Micky, Ash, Daz, Phil, Lewis, Sparkles & big Pat.

Neil J Moore

THE BITTEREST PLC
TO SWALLOW

AUSTIN MACAULEY PUBLISHERS™

LONDON ★ CAMBRIDGE ★ NEW YORK ★ SHARJAH

A CIP catalogue record for this title is available from the British Library.

ISBN 9781035809301 (Paperback)
ISBN 9781035809318 (Hardback)
ISBN 9781035809349 (ePub e-book)
ISBN 9781035809325 (Audiobook)

www.austinmacauley.com

First Published 2023
Austin Macauley Publishers Ltd®
1 Canada Square
Canary Wharf
London
E14 5AA

Chapter 1

When Did Pubs Become Assimilated...?

Yes, I know I know, my geek side is showing through, using a Star-Trek Borg reference is never cool, but telling the story of what has actually happened to the Great British Pubs of the 80's and 90's needs a hook, assimilated is the hook I have chosen.

A least one local boozer featured on every town housing estate, high street, village, city centre and sea front.

Nowhere in the UK was without a public house, a proper pub, a boozer if you like.

What do we have in place of traditional 1980's hostelries in 2022?

We certainly don't have proper pubs.

Where have all the pubs gone?

Drinking dens that were once busy social hubs full of working-class men every evening and all-day at weekends?

When I look anywhere in the UK for proper pubs, all I find is tacky themed family food bar/tavern/grill/smoked/sizzle/kitchen/BBQ/eatery/canteen/burger or steak house family food pub-restaurants...

Are you lucky enough to still have a great local where the focus is still on the people, and their conversations about local life, near to where you live?

If you do have a great local pub near to your home, cherish it, just like a dog, a pub is not just for Christmas. If you don't use it or feed it for the other 11 months of the year, don't be surprised if it becomes a HornyPony family pub, a Tesco Metro, or even a row of 10 modern tiny houses with even smaller numbered parking spaces by next Christmas.

So back to my Star Trek analogy where I used a Borg line of speech from the film Star Trek First Contact...

You will be absorbed into the collective, assimilated, resistance is futile, OR DIE…

Pubs should be, and at one time were, all about the infectious personalities of the people that made their pub special, alive, it had its own heartbeat that connected people on a very personal level.

The bond between landlord / landlady, their team, and the building itself, was the driving factor behind the family atmosphere. The buildings were often beautiful, old, with stunning plaster roses in the ceiling, leaded stained-glass windows, stone fireplace, Victorian ceramics in the toilets and very old wood carved into intricate patterns, the history and splendour of the building alone earning its place in the community.

The first pub I ever worked in as a glass collector was the Old Ship Inn.

A building with huge, painted wooden beams running in box shapes framing the small wonky windows on the exterior.

The walls were rendered white, the beams painted black, the steep roof line and low doorways, The Ship Inn was a gem, a beauty, cramped, hot and sweaty, no ventilation except for a propped open fire door during the summer, but as young locals in our small mining town, we loved it. Stunning as the Grade II listed Ship Inn building is, it has been closed for a couple of decades, it does not fit the modern model of what a pub needs to be in a working-class town, and that is such a shame. As teenagers (16+ as most of my old friends will confirm), we had some amazing times in that place, dancing, scrapping, snogging, playing pool and drinking together.

I remember the very first comic relief event, Pudding and myself based ourselves at The Ship for our day of fund-raising frenzy, him wearing a giant nappy, laid in a shopping trolly while I pushed him around town while wearing a gorilla costume.

The Old Ship Inn was a place where the public were more than data dots on an excel spreadsheet, we were friends, and foes, we had fun banter without screaming "oppressed", we flirted desperately without fear of arrest, there was fun, and tears, it was real life without the judgement of social media, no trip advisor reviews and no camera phones capturing images to be posted to an uninterested world.

Everyone in your local pulled together, there was always a shoulder to cry on, support we knew was just a shout away from the amazing extended family that surrounded you in your workplace, your second home, your favourite place to be outside your family home.

Whatever the local pub was to you, you genuinely felt it was partly yours, you felt safe, welcome, even if just having a quick pint, working behind the bar, or managing the whole place, you felt a sense of belonging.

Local pubs in communities were like second homes, you drank, you socialised, you joined in, even helped if needed, and in many cases, spent more time there than your actual home.

Friends in local pubs often became your closest family.

In the good old days of long-ago past times, pubs were managed from the bar, the snug, the family room, and yes on occasion, the back yard!

Someone was in charge, a governor or a tarted-up landlady who commanded respect, everyone knew who the boss was and very few crossed their path or disrespected their authority because running a good local pub really meant something, most landlords and landladies were looked up to as well as gaining respect from the local community.

The office work to be completed was minimal, we didn't have the 10 different tick-box forms to fill in daily as they have today.

We knew how to run the pub, maintain safety and hygiene to the standard that was required by the loose, and far too flexible, legislation of the times.

In 2022 the new breed of "licensed retail" manager, or pub gaffer as they were known, needs to be guided by their hand and told what to do, anything and everything has to be done by following written instructions that must be executed at pre-set times of throughout working day.

These days the basic knowledge and experience is far too often missing when it comes to new, first-time managers, most have certainly not worked their way up from glass collector to manager over many years, learning every task that running a pub throws at you, on their way to successfully becoming a licensee and general manager of their own establishment.

Any idiot can be given a pub to manage these days, even those void of any personality what-so-ever but hold a bachelor's degree in gender studies who interviews well because they spent just a single summer behind a bar in Zante can become a pub manager in the branded pub world of today. In reality a degree qualified tosspot is no match in ability, skill or knowledge to the assistant manager applying for the same pub manager's position.

The assistant, who started aged 17 in the pub as a pot washer and has just completed their 6th year working full time in the pub, the last 2 years as assistant manager in a very busy and successful pub does not have a degree, but has completed extensive vocational studies and training, they know the pub business inside out.

Who would I hire to run a busy pub as GM?

I would promote the assistant with the experience and support network they have built up over the years rubbing shoulders with brilliant managers, quality chefs, door-staff, cellar experts and bar teams to the position of GM.

Who would the new into the position, first time appointed, straight out of Uni idiot area manager appoint to the vacant GM position?

Of course, the choice is so obvious, he will hire the tosser that worked in Zante, a dope smoking ex-Essex Uni graduate because they have earned a useless degree.

Much more the new area managers type of person than a blue collar hard-working experienced pub professional who has been training for the role for 6 years.

A degree in gender studies far more useful when managing 20 staff members serving shots in a packed solid bar at 1am when a fight breaks out than experience, isn't it?

The tick-box process has taken over the management of modern pubs, each business and brand becoming more reliant on the clip-board compliance management style year on year. This is due to poor recruitment by people who themselves are poor appointments into mid-level positions.

The current hiring trend in the "assessment process" is using the phycology deep-dive questions that are used to discover the personality traits of potential managers.

The results are analysed, and we place individuals into categories with heading such as Reflector-Theorist-Pragmatist and Activist.

I've been called Tough Minded, but I don't know if that is good or bad thing?

When I asked the assessor, she didn't know either.

What I want to know at your interview is if you can change a barrel, pull a quality pint, talk banter to others, how do you book a live band, cook a steak, have you ever un-blocked a toilet, what do you know about COSHH and manual handling risks, and what HR training you have received up to now?

When I interview someone, it rarely lasts less than 45 minutes and often passes a full hour because I want to understand the person sitting in front of me, how does the interviewee react to my questions, are they a quick thinker?

No, I do not want to know what mark they received for their dissertation on salt concentration in the Dead Sea for fucks sake.

A lot of modern pub mangers I have met are often qualified only by "passing exams" to ready them to be a manager and licensee, many have only briefest hands-on experience.

Far too many have no personality, they are just following written instructions of the basic rules required to be implemented and maintained to remain open, keep the beer flowing, how to protect the money and then bank the cash.

I don't normally call someone a "manager" who has not spent years in pubs learning how the job is done properly, I call them a "key-holder" because that is what they are, they open up and lock up, they are certainly not a seasoned landlord or landlady with skills.

The problem with the modern manager appointments by a child-like area managers is, they normally lack a public character, the ability to be a showman and engage, and this means they have almost no interaction with their, lonely, neglected, friendly locals and regulars. Even the older pub users, who are witnessing their circle of drinking friends diminish yearly because they are drinking in the tap room above the sky, and basically ignored.

Let me explain the difference between my recruitment interview process and a recruitment agency screening.

I recruit an attitude, a bounce, passion, and the chance to tap into yet to be discovered skill sets and potential.

Recruitment agencies recruit by asking potential employees to answer questions on a form that is then marked and given a score value.

If the applicant scores high enough to reach the benchmark score, they have passed.

These are two very different systems of achieving the same goal, but what I will understand about the actual person by doing it my way is actually very different to the agency result:

I can teach someone with a great personality to do anything they need to do, but if they don't have a flare or spark that I can develop and help grow, it is not possible to give someone a personality that they can then use.

Modern pubs are so disconnected from real people, and they often treat their regulars really badly, even the decades long locals who kept the pub going long before a brand had even been dreamt up by marketing boffins.

I'll go as far as to say that many of the agency recruited staff and recently left University newly appointed managers treat old regulars as second-class citizens because they are seen as an old stain spoiling the look and feel of these reinvented, modern, hipster, clinically branded theme pubs.

Indulge me please, I want you to imagine you are long term regular, let's call him Bill.

Bill has been drinking regularly in his local pub for 50 years, but in the last 10 of those years Bill has been forced further and further into a small corner where drinkers who are not eating are still allowed to enjoy a pint without buying food.

Bills local pub, The Cannon, is now branded as a "Pasta Kitchen and Grill" family food pub with a kid's soft play area and kiddy swings dominating what was once a great beer garden that overlooked the pubs now dishevelled bowling green. The bowling green area is fenced off due to a risk assessment, apparently the rose bushes surrounding the green have thorns that can scratch children's skin!

Bill has smoked for 60 years and will never give up because it's one of the few pleasures in life he still enjoys. He can no longer smoke indoors and over time he has got used to wandering outside to the basic smoking shelter twice every hour. Then suddenly and without warning the brewery recently knocked down the smoking shelter that was installed in 2007 because it is not conducive with the modern family eating image the "Pasta Kitchen and Grill" brand demands and wants to project outwardly to potential new customers.

After all, who wants old customers when there are new ones out there to tempt in with spatchcock chicken and vegan burgers served on brioche…

Bit harsh you say, the pub is just trying to survive in changing times.

You may think I am being harsh on the pub for ignoring Bill's needs, and if you do think that way, let's take a closer look at Bill as a long time regular and how he fits into the modern "so-called family (food) pub".

Bill is a man who has spent 50 years drinking in the same pub, 25 of those years drinking in the same spot by the bar counter 5 evenings per week, 6pm till 9pm, plus Sunday 12pm till 6pm.

Bill spends every Saturday fishing, it is his passion, coming second only to his family who always come first. Bill loves to fish and spends his time in the pub entertaining his fellow drinkers with hour upon hour chatting about his escapades while flicking his rod and yanking at every bite. These fishing tails are regaled from that same spot every time, Bill's spot, where only Bill stands in The Cannon Pub.

After 25 years of "owning" that spot by the bar, Bill was told he had to move away from his spot at the bar counter because a new "no standing at the bar" rule was being brought in by the first of many revolving door personally void youthful managers who are all hand-picked by the new area manager.

The reason that a never-ending stream of new managers is required for The Cannon is because the highly successful couple who had run the pub for 15 years and intended to retire after running it for a further 10 years, have quit because of the disappointing appointment of the new youthful area manager.

More on that and the "area manager effect" is coming in later chapters.

The new, young, university educated prat we now call the pubs general manager is someone who thinks he shouldn't have to talk to regulars, he's not paid to that, he is only there to tick-boxes and enter numbers into the master control computer. He certainly does not appreciate what a great pub means to a regular punter, and this new prat of a manager has no idea what a regular customer means to a local pub.

A further 10 years slip by, and Bill settled on a high table near the fireplace as his new spot.

The new "spot" is central, 8 steps to the bar, 12 steps to the bog, he can see the main entrance door and a large window is to the right where he can see the car park.

Bill has spent the last 10 years drinking, sadly, with fewer and fewer friends as the years role by, but by making that spot, his second spot, his very own, drinking alone or with friends, that is where you will find Bill, but never on a Saturday.

The time has come for yet another refurb of The Cannon, no consultation or consideration for the regulars' views or local community impact, why would a big PLC company run by venture capitalist, they now own the brewery, care what local people want and why would they care that Bill has now been drinking in The Cannon for over 35 years, these regulars are just people, they are not share-holders or anyone else special.

Yet another new area manager is now in place, a nice university leaver with a 2nd in humanities from Hull University has been appointed and he will be deciding the future for The Cannon from now on.

This new area manager is someone who has never socialised outside his Uni and private school crowd, he has never been blind drunk with working class people, had a date with a girl who doesn't own a pony called Buttons, or ever watched sport in The Cannon, or any pub for that matter, because he only visits bars that specialise in Prosecco and artisan spirits.

He has decided unilaterally, but only after reading a Waitrose magazine while sat on the throne, and enjoying a big night out with his wealthy uncle in Richmond at the local Michelin Starred uber cool thatched roof Italian grill restaurant, what the future of The Cannons Pub looks like:

"Let's turn The Cannon pub 98% food and family orientated."

He wants to bring in a new youthful general manager from a restaurant background, just find a cheap assistant and promote them to be the general manager, that seems simple enough.

You may be thinking "why would the brewery listen to this first-time appointed area manager about the direction of a long-term existing pub?"

Well, it's really simple when you realise that the rich uncle from Richmond is a major shareholder in the offshore financial company that now owns what once was the brewery, but is now just a licensed retail pub company because the brewery was sold off to an international brewing giant to deliver the shareholders' huge dividends.

So, Bill's second drinking spot by the fireplace is now consigned to history as was his original spot by the bar. Bills second spot will become part of the extended dining area, Bill and drinkers like him are once again relegated, but this time to two small tables under a window that overlooks the bin storage area.

These are no longer high tables and chairs, just standard height tables with normal chairs.

What was once The Cannon Pub is now called "Pasta Kitchen and Grill", has 100 tables in total, 98 are dining tables, just two are reserved for drinkers like Bill and his fellow regulars.

Bill and his ever-decreasing number of friends continue to drink at The Cannon Pub for the next 15 years, the pub has countless managers come and go, paint refreshed every 5 years, turned no smoking in 2007 and now has 20 more baby highchairs that drinkers' seats.

Welcome to the modern pub, and what's wrong with it you may ask, it sounds like a lovely place to pop in with my family for a mid-week meal deal?

Let me explain something about Bill and the 1 million others just like him and with a similar story.

Bill is dead, has lived in that town all his life, he drank 1 pint per hour for approximately 21 hours per week for 50 years, that's around 54,500 pints, the price ranging from when he started drinking in The Cannon Pub aged 20 years old, just before the hyperinflation of 1973, a pint of Courage bitter was yours for just 17p. In the modern Pasta and Grill Kitchen a pint of John Smiths in 2022 costs around £4.50.

All the money he spent in that pub should have earned Bill a little bit of respect wouldn't you think?

It's complicated I know, but let's try to imagine just how much money Bill spent buying 54,500 pints over 50 years?

Firstly, I think Bill deserves a plaque on the wall, but I'm an old, grumpy, time served landlord and I'm always going to appreciate the older regular drinkers.

A member of Bill's family wants to throw Bill a wake in his favourite pub to celebrate Bill's Irish heritage and life, so in he goes to speak to the youthful manager and asks if they can hold the wake in the pub Bill used for over 50 years, and because Bill was without a doubt the longest continuous regular in the pub's history.

What does the pretentious manager say—*WHO?*

WHO for fuck's sake, this tosser of a manager, who has been "managing" Bill's local pub for over 18 months has no idea what that old "waste of a good table" fella's name was?

So, this bell-end of a manager decides to call the area manager to ask if a wake should be held in "Bill's" memory at this local because he is far too wimpy to make a decision himself.

The area manager instantly says no: *"we don't do that sort of thing because it could affect our regular diners, sorry but that is the policy."*

The area manager doesn't even ask the dead man's name… Bill.

What a load of bollocks, fuck the policy, Bill deserves better!

This is a bad decision by 2 wankers with zero people skills and no community understanding.

And **THAT** is what is wrong with modern branded pubs right there in a nutshell…

Bill was made a second-class citizen by career hungry uncaring pub company pole climbing paper shufflers, the very same people who should have been rewarding Bill for his support, and cash, over his 50 years of loyal drinking, but nawh!

The Pasta and Grill Kitchen branded food pub is targeting faceless repeat family diners who spend money on food at least once a week.

Two adult and two kids' meals bought from the meal deal food menu, add a couple of drinks, the family spend a healthy sum of £32.50 during their 90 minutes visit.

Thank you so much for your huge spend of £32.50, we couldn't survive without you spending so much ever week.

According to idiots this monetary income is much more valuable and creates a better return for the financial market pub company owners than a few regulars sitting in a corner 5 evenings a week and most of the day on a Sunday.

If you think family man spending £32.50 is a great benefit to the pub, I'm about to kick you firmly in the nads… *HARD.*

Bill was buying 21 pints a week at £4.50; that's totals £94.50. That is £62.00 MORE EVERY WEEK than the family spend during their once per week family dining visit.

Yes, yes, yes, I know the family was only in for 90 minutes and the pub wants that family scenario to repeat hundreds of times per week, I am just pointing out that Bill was not worthless, the pub has just Bill's guaranteed spend of £4,914 yearly spend.

Bill deserved much more respect, drinkers like Bill are one of the most ignored and marginalised assets to the UK leisure business, modern pub companies are using them to sustain a business during slow seasons and cost of living crisis pressures, but they are offered little to no reward, not so much as a thank you.

Do these stupid, youthful, robotic university educated so called general managers and gormless idealistic over promoted area managers understand the real-world value of a genuine pub regular?

I very much doubt it.

They should be celebrating a pubs regular's and kissing their arses over and over again for paying their wages year in year out without asking for anything except somewhere to sit and have a pint in comfort with their friends.

Anyway, as I was saying before my Bill rant, there was very little book work needed to run a pub for a brewery, all the legal stuff was completed in head office, as pub managers we spent just three or four hours on a Sunday morning "ending the week" and balancing the books.

Stock ordering and delivery was mid-week and banking was performed on Mondays and then when we felt it was necessary.

Running pubs in 70's, 80's and 90's sounds easy, very twee, and almost a little quaint.

It's often referred to as the good old days by those who were there.

Licensees enjoyed the lifestyle and culture created within and around local pubs.

The most important part of pub life was constantly reminding yourself that the pub is nothing without people and ensuring those people were kept at the very heart of the community.

It's now 2022, modern times with branded pub chains, or should we just call them restaurants, super bars and uber clubs.

But do you know how, and more importantly, why things changed?

Pubs have slowly changed from being the local focal point of every housing estate and community in the UK and have been turned into the disconnected licensed retail shops we now call branded family food pubs.

Within these plastic pretend pubs, it's all false smiles, trained robotic teenagers working for managers without any personality and absolutely zero understanding of genuine customer service.

Should we really be calling these sizzle roast pizza pie carvery steak grill pasta burger kitchen branded family-based restaurants with no room for drinker's pubs at all?

NO, I don't think we should be calling them pubs, they are more like restaurants.

Now is the time to ask you once again.

Do YOU know how and why pubs changed so dramatically, the 50-year-old drinkers from 1980 wouldn't recognise what a modern pub.

I do—*GREED*

I really hope this book will go some way to explain why the Great British Pub has largely disappeared from the high street, housing estate, town centre, village, and waterfront.

The old local pubs have been consigned to history by financial power brokers, not because the public and regular customers were asking for them to be changed, but because the pub companies, with new city owners, saw big opportunities to make more money by changing the local boozer into something radical at the time.

Instead of the local hostelry being a place to spend a bit of spare cash on a few pints and a game of darts, almost all the UK's pubs were about to take a significant slice out of the weekly household budget by targeting each and every family member as an individual contributing spending unit ready to be rinsed.

The only way this could be achieved was by replacing the weakest link in their grand money-making scheme, locals like *YOU* are out, from now on they only want families looking for food matter from now on.

In those good old days, the financial week ended on a Saturday night when the pub called last orders at 11pm and everyone filed out heading towards Dandy's, Annabelle's, Roxy's, Climax or Josephine's nightclubs in every town and city across the UK.

Except York, I will come back to that later.

The new financial week started on a Sunday morning as you opened the pub doors at12pm for the lunch time drinking session.

If you wanted a Sunday Lunch back in those days you stayed at home, went home from the pub at 2pm for a late lunch served at home, or queued at a Toby Carvery with a plate in your hand while following the zip-zag line of hungry guests in front of you.

As a pub manager what sights would greet your eyes as you open the doors on a Sunday? Hungover regulars who were still drinking at 2am last night looking for hair of the dog because their other half made them sleep on the sofa.

Or maybe this wreck of a human being is avoiding going home because their husband/wife has no idea where they have been for the last 18 hours?

Oh, the joys of the pre-mobile phone times and "find my iPhone". No one had any idea, except the guilty themselves, where, when, or who you woke up with, hands up, are you on this naughty list? If you are guilty, was this you?

It's 12pm Sunday and you need a drink before returning home to face a very angry other-half.

The pub office, or spare bedroom as it was also known under its real name in most pubs, contained a type of speak and spell basic computer that had a greenish screen with a flashing curser.

We completed the book work with a pen, land-line phone, a ledger (for the young, this was a handwritten A3 spread sheet with a carbon copy page) an ink stamp and a big envelope to post last week's bookwork, banking slips and till rolls off to head office.

The office almost always had a compulsory overflowing ashtray, 4 or 5 dirty cups and at least one near empty pint pot with the left-over dregs of a three-day old pint that was once Stones Bitter swilling around in the bottom, often with a floating fag butt soaking up the last few drops of liquid!

Pub managers had a one-hour phone call from their area manager, he would discuss the good and the bad of last week, this week's plans, goals, and actions, and lastly, next week.

"Are you showing the racing at Aintree or the Man Utd match on Saturday?"

We only had 3 TV channels and just one wooden box housed TV set.

Every Saturday the BBC ran with Grandstand and ITV showed World of Sport that always had wrestling on about 4pm. I'm fairly sure I was watching wrestling on ITV when the news about the Hillsborough disaster became breaking news…

Big Daddy flattening Giant Haystacks with a belly slam no longer mattered that day…

Pubs could only show one sporting event at a time on their 27inch cathode ray tube TV set perched high on a shelf in the games room or snug, and that was it, we had choices to make, rightly, or wrongly in some cases, what sport we decided to show could be the difference between a busy pub trading session, or a really bad one meaning we would have to explain to the area manager why the sales had dipped so much.

Managing the stock, the people and the money was so simple.

We managed our pubs by using hard earned skills, passion, knowledge, and our experience. The area managers who had themselves once been general managers, knew exactly what they were doing, and what we should doing. We could learn from them, they were our support network, a 1980's version of Google specialising in pubs at the other end of a phone line.

Not all area managers were nice people though, I remember one time when a female manager had been punched full on hard to the face by a man in her pub in a tasty part of Sheffield.

At the time I was this poor manager's mentor, and I was horrified to see the dark purple and off green deep dark bruisers around her eyes and nose. I rang her area manager to let him know what had happened, and his reply: "*So, what, it goes with the job.*"

What a knob head, this nice middle-aged lady has been hit in the face so hard, over half her face is black and blue and he thought that was just to be expected as a pub manager.

I reported him to the personal department, and they did do something by stepping in, helping her, and acted against her misogynist fuck-wit area manager.

We reached 1999 and new employment strategies were ushering in trendy and modern hipsters bringing with them new ways of working. The old dinosaur pub company head offices all around the UK didn't know what had hit them and little did we know just how far these changes, the modern thinking, new ways of working, better communications and tighter rules would set us apart from the last millenniums people focused pub culture.

None of us basic, but happy to modernise, welcoming of change general managers saw the crazy new world of shareholders, management speak, digital control, marketing teams, diversity departments, audits soldiers of doom and leadership without any direction what-so-ever coming and taking hold as it has done over the last few years.

We just knew that change had started, but no one could see that far ahead or imagine the good days would ever come to an end.

20 years after the big revolution started in the 90's I found myself an unwanted fossilised turd and all traces of my very successful pub history seems to have been removed like a poison colonial legacy.

But this turd is hard to flush and I just keep floating back to the top over and over again.

Old school managers were out of fashion.

Yes, we did things differently just 20-25 years ago, massive mistakes, monster cock-up's but we learned the lessons through first hand and on-the-job experience.

But crazy as it may sound, no one wants to learn from the old days and not repeat the same mistakes again and again. The old timers who spent their lives learning the job through decades of hands-on experience are just dismissed as uneducated fools, what could old duffers teach the head office boffins even if they did listen?

Modern pub companies: *"let's bury our heads, remove all the experience that was learned over two decades by simply cancelling the people who were actually there and helped build the foundations of what the modern hospitality pub trade is today."*

I will talk much more about cancelling people much later in this book.

Pubs were at one time focused on people, not only the customers, but the team that worked within those warmly supportive walls.

Families and friends intertwined, in a local community pub we respected our elders, looked out for the regulars, understanding the characters was key, keeping an eye on "jack the lad" and telling his mum if he stepped out of line.

As the landlords of pre-millennium times, we could spend so much more time doing the "day job" because we spent so little time number crunching.

Managing our pubs included paper shuffling in the office, but once it was done, we were with the punters out front in the pub and leading the way, setting the tone.

We did the same tasks every week, all 52 weeks, 12 periods, 4 quarter's and 1 full financial year, we filled in paperwork for just 3 or 4 hours a week, the rest of the time we were with the public, serving, policing and laughing along with them, or we were with our families because pub companies respected family life in those days, they hardly ever recruited single managers, it was all about couples who were living their family life in the public's eye, and because they were often under public scrutiny, leading by example.

The simplest part of manging pubs was this, if you made a balls-up, your area manager would visit, shout, and swear, stamp his feet, and tell you what you needed to do to put it right!

Then he bought you a pint at 10:30am, a quick one before you opened at 11am…

While things were so simple, more importantly to the manager, their teams, and the punters, working in pubs was full of fun and a way of life.

I look back at the years I worked for Sam Whitbread, a member of the original Whitbread family who had founded the brewery centuries ago in the family name. Yes, by the time I started working for Whitbread the remaining family member, who still sat on the board, was just a figure head by the time I started in the 80's. There was a senior team of people making the decisions in a board room, but the values of the Whitbread family still meant something to everyone working under the family name.

We were working with leaders who said things like JFDI (just fucking do it) because it was a great idea, it would impress customers, make our teams working conditions better, and deliver better sales and profits…

The vast majority of pubs in the UK were owned by breweries and many of the breweries still had a connection with the original family dynasty that started the brewery many years before to fill the need in the community and support local people.

People were far more important to brewery owners than today's data uploaded into financial spreadsheet by the company accountants…

What do older 80's and 90's pub punters reminisce about?

They tell tales of the good old days, Stella for £1.25 a pint, 20 Bensons for £1.76 sold from behind the bar, pool games for 20p, condoms in the bogs for 50p, ashtrays on every table, a jukebox with 5 tunes for a quid, toilet troughs with big yellow and blue blocks to aim at, piss powered blow football really was a thing between mates wazzing at the same time.

Do you remember soda bottles on the back of the bar, a choice of just two lagers, Stella or Carling, a strange dark beer called "mild", a choice of either Gordon's or Plymouth Gin, Bells or Grants whiskey, and if on the 1st date with a new bird you would splash out and treat her to a Babycham with a maraschino cherry plucked for an 8 year old jar that hasn't been opened for at least 2 years, oh yeah, and a bag of Scampi Fries because we all wanted to snog a girl that tasted just like a Grimsby docks prostitute undercarriage.

Pub dining was mainly in hybrid pub/restaurants called something like Beef-Scoffer, Bernard Inn, and Toby. Wonderous new foods could be bought as a starter, a real treat was the prawn cocktail smothered in Marie Rose sauce.

Marie Rosé Sauce was one of the very first lies the pub companies used to trick guests into thinking they were paying for exotic foods.

Dining pubs of the day relied on the fact that people had no idea how exotically named foods should actually taste like, so in those days we could create "our own" Marie Rose sauce.

It was really simple; just mix 3 X wholesaler cheap own-make mayonnaise with 1 X Kwik-Save own label ketchup and dust a tiny amount of the red dust called paprika on the top.

Add a slither of lemon, bobs your uncle, prawn cocktail made with an exotic and expensive Mediterranean sauce.

The best bit, because it's sounds foreign, we could charge an extra £1.00 for each serving, the British pub user will never know the difference.

Scampi Fries, do they still make them?

In my humble opinion they were the only snack created to smell exactly the same as the pungent aroma from a three-day unwashed minge of a Rotherham scrubber.

But for some reason we ate tons of Scampi Fries from small green and gold packets, then if they were really lucky, the boys found themselves licking actual unwashed minge after it had danced and sweated for three hours on the dance floor at Dandy's nightclub, and to this day, no one can categorically tell me which one tasted the worst, the crispy snack from a packet or the exposed and sweaty chapped lips surrounding the crunchy prawn?

Late night sexual shenanigans, you knew it was always a bit nasty, and once sober we swore to never do it again but come next weekend after 6 pints of Harp lager you find yourself eating Scampi Fries and looking for a sweaty snatch once again, and we repeated the same routine every weekend.

The politically correct woke world is everywhere, we cannot avoid it, you may, as I do, even welcome, and applaud parts of what wokeism it hopes to achieve in society.

TV, social media, papers, I agree with every change in society that has led to increased respect for women, men, equality, race, our bodies, and the banning of Benny Hill style bum spanking sketchers that encouraged men to do the same thing in the pub, swimming baths or even on the bus.

It has also led to shagging in the pub bogs as no longer being acceptable and this is such a shame.

Only joking…

Getting your end-away in the shitter was a rite of passage for the 80's young stud and a reason to celebrate.

Everything from the 80's and 90's is now outlawed as unthinkable in these modern times, and rightly so to be honest, we were just filthy animals with no access to Porn-Hub.

In the 80's and 90's, it was a badge of honour to finger a bird against the bar, be tugged off in a bus stop, doorway, or even back seat of the night bus. If you were really lucky you were having a knee trembler in a high street shop fire exit or car park behind Blockbuster.

Come on girls own up, a lot of you have done it, we have seen the CCTV from your night of lust, that moment of madness when you dragged Gary from the dance floor into an unused cubicle, ripped open his zip and lifted yourself onto his knob without speaking for a full 90 seconds of sheer bliss.

If you were a disco bopper in your moccasin slip-on's, Burton's strides, and a Freeman's catalogue shirt of the 80's or 90's, did you find yourself trying to dance to Frankie Goes to Hollywood's Two Tribes? That was one seriously hard track to dance to, especially the 12-inch version, unless you were super fit. After two minutes I was knackered every time.

It was best to stick with Wham tunes, slow and swinging hips movements was the way to a girls' heart, and third base if she was easy and drunk just enough…

Pour yourself a gin, sit back, close your eyes and smile while remembering all the sexual fumbles you enjoyed, or regret, 30 to 40 years ago.

Have I brought back any memories from your younger days?

Concentrate please, never mind the sexy fumbles, think back to those heady days of synth music, double breasted shirts, men wearing make-up on music videos, Mad Dog 20/20, Blue Nun, Dusty Bin's 321 and lying on sunbeds for hours for a George Michael "life" T-shirt tan.

Most of you will have a secret smile going on right now as you think back to waking up in Park Hill flats with a boy or girl whose name you never knew and didn't ask.

Add your own unknown boy or girls name and address that's fits, and now smile…

I hope you are not blushing to much while remembering catching the night bus home without wearing any knickers because you used them to wipe yourself clean after having sex on a car bonnet with "what's his name" or whatever memory is emerging from that dark corner of your mind marked "need to forget I ever did that."

We all have a past that we like to bury deep, but at the time, oh what crazy and colourful fun we had in the late 80's and early 90's.

So, with all these memories flooding back of your younger days, the debauchery and scandal, the fumbling and fingering post hot sweaty nightclub smooching, I bet you can now remember exactly what Scampi Fries, dark alleyway cunnilingus, or fellatio tasted like…

I hope I have opened a pandora's box of memories for you to smirk at or sit in shame.

My strangest night was going out in Sheffield, hooking up with a girl called Mandy and waking up in a guesthouse in Ingoldmells.

I remember waking up, not recognising where I was, opening the curtains and seeing the sea in the distance, it looked like miles away.

Where the fuck was I, then I saw the road sign: Ingoldmells 2 miles.

What a night, and expensive train journey home, but what the heck, we were young.

Some of you are all now thinking back at how much fun you had in the pubs as a young stud, a sexy fox, a macho man, or a right easy slapper who enjoyed random cock a lit too much.

I don't judge.

Whatever and whoever you were in those heady days is what has made you what you are today, I'm sure we all had some amazing times in fantastic pubs and clubs all across the UK.

These were the great days of UK pubs, right?

or were they really?

Chapter 2
The Good Old Days

Were The Good Old Days really as great as we remember them?

What do you really remember about those dark, smoke stained and poorly lit buildings that we spent so much time in with our mates and trying to pull?

The human condition has a peculiar way to protect itself from future self-loathing, regret, and mental long-term damage.

For some very odd reason we forget the very worst of things, or we edit the details and clean up the memory until it fits the heavily sanitised filing system that is our brain.

You only "think" you remember pubs how they actually were 40 years ago.

Let's test my theory of how we look back at the past through your mind's eye…

Nothing proves this theory more than thinking about a nasty and good riddance Ex.

When you split up, for whatever reason there is bile, hatred, anger, tears, shouting and relief it is finally over.

You tell yourself that you will completely blank them in the street, you wouldn't piss on them if they spontaneously burst into flames, all the usual reactions we experience when exiting a toxic relationship, just thinking about that Ex boils your piss…

Six months fly by, and your life is back on track, no stress, no rows, and no more cleaning the bog bowl with their toothbrush just for fun, life is once again smooth, relaxed, and great.

Until 2 things happen that changes the memories of your time together from bad to GOOD!

FIRST: you see your ex in a pub laughing and joking with a new partner and your friends… "I introduced her to my friends and now they are spending time with her instead on me, she must be goody two shoes after-all, oh god what have I done!"

SECOND: You have had a bad day, feeling a little lonely, 3 quarters of a bottle of red downed in the last 30 minutes and your phone is in your hand. You begin scrolling through photos of last year's holiday with your Ex, "one little text message won't matter, after all we did have some good times."

Your mind "removes the bad, the nasty, the details" and leaves you with a PG rated "roses around the door" edited memory of something that, in reality, was terrible.

"Ohhh but I miss them SOOO much, will they text back, maybe we could have sex just one more time?"

Many of you reading this have done exactly as above, I know I have.

So now we understand why we look back with such love and fondness of the Good Old Times in pubs, but it's time to awake those deep-seated memories of what pubs were really like between 1980 and 1999.

Many of the branded pub chains have become themed manipulative money grabbing extortionist pickpockets for their stock market venture capitalist owners.

I have an argument that we shouldn't call them pubs anymore.

"Pubs" as an abbreviation of "Public House".

I think we should use the new abbreviation "Vic's" because we are all:

"Victims" of their trickery and bare faced ripping us off!

Modern pubs are no more than giant cash rinsing machines taking the piss.

More often than not the food portions are so small you will need a kebab two hours later on the way home to stop the hunger pangs.

If fashionably overpriced and badly poured beer wasn't bad enough, what about the wine brought into the UK in huge foil bags and bottled in the UK?

Oh dear, have I just popped a bubble by telling you that your favourite white zinfandel is not bottled by an historic winery in the south of France or South Africa?

Why isn't it bottled by experts in France?

Maybe it's because the French wouldn't want their winery name associated with cheap bottles of wine sold in UK branded pub chains.

These cheap pub wines are often bottled in places such as ex-mining town Worksop, using large, unmarked warehouses. Don't get me wrong, what they do is all above board, perfectly legal and completed to a high standard, but don't forget the big foil bag.

Some people think we have moved on from the days of Liebfraumilch and Blue Nun, but house wines in pub chains are often bottled by the pub chain owner to keep costs down and help create huge profits.

How is the profit actually made on reasonably priced pub wine?

Surely cheap and discounted wine is a loss-leader just to get customers into the pub in the first place, isn't it?

You have all seen this deal before:

"Buy 2 large glasses of wine and get the rest of the bottle free?"

If you visit branded pubs, you will see this sort of deal and you think "oh yes I'll have some of that."

You pay £7.00 for 2 large glasses, 250ml of wine in each glass, then you receive the last 250ml still in the bottle for free.

You are onto a winner; it's smiles all round.

But let's break it down a little, it's an own brand wine, let's call it Grape Juice Grigio, and it sounds Italian:

It actually comes from the famous vineyards of Bulgaria, surely you have heard of Bulgarian fine wines.

The bulk wine was bottled in a warehouse near Fleetwood docks.

The storage and transportation have been in non-temperature-controlled containers for at least 7 weeks across various ships and lorries, and then stored in a warehouse.

So, what is the real value of the product you are so pleased to be buying for just £3.50 per 250ml glass?

For the moment let's forget about VAT and alcohol duty, let's just talk in plain English while rounding up the real costs.

The bottle you now have on your table containing the extra 250ml of "FREE" wine for a steal at just £7.00 per full bottle in total is actually worth around £2.00 a bottle, and that means the liquid in the bottle is worth less than £1.00.

I went on Amazon today and found I could buy 5 litres of Sarsen's malt vinegar for £6.99

Enjoy your quality wine for the "bargain price", and remember, it is defiantly YOU that is taking advantage of the pub chain at this price, or so you are led to believe.

Before you know it, you are saying "let's have another bottle, at this price it would be crazy not to have another."

The BIGGEST pub companies rake in the profits from one of the oldest tricks in licensed retail.

I call it, *the perception flip.* The customer perceives they are onto a winner.

The truth is, they are being tricked into buying crap wine, and then buying double the amount because they are so pleased with themselves and the great bargain they have stumbled across.

The end result of this "buys 2 glasses and get the rest of the bottle free deal is":

The bottle of wine only cost £2.00 to produce and to reach your glass.

You pay £7.00 for the deal—take off 20% vat = £5.83.

Using the £7:00 bottle, BIGGEST pub companies make £3.83 cash profit or about 65% margin as it is called in the accounts department.

That's how they make money from cheap house wine, and this is just one of hundreds of products sold in ways to deceive customers into believing they have found a perfect deal.

If you come across a pub deal on drinks, or food, that seems too good to be true, it is definitely the one deal to avoid.

Breweries started pub chains without any real intent, they just wanted to put their own brewed products into their own pubs to sell more.

The pub chain was born.

The idea of pub chains was started by the pub users to be honest. All it took was for the public to start referencing to a pub as being a "Bass House" because it sold Draught Bass, a "Stones Pub" because it sold Stones bitter, Tetley, Courage, Trophy or Smiths, people picked their watering hole by the beer brand they enjoyed drinking.

Pub companies quickly got their heads around how many of the regular drinking public, but especially non-regulars, picked a pub to visit because of the unintentional branding slapped onto the pub by the punters themselves.

Modern signage had begun, traditional pubs had always used old fashioned signage displaying the owners' names such as Tetley's, but now branding was becoming a fashion.

Carling and Heineken were now being displayed prominently on the exterior of pubs and signage was becoming colour co-ordinated to match the beer branding.

The American style of marketing had arrived in the UK hospitality industry, subtle identity plaques were about to be replaced with brash, loud, and illuminated branded signage.

A non-regular does not pick a pub to visit because it is called "The Kings Head", they choose to visit a pub because it sells Carling Lager and is known as a Carling Pub etc.

As pub companies began the wake up to the commercial power of brands, they also began to evolve from using a small office in the corner of the brewery to oversee the pubs they owned. Now they needed head office operations with corner offices for the soon to arrive commercial thinking marketing and revenue departments.

So started the hiring of new types of employees into these large head office buildings, the hiring of marketing managers, strategists and brand managers became the normal very quickly and this was just the beginning.

These new additions, with their never seen before skill sets, joined old fashioned and antiquated family-owned brewers, and developed, at pace, the pub chain revolution.

Selling the idea of expansion, never ending growth and brands that could become part of the fabric of a modern consumer society, to the brewery owning family was easy. The family thought it would be able to sit back and enjoy the success achieved by the new department managers they had employed, but it didn't end well for most of the family owners.

The new head office departments, led by slick people who were by now fluent in the new language that was to become "management speak", were working together to convince the owning family that pub chains and brands will lead to higher sales and profits.

What they needed to achieve this was huge amounts of money provided by the city.

This will be a huge win-win for the family name, but they lied…

The revolution started with branded pubs that people soon recognised and trusted.

The public appreciated rare brands such as TGI Fridays, I'm not kidding, they were at the times I'm talking about few and far between, and Beefeater, these were something special that the public travelled to, searched out and made a special effort to visit.

Brands were seen as "Top-End".

The pub companies had seen the future.

Names like Toby Inn, Brewer's Fayre and O'Neill's started popping up in every town and city, the time of replicant pub chains had begun, the future of independent pubs was thrown into question, brands within brands were the future and the financial city could see a new opportunity opening up right in front of them, brand *plus* brand = double the profits.

Pub companies and breweries don't really own many pubs anymore, they are almost all owned by the financial institutions that control huge amounts of venture capital around the world, businesses that appear on stock markets and are traded in financial hot spots around the world like Frankfurt, Hong Kong, and Tokyo.

The vast majority of pubs, bars and restaurants in the UK are owned by financial institutions. These huge conglomerates are steered by people who have never been in a British pub, have never stepped into a cellar, been behind a bar, commercial kitchen or even pulled just one pint for a pub regular.

Many of the "financial-over-lord" companies are based overseas and don't even care if a British Pub company sits within their business model. With portfolios that include international building contractor, aviation investment, shipping lines and pension funds, why would they want a pub company?

It's about UK property value, the food and drink doesn't really matter, that is a biproduct, the real interest is in the bricks and mortar that sits on freehold land.

Banks certainly don't understand what a British pub is supposed to be, they just see potential real-estate profits.

Number crunchers are put in charge of the pub company so that profits can be maximised, but at no point have the investors behind this venture capitalist financial conglomerate that has bought a working pub business taken the time to understand that you, as an employee, has worked for that pub company for over 20 years, or that pubs are a people centric business and that people do actually matter.

That family name that was etched into every fibre and drop of beer produced, had spent decades, even centuries, carefully building a legacy, were fooled by marketing puppeteers and city slickers that what they had created in the past was going to become so big, revered in history as it grew with city investment.

But sadly, the family name matters not-a-jot anymore, they family name falls away, become nothing more than a footnote in a long-lost history as the city takes full control using its power to acquire more and more chunks of the old and once loved family business.

Welcome to the new shareholder owned "family" brewer and pub company.

At no point, when buying this old-fashioned British Institution, has anyone on the new board or directors, appointed by the new city owners, had any thoughts, or regards for you, the customer, the manager, or the team members.

Front line workers are now just employee numbers and customers are just doners to a financial war chest, both are part of a demographic being used for profit calculation enabling the critical return on investment payments payable to the shareholders.

I worked as a manager for a pub company that was aggressively growing to match the CEO's ego. No really, it was his ego that was driving the decisions that would eventually hurt the 1,000's of staff who have worked for that company for many years, one man's ego was forcing labour budgets cut, quality cut, training budgets cut, and forcing manages to reduce staff pay per hour by using MW rates, it was wrong, so wrong.

But why should he care, he was the darling of the financial and trade publications…

what a tosser.

I once asked this CEO a question in an open forum where managers could put questions to the top boss, but only if the question was pre-approved, it was all very civilised.

Our company's customer engagement scores were slipping badly, every survey, every mystery visit, scores were dropping like a stone down the league tables on customer service, something had changed dramatically and needed to be addressed.

About a year earlier our company had moved from the hugely successful face to face induction sessions where all new starters engaged with their new manager through the whole induction process, to an on-line only unsupported induction process.

The training courses about safety, allergens, fire risks, and even customer service were all being completed on-line. This meant all new starters have lots of sessions to complete, staring at a screen without an ounce of engagement with another human being.

How very convenient.

Apparently, there was no reason to have a face-to-face induction with "your" new manager, new colleagues, and future friends.

The face-to-face coaching, where a new starter would get a feeling for the pub, the people, the passion needed to continue to make our pub special, none of this was needed anymore apparently, a device had replaced the personal touch.

It had always been the one-on-one training that made the difference when "on-boarding" a new starter, they immediacy became one of the team, they were paid for the time taken to complete the training and rewarded with a personally presented certificate to say you are now one of us.

Our company and CEO decided, it was done to reduced costs, that from now on all new starters in our pubs were to complete all their induction, safety, and customer service training on-line and alone.

Oh yeah, and they were no-longer paid to complete the mandatory training required before they can start their new job in customer service.

Get your head around that, 5- or 6-hours training without pay, how much notice would you take if you were not being paid for something forced on you by a new employer?

The irony that this "customer service" training is completed in the most sterile and unengaging way possible is not lost on anyone, I hope!

What does happen to a potential new starter who has attended an interview?

Following a successful interview, the next day we offer the candidate a job and explain that we will be sending email links to them for them to complete their induction training.

The email explains that this should normally take no more than 3 hours, most of which is based around H&S questions and videos.

All very efficient and not a problem, you may think.

Not true, it's a huge mistake because many candidates interview really well, but then they treat the on-line induction training as a jobs-worth exercise and decide to play FIFA on Xbox or watch TikTok videos while filling in the online forms and "not" watching the videos.

What happens if really early into the on-line H&S induction process our new starters sister walks past and he asks for help as she was once a supervisor in a pub.

His sister finishes the on-line induction for him while he is playing fantasy football on his phone.

So, what we have now is a badly prepared, poorly trained, unaware of safety risks and disengaged new employee because they are not being paid for the time that they "say" they spent working through the online induction process.

How does this new starter feel about his first shift in a couple of hours?

He has no relationship with his manager, work colleagues or surroundings, and they have no relationship with him.

This has now become a very poor induction process that will cost much more money in the long run than the old face to face paid induction system.

Why will it cost more?

Inducting team members using the on-line process leads to higher staff and manager turnover, poor standards, waste, a breakdown of teamwork and lower customer care scores.

By pushing through the on-line induction process by falsely claiming that it will raise standards of training to the bigger bosses who have no idea of just how important a quality pub induction is, the new "Training and Engagement Manager" has set the standard of training to a default position of compulsory awkward working relationships in every pub the company owns because that new starter walks in on their 1st day as a complete stranger.

If the team were people the new starter had already met, had been introduced to other staff members last week while they were being inducted, they would instantly become a team member.

If you had met him last week you would be looking forward to greeting them again and making them comfortable because the fear factor has already gone.

The difference between someone joining a team after 3 hours unpaid tick-box on-line induction training and a one-to-one induction that includes introductions to senior staff and general team members is beyond measure.

But the new "Training and Engagement Manager" has never worked in hospitality or had any dealings with face-to-face customer service. Their background is as a HR manager in a telemarketing company, so they don't understand the need for doing anything face to face.

To them it just seems pointless, to me it means they are out of their depth...

The company have now laid down a new lower benchmark for staffing investment.

By removing the human element and creating an on-line world of training that is only there to mitigate any risk to the company, and nothing else, they have reached their main goal, self-protection of the senior people and brand names owned by the company.

Through bad advice and poor leadership, to saving money and removing all personality, killing off teamwork and individualism from your front-line teams, your company now has robotic staff who just repeat set spoken lines, training manual phrases such "may I help you today" or "will you be dining" to the annoyance of every customer they speak to.

If you have ever ordered at a fast-food burger joint counter, you will know exactly what I mean…

Well done Training and Engagement Manager, you have created a pub chain where the location no longer matters, North, South, London, or Carlisle, you will receive burger brand style service, the same phrase said every time, by every staff member, anywhere.

It is so sad when hospitality teams have their personality taken away.

Is this what you want from a Traditional British Pub?

Back to my question to the PLC Pub Company CEO, which was:

"Do you think there is any correlation between falling customer satisfaction scores and the introduction of on-line induction training and did this fall in customer satisfaction start when we ended face to face paid inductions?"

The room went pin drop silent, and I realised that every bigger boss in the room was staring at me without blinking.

To save the CEO's embarrassment one of the Operation Directors stepped in and said, "Can we come back to you on that?"

The meeting ended and we were all filing out when I heard my name called so back into the room I walked to where one of the CEO's chief advisors was waiting to speak to me with the Operations director and my area manager.

The first thing I thought as he introduced himself as one of the CEO's advisors and told me his name was:

"Who the hell are you and if you have such a big influence on the end product, the actual way our customers feel about us as a business, why have I never heard of you before?"

Firstly, I was asked "did you get approval for that question?" *errrrrr no—* What the fuck, are we now suddenly living in 1984?

Then this advisor went into management speak about the lowest common denominator and something about how we cannot expect everyone to train to the same high standards that I do so we are doing it online to make it achievable for everyone.

A blank and puzzled face was my response!

So, I then asked *"Instead of raising the training standards throughout the company and delivering better inductions you want good trainers to accept much lower standards from their new staff?"*

His answer was something about being legally protected from prosecution because we will have an on-line record for all the new starter training and that releases the plc from risk.

I really wanted to tear him a new arsehole, but I stood silent, shocked…

What utter bollocks from a man helping devise the future for our people-based business.

A man who obviously has no experience in hospitality or customer care.

If I've understood this correctly, as long as the company is protected from financial risk if someone gets hurt due to poor training standards that is fine in the eyes of the company because the HR department has detailed records that show the necessary training was completed.

The team member, by ticking a small box on a screen, has accepted that the company has mitigated any risk to themselves if that team member is hurt while performing their duties.

What The Actual Fuck!

To boil this down to the real reasons the company do things this way is very simple:

If an employee is injured at work…

A: the company can sack the team member and say that they have acted quickly to remove any further risk because we have removed the risk factor, or in other words, YOU!

B: it reduces the costs to train any new team members and removes the cost of senior employees delivering the training to new starters that may not be consistent.

Surely if we just trained people in an engaging, congenial, and personal way we would reduce the risk to everyone, public, the team and the shareholders?

Oh sorry, I forgot myself for a moment, this is not really about protecting the public or the staff, oh no no no… if only On-line training is about protecting the company from the risk of litigation that could risk reputation and ultimately affect profits and share price.

It was at this point in my pub career, after being told by a company advisor wanker it was all about being fair to everyone, but I was not eating his bullshit, I had just moved myself into 1st gear and released the handbrake on the road to my forced removal, at any cost, by higher management... or as I like to call them: Bigger Bosses...

I was no longer a drone, I was refusing to be assimilated, I had become a rogue manager and placed an enormous glowing bullseye target on my own back...

What I do know is, we had a really good working system for introducing new team members in our businesses and making them feel valued, and then, just like that, we didn't care about the quality of the induction process anymore.

It was gone, ripped away, we were taking a huge step backwards in our customer care journey, but the bigger bosses didn't care about that, how could they know because they defiantly didn't understand.

Every time the bigger bosses turn up at one of the pubs the area manager has ensured that all the best staff are working that day, extra staff are working and the service the bigger bosses receive is just about perfect.

Bigger Bosses think it is normal to have their arse kissed by terrified young underpaid managers after being threatened by the area manager to "not fuck it up for him."

Bigger Bosses never see the real business, short staffed every shift, staff shouted at by thirsty customers, stressed team members not allowed to take a break because it's so busy, this is what bigger bosses policies do to hard working pub teams, but they never see it...

My concerns had been dismissed out of hand because someone with 35 years' experience of inducting people into award winning teams knows absolutely naught about the team training process, compared to a pompous dick CEO advisor.

My working life started to become much more difficult.

Surely not because I dared to ask a question about how induction changes are affecting customer service and team moral?

Bigger Bosses wouldn't victimise, would they?

The end for my PLC pub life was now clearly on the fast-approaching horizon...

Many of the pub owning venture capitalist financial conglomerates are nothing more than players gambling with someone else's money. They use money from the financial markets to buy a pub company, then they load the debt they borrowed to buy it back onto the acquired pub company against its assets.

It's genius, you borrow billions to buy "something" and then use the "something" to off-set the debt.

If the "something" that has been bought losses money, that goes against the "something" asset value.

But if money is made, it is paid out to the people who borrowed the money to buy the "something" in the first place.

No doubt I will be told that is not exactly how it works, but it's not far off the model venture capitalists use to make even more money without lifting a finger themselves.

The modern pubs, or "bars" in modern speak, are trendy glass and steel monoliths, shabby chic overpriced city bars, pizza theme pubs, poor quality grills themed around sport and tiny portions, or BOGOF food pubs that push the humble drinkers into one grubby corner.

Even the super-sized carvery monster food factories that serve wafer thin meat, mountains of overcooked vegetables from a scruffy hot plate manned by an ex-Debenhams toilet cleaner on minimum wage, are just huge cash cows accepting your money for rip off prices.

You buy a carvery that is 90% vegetables, then they have the audacity to sell you a slice of cake to take home that cost pennies to make, but many many £££££££ to buy.

I'll come back to cake to go, that's a story all in itself, but for now let's get back to The Good Old Days…

Old pubs were individual, many were unique. Pubs stood at the centre of a housing estate as the social hub, bright and bold on the high street with vivid colour schemes and etched windows, and on busy road junctions where they became a local landmark.

I'm pretty sure that most people giving directions use pubs as the guide.

"Just past the Dog and Duck, turn left, go down there until you see The Cross Keys."

Most village pubs were the place to meet, a focal point, somewhere to conduct business, appreciate family and friends and celebrate agricultural and rural life.

The landlord and landlady set the tone, the locals were the theme, and pubs had their own, often daft, and steeped in history, names like "The Jolly Taxpayer"; "Three-Legged Mare"; "The Drunken Duck" and the classic that still makes me childishly smirk whenever I say it out loud "The Cock Inn" …

When I was an 80's bopper I was a regular visitor at the infamous Fannies nightclub that sat on the same roundabout as a pub called The Cock…

We did giggle just like we had many years before when we sat in our school's sex education lessons, aften a boys first talk about boobs, and really not wanting to stand up if you know where I'm coming from…

Why was it always me who had to put the Jonny onto a banana while everyone else in the class were falling about laughing.

Every pub came with its very own local idiot, local hussy with knickers to keep her ankles warm, everyone knows she shags approximately 10 married men and two 18-year-olds per year in the gardens, bushes, car bonnets, bus shelter and behind the kebab shop between the pub and her house.

It's funny how no man has ever admitted to it?

There was always a quiet hard man, a loud tosser who *thinks* he a hard man, a Dell Boy, and a pathetic sexual predator who believes he looks like Beckham.

His poor oblivious wife at home with his 5 kids, you have all met this one, haven't you?

Were you the underage 16-year-old who hit puberty early and supported a full beard and deep voice? All your mates who were still under 18 sent you to the offy or bar to get the beers in.

And finally in my list of "every pub had one", the piss head 45-year-old adolescent divorcee whose dress is a little too short, make up a bit too heavy, at least she always puts on a great show after 7 GandT's while dancing around her handbag to "I will survive" that will be played at least 5 times tonight on that bloody juke box.

There was also something else I can vaguely remember, a man with a white lab coat selling warm shellfish and something called "Fish Sticks" from a basket.

Or did I dream that after knocking back my first every double whiskey from a huge bottle of Bells hanging up behind the bar at The Lord Byron. I was only 16 but I had a pretty decent moustache that helped me purchase booze, but it didn't help attract the girls.

A 16-year-old who looks at least 20 had a choice, or at least I did. I could be the pretend big man and enjoy the naughty underage booze that gave you a buzz and bragging rights because you can get served in a pub or choose chasing girls your own age who cannot get away with being in the pub with you.

Tough choice?

What happens if you chase the girls?

If you are lucky, you get to feel one left boob, inside the coat but on top of her jumper in a freezing cold bus stop somewhere near cement city housing estate.

I had already felt up a few boobs through thick Arron cardigans, so unless second base was a sure thing with one of the Manton youth club slappers, the one boob just didn't seem worth it.

I picked the warm pub with a pool table in the games room.

It was always quiet in the games room on weekday evenings, the only person serving was the landlord's daughter who was one year ahead of me at school. She was in the 6th form and new that we were underage, but because she fancied my mate see never grassed us up to her dad. Winner…

At 16 years of age, I chose the booze in a warm pub over a quick boob squeeze while leaning on a garden gate.

This was the beginning of my 35 plus years having a troubled love affair with pubs.

Even at 16 I needed things I could be sure of, and I could guarantee a beer buzz in the pub, but 3rd base, and often 2nd base depressingly, was often the unreachable destination for a lanky, stuttering, and spotty teenager with a bum fluff moustache and deep voice.

The Lord Byron was a big local pub, it had an offy (off license) counter to dispense sealed alcoholic drinks, bottles of Corona pop, fags, and crisps. This was the place dads sent their kids to buy two bottles of Mackeson and 10 Player's No 6 cigs with the exact money.

If dad was feeling a bit flush, you were allowed to buy a bag of Smiths crisps to eat on the way back home.

Licensing laws were largely ignored in the off license back then, if a 12-year-old turned up with their dad's order written on rizla fag paper, the landlords only comment was something like *"Make sure you get them home untouched; I will ask your dad when I see him."*

Draught beer was delivered by a lorry tanker and pumped into either 90- or 180-gallon tanks through a long fat pipe.

Lagers and Bitters, the mainstream draught beers of the time we're all treated and delivered in the same way, slopped around in a tanker under the heat of the sun, pumped through a 6-inch pipe that had been fed through the cellar drop and into the open hatch of a huge metal tank.

Beer was delivered like this every week, and if you were lucky enough to have a good landlord who cared about quality and reputation, the tank had been cleaned out and sterilised before delivery, or had it?

Landlords varied in ability and in terms of the amount of effort they would put into running the pub properly. Far too often the landlord couldn't be bothered with "all that cleaning shit" and still had 2 or 3 pints of 2 weeks old stale beer swilling about in the bottom of the tank giving off a dank and musty smell, similar to the smells of old yeast damp sweaty socks.

Let's call it what it was, slops, a liquid that was slowly turning into vinegar in the bottom of the so to be receiving beer tank.

These slops would be 16 to 18 days old, maybe more!

To describe what I saw swimming around in the bottom of beer tanks in the 80's I'd say it was similar to the old stale beer that was as flat as the over-poured Mild spilled by the over enthusiastic teenager bar staff and found in a drip tray at the end of a night.

And what happened to the drip trays in a lazy landlord's pub?

They were all slopped into a bucket along with all the other drip tray spillage.

These are the very same slops that we're then poured back into the beer tank or cask ale barrel to "top it up".

Oh well, the tanker delivery is here, so clean, or not, into the beer tank goes the transfer pipe and the beer gushes in mixing the old dregs with the new 90 gallons of bitter.

No one will notice 3 pints of stale, flat sour beer when it's mixed with 720 new pints will they?

Why were the slops swilling around in bottom of the tank for as long as 16-18 days instead of just 14 days you ask?

Breweries are clever, if they always have at least 10 days' worth of beer available in the pub after every 7 days' worth of booze has been delivered it removes risk.

If the beer tanker breaks down on the way to the pub on the 7th day since the last delivery, there is now at least 3 days' worth of beer still in the tank allowing time to the brewery to arrange a replacement tanker to deliver within 3 days to make sure the pub doesn't run dry.

This is why there was always 2 bulk tanks for each draught product in the cellar, each holds 7 day's volume of beer sales, but you didn't start using the second one until the other tank is empty in around 3 to 5 days.

Before you start thinking how nice it is for the brewery to make sure we don't run out of the thirst-quenching brew, it's was never about YOU as a customer and your needs, no no no…

It's to make sure you don't wander down the road to another pub nearby only to find that the beer and atmosphere is far better, it's about sales and profits through maintaining a customer base.

The tanker beer story is not quite over, there is a little more to add!

Many old-style landlords liked their beer, their size and shape was a tell-tale sign of, without any doubt, how much they liked a lot of draught beer.

Think back, it is early1980's, well before the big revolution that changed pubs forever, you had met more Unicorns living in your back garden than a slim landlord.

We know landlords enjoyed their daily quoter, but they didn't like paying for it.

Many old-time landlords thought it was their god given right to consume vast amounts of beer and it should all be free!

50 years earlier some breweries did give a landlord an allowance of beer, it was seen as a perk of the job. But as companies grow in size, going from 10 to 100 pubs it made a big difference in cost.

If you have 10 pubs and let each of the 10 landlords have 2 pints each per day that totals 140 pints, or 17.5 gallons, per week.

But after time and the business grows strongly, you now have 100 pubs.

If you let all 100 landlords running your pubs have 2 pints per day, that now totals 1,140 pints, or 175 gallons of beer every week.

No brewery can afford that, can you imagine giving away 59,280 pints in a year? NO So this practice it was stopped by all the breweries.

The problem that breweries had with stopping free beer allowance is that the old ways of working take decades to change from being the normal practice.

Old-Time landlords still want their beer allowance and so much more.

Many of you reading this have known a landlord or manager who regularly drank 8 pints every day 7 day a week.

That's 7 gallons of beer a week. Even if this was 25 years ago when a pint of Trophy bitter was just £1.45 a pint, that still totals £81.20 per week, or £4,222.40 per year.

How the hell could anyone get away with drinking all that beer without paying for any of it?

This is how the old guzzling landlords made a tank of beer go much further than expected so they could still sup to their hearts content without paying a penny for a single pint.

The beer tanker is parked outside the pub, the cellar hatch is open, and the beer is following down the pipe into the empty beer tank.

The tanker driver is having a fag on the roadside, he has no sight line of the beer tanks.

By pour coincidence it just so happens that the landlord is cleaning his cellar floor using a hose pipe connected to the cold-water tap. Hose pipes can be tricky to handle, the cellar is a bit chilly, and the nozzle of the hose pipe just happens to slip into the beer tank without the landlord noticing. Even the sound of spraying water hitting the side of the beer tank does not alert the landlord that clean, fresh water is running into the tank at hight speed.

I hope the landlord notices soon before too much water is accidentally mixed with the fresh beer about to flow from the tanker.

The tanker driver is waiting for the all clear to open the taps and deliver 180 gallons of lager to the huge tank.

The landlord makes one final check before he signals the-all clear to the tanker driver and surprise surprise he sees the hose pipe dangling into the empty tank, he shuts off the cold water tap and completely by chance, approximately 7 gallons of water has accidentally been poured into the beer tank, the exact same amount of beer that the landlord will consume over the next 7 days…

Have any of you may have wondered how you could drink so much when you were young in the 80's, but these days, in your late 40's you have just 3 pints of pilsner and you are wankered…

So now you know… pubs don't use tanks anymore, so this practice had all but died out by the early 90's, and to be honest, it's is far too bloody dangerous to open a pressurised 22-gallon keg to top it up with a hose pipe, but a few dozy landlords have been maimed or died trying.

Recently I have seen a few of the latest Uber Cool city bars bringing beer tanks back from the dead, but they are much smaller, polished bits of theatre to dispense the latest craze called "Tank Fresh Beer".

Don't be fooled draught drinkers, if beer is being stored in a tank, and if that tank has a cleaning hole in it where a pipe will fit, someone will be up to the same old tricks and drinking free beer at YOUR expense.

Someone will be topping that tank up with water, and water contains no alcohol, so topping up reduces the alcohol strength because beer is basically being "watered down".

If a beer tank is a highly polished metal vessel hung high above the bar, and all the pipes going in and out the shiny "Fresh Beer Tank" are also highly polished metal tubes, what magical power is being used to prevent the beer from becoming room temperature?

Makes me wonder if there is any beer sloshing around at all in this latest trendy city pub gimmick.

Beer is normally kept in a cellar, stored between 10° minimum to 12° maximum.

If a cellar is too cold some beers, such as real ales and craft beers can become cloudy due to being too cold. That's right, the yeast in the beer gets a chill and shivers when it's really cold.

If cask, or real ale, becomes too cold it can go hazy enough to look cloudy.

This is called "chill-haze".

Beers and lager's that are served super chilled, I will offer Menabrea Birra and Heverlee as examples, are fed through a cellar chiller that sends the beer through an ice box containing a thin metal pipe that takes the golden liquid on a long and twisting journey allowing the packed ice to suck the ambient heat from the beer until the temperature hits almost zero.

Beer travels from the cellar in a thickly insulated pipe called a python. The python contains a recirculating fast flowing cold water feed continually pushing ice-cold water its full length where it ends up under the bar counter.

It is this very cold piping that delivers the ice-cold lager to the beer font and finally to the tap.

This carefully installed and expensive python ensures the beer is reaching the bar in perfect condition, the only heat soak that can affect the beer between the cellar and your freshly poured pint is a tiny length of uninsulated piping that runs into the beer tap itself. Less than one centimetre of un-chilled python holds only a few millimetres of liquid, not enough to make any difference to the temperature of the beer being poured into a cold clean glass.

The only damage a tiny drop of warmish beer can do to your pint is make the head a little bit too big because, no matter how small an amount of liquid, when beer warms up the gas absorbed into the liquid escapes and creates froth.

If a lot of froth is being created when pouring a pint, you now know that the installation of the cellar cooling, the python and the beer chilling equipment is not as good as it should be. Draught beer is expensive and deserves the equipment and handling to match the price you are paying for it.

There is a huge amount of engineering and equipment that extracts beer from a keg in a cellar and allows it to be poured into a glass in perfect condition and at the perfect temperature.

Take another look at that new "in fashion" shiny metal beer tank hanging above the bar, can you see any condensation?

Can you see any foam or material insulation of any kind?

Pub companies are very much the snake and oil tricksters of modern times, just like in the olden days, cheating the public with potions to cure baldness, treat leprosy, and could remove evil spirits from a godless soul, all for just crossing a palm with 5 groats.

Dumb suckers out on the lash see a fancy tank, a continental product name, complicated pipework and a premium price tag and say, "I need to pay an extra £2.00 per pint because it is the TANK beer". They actually think the extra £2.00 is worth it because they believe it is coming from shiny tank hanging high above the bar.

If that very same "tank" beer was served through a normal beer tap it would cost £4.50, not the £6.50 you are being charged IDIOTS, you have just been mugged by an expert bandit, a branded pub chain…

After what I have told you about beer tanks in the past, say NO to tanks in pubs.

As I said, no condensation on the tank means no chilled liquid inside it, so by simple deduction, it is all smoke and mirrors to add £2 per pint.

The quality of pub drinks was not great in the last two decades of the 20th century.

Heineken was only 3.4% volume alcohol in the UK; in the rest of Europe, it was 5%!

The Heineken in British pubs was so weak we chucked it down our necks like it was no more than a can of shandy bass pop (Google it).

Let's imagine, one day you find yourself in Berlin during November 1989, the wall has just come down and you want to celebrate.

Heineken is on the bar, you are a British tourist in the 80's, you will only eat or drink what you recognise, so you have 3 pints of real Heineken at 5% strength, and now you are wankered because this is not the watered-down rubbish we served in the UK.

If you wanted real Heineken in the UK back in those days, you had to order Heineken Export.

In Europe there was no such thing as Heineken Export, it was just Heineken.

But nobody ordered Heineken Export in the 80's, if you wanted stronger lager, you went reassuringly expensive and ordered a wife beater, sorry, I mean pint of Stella.

No Dutch or German bar owner insulted their European drinkers with UK Heineken, that dishwater was reserved for just us Brits.

Some drinks may bring back some pretty vivid flashbacks, tastes you buried in dark and deep recesses of your mind long ago, hoping to never taste, see or even think of that poison ever again.

Just by reading the names of drinks you never want to pass your lips again may awaken your subconscious, bringing those tastes flooding back, worming their way from deep hidden corners where your taste bud memories are stored…

Are you ready?

Liebfraumilch wine, Glass Soda Siphons, Mad Dog 20/20, Trophy Bitter, Hooch, K7, Labatt's, Skol, Harp, XXXX, Barbican, Hoffmeister, Lambrusco, Advocate, Babycham, Mateus Rosé, Benedictine, Pernod, Cherry B and finally Corona Pop Limeade and Cream Soda flavours.

Which ones do you remember and what would you add to that list?

We have all done it, abused a certain drink in the 80's and 90's, and you still cannot face, sip, or taste it ever again 20 years later without it making you want to chuck up a little at the back of your throat…

Mine is Southern Comfort and OJ…

While in Tenerife with Pudding, Tablet and Kev, I was downing it by the half pint glass… we were on an 18 / 30's holiday and even now, 30 years on, the smell makes me rush to the big white telephone barfing …

Oh God Oh God… Ugh Looking back at pubs from the 80's and 90's, we tend to look back through rose tinted spectacles, those fond memories of snogging in a corner, struggling to slip your fingers in under the table because in those days it was normal for all the birds to have a thick hairy growler, while she tries to keep a straight face. Playing pool using a yellow ball as the cue ball because someone lobbed the cue ball into the men's bog trough, and no one is putting their hand in there to retrieve it, no fucking chance. Juke boxes with a choice of 30 records, but only 10 tracks were ever really played. I hated any jukebox; it allows loud dickheads to control the atmosphere by playing their boring choice over and over again every night.

"Oi, knob-head, quit holding onto your youth by listening to Beech Boys, Kinks, Abba and Slade, let's get some MJ, Prince Specials and U2 on ffs."

In reality we should be looking back at pubs through nicotine-stained beer goggles laughing at badly dressed people drinking poor quality drinks in establishments similar to what we would now call old man boozers in 2022.

Pubs were actually boarder-line slums, un-healthy and filthy.

Everyone smoked, the customers, the bar staff, the landlord, even the cleaner mopped the floor with a dog end smouldering in the corner of her mouth.

I remember standing in the bar flap gap, smoking away, then a customer approached the bar, I would take a big draw on my fag, balance it carefully on the edge of the bar and off I go to pull them a pint.

Without a care in the world, I would serve drinks while breathing out the toxic smog all over their drinks, the customer, and the clean glasses nearby. Smoke just hanging in the air.

WE WERE DISGUSTING…

The smoke got EVERYWHERE, the walls, the curtains, the furniture, carpets and lamp shades, everything had the greasy sticky coating, it looked like someone had mixed marmite and diesel together and painted every inch of the pub with a 5-year-old dried out and grizzled used toilet mop.

Every local pub ceiling could be compared to the lungs of a 30 year hard grafting coal face minor suffering with emphysema, coated in filth.

In the 80's and 90's the vast majority of pubs-goes went out to the pub smelling of either Brut, Old Spice, Tweed, or Charlie, but everyone went home smelling like a dog end filled ashtray. The smoke would visually swirl around as you opened the pub door, you could see it hanging near lightbulbs and rolling along the floor, no one entering a pub could avoid it, the fog of ciggy smoke sticks to every strand of your hair, inch of your skin, your clothes and even the back of your throat. The bigger your flares, the more pleats in your trouser waistband, the bigger your shoulder pads, the longer the collar of your double-breasted shirt, and even the bigger your hair, the more this thick smog will stick, stain, and contaminate.

Ladies opening their handbag next morning, puff, out comes a whiff of last night's sweat, smoke, stale beer, and any shenanigans she may want to forget, all collected in the sticky smoke that settled inside your bag while dancing around it to a classic by Duran Duran.

The smell emulating from the bag brings back Campari bleared visions, memories of attraction, dancing, snogging, and calling into the chippy while staggering home. As the whiff pours from the bag, you breath it in, do you smile, or turn away and gag?

It all depends, was it was good or bad night, where have you have woken up, who have you woke up with, have you got a black eye, are you still wearing underwear or are your knickers in your pocket?

You are still dressed for a big club night out at 9am in the morning, in a strange part of town, one broken heel, a thread bare feather bower and panda eye make-up.

Sounds like a good night out for many in the 80's.

You now need to steady yourself for the long, but necessary, walk of shame… no mobile phones in those days, hardly any cash machines, so you have no choice but to walk while desperately trying hide your identity.

Girls who have been out all night are easy to identify the next morning, even if wearing a big coat, because they will be carrying their shoes.

You will be doing everything possible to avoid people, no eye contact of any type and you are almost crouching over as you try to shrink and become invisible.

And just to top everything else, you absolutely STINK OF SMOKE Time to honest, have you ever had a morning similar to what I have described?

The time would eventually come round to when the local pub needs some TLC, an upgrade, modernising, a fresh image, so the brewery would repaint a pub, hang new curtains, new lamp shades, new carpets, and new artwork…

It's seven years since the last paint job, surely that is too long between slapping a bit varnish on the wood.

Breweries by now were beginning to count the pennies, shareholders had arrived and wanted their pound of flesh, so how could the breweries extend the time between refurbishments so save money?

Easy: repaint the whole pub covering every inch of the greasy, dirty nicotine-stained walls and ceilings with an industrial emulsion and gloss leaving all the dirt, hairs and dints showing under this fresh coating of paint.

The pub looks fresh, even cleanish if you don't look too hard, but this is not the new look in its fully finished form, and yet, there is more to come.

It has just been freshly painted, is that not enough?

Every inch of the new paint job was now rag-rolled with a brown, oily staining solution that looks exactly like thinly spread marmite mixed with diesel. This brownish fake nicotine coating is wiped on to cover every inch of the new paint job the decorators have just spent two weeks applying to hide the old nicotine-stained paint.

Covering every inch of the walls, ceiling, door frames, windowsills, just about anywhere that the cleaner will not be wiping daily, this artificial "mucky" odourless stain job will last for years and years because freshly smoked nicotine will not show up and make it look grubby…

Making it look grubby in the first place, that was the designers and decorators' job.

Seriously, this is the truth, this is what happened to working class blue collar local pubs, they were made to look grubby from re-opening day.

A fully refurbished pub reopens wearing new grubby clothes, and dressed exactly the same as it was before:

The stench of cigarette smoke, the acrid taste of nicotine sticks to the curtains, the furniture, the carpet, and every other surface.

No one, including the customers, the brewery owners, staff, landlord or landlady realised just how dirty, smelly, sticky, and poisonous the effect smoking had on the inside of pubs until they went smoke free mid-2007.

Designers no longer needed to stain the walls with artificial nicotine because there was no longer any nicotine to disguise.

Think back to 2007 and the refurbishments that have happened to pubs since the smoking ban. You now see pastel colours, white is everywhere, quality wall papers, fabrics with bright shades of gold and silver woven into the pattern, and mirrors that no longer distort your reflection making you look like you have an all-year-round Benidorm tan.

The reason why the lingering smell from a night out no longer brings back vivid and colourful memories making you want to smile, or barf, is due to a couple of things that have changed since the 70's…

1. Ventilation
2. Smoking Ban
3. Drink Quality
4. The crazy days of taking acciiiiidd and eboneeeza are in the past, most people gave them a go, then we grow up, well most of us did.

Let's take a look back at ventilation in smoke filled pubs, that invisible movement of air you relied on to keep you cool, fresh, preventing your groin area from become the equivalent to a stagnant cesspit pumping out the smell of a stink bomb let off in a tramp's jockstrap. Ventilation didn't really exist and to be honest, no one cared if their sweaty nether regions smelled like the 7-year unwashed whores' flaps because all we could smell was fag smoke anyway.

The pub was where you would spend all your hard-earned money trying to impress a willing stranger to bump and grind with you at the end of the night, but a pubs ventilation system was not your friend.

In most old pubs air movement was overlooked, or just plain ignored by the brewery because how could air being swirled around make them any money?

So, what you got to meet the needs of air quality management was a 6-inch diameter window mounted Xpelair fan covered in dust balls, hair and spider webs turning at the mind-boggling speed of 7 revolution a minute. This fan couldn't remove a wasp fart in 24 hours never mind the haze coming off 300 heavily breathing hormone driven teenagers wearing nylon, polyester, and fur-edged hooded parkers.

These sweat-dripping and smoke-filled rooms were classed as a healthy environment in the good old days, but let's be honest, we now know the pubs of the 80's / 90's was the complete opposite of a real healthy environment…

Pub Toilets in the 80's and 90's was often a place to fear and avoid. There was some really dirty boys and some very nasty girls in those days, and if we want to be honest and current, right up to date, there are still feral people with hygiene standards that could stun an experienced abattoir offal cleaner into silence.

Let's start with that smell: come on you remember the eye watering smell that would hit you as you passed to gents' door, and someone suddenly opened it. The smell rushers out, hitting you by surprise so there was no way to prepare. It's in your nose, in your mouth coating every taste bud with a toxic so bad that your taste buds are committing suicide rather than taste that stench again... Uuurrgggghhhhhhhh.

So why use this pub if the bogs reek so bad?

You are in this pub because a girl who once looked you up and down over a year ago is there with her mates and you want to catch her eye, you are hoping to make her moist as she stares at you, is she imagining your body under that Burtons polyester shirt, black bray nylon trousers and Freeman Hardy and Willis moccasins. You are a god amongst boys, acting cool, knocking back the pints with the lads, throwing back a few vodka jellies. You are having a great night; she has targeted you for sexy times and your eyes have met a dozen times but drinking to show off and trying to make yourself look cool only makes that dreaded bog visit inevitable as your alcohol pickled kidneys fill your bladder to the point of bursting.

Sooner or later, you will have to go to that bog!

Rumour has it that men have visited that shit hole and never returned...

You approach, the zesty smell of cheap bleach mixed with alcohol infused stale urine is oozing through the door. As you get close you take a deep breath, you push open the door, you smell nothing with your lungs full of pre-toilet smoke filled air, but you do feel a stinging in your eyes from the toxic vapour emitting from the porous grout, the crack tiles, ripped vinyl flooring and leaking waste pipes that has absorbed years and years of drunken splashed piss, festering, matured and concentrated into something resembling a living fog of foul nastiness that sticks to clothes, to skin, lines your nose and seeps down into your throat ready to make you gag the next time you dare breath. You know it's waiting, there is no getting away from it, the odour of a 1980's pub bog is going to hit you with the force of an invisible diorama smothered nappy slapped square in the face.

You are at the urinal, clenching and straining every muscle in your groin, desperately trying to make yourself piss faster and faster, so fast the yellow liquid bouncers back like a fully depressed aerosol nozzle spreading urine onto your trousers, shoes, and hands.

The powerful piss blast is bouncing back off the vertical porcelain, spreading far and wide beyond your legs standing just 10 inches' away, and is yet more food to the living foul fog monster that has been created in this cesspit over the last 10 years.

Fine urine spray, badly shaken todger's dripping onto the floor, the drunken beer goggled eyes aiming, but missing the porcelain, streams of piss running down the walls, splashing down and running under the lino floor, turning the dried piss lake back into a wet slime that can release its fermented bilge once again as it does every day.

And every day the odour monster grows and grows, attacking every man foolish enough to venture into this den of hellish man waste…

At least you don't need a shit, small mercy's eh You are 75% through, butt cheeks clenched so tight a rubber glove wearing sex-kitten dominatrix couldn't slip a cigarette paper between your arse cheeks with a gallon of KY Jelly and a crowbar, pushing to finish emptying a bladder that has surely doubled in volume tonight of all nights. You are getting ready to sprint to the relative smell free zone the door is teasing you with, clean tasteless air is cruelly just out of reach on the other side, your lungs are bursting, red faced, veins in your neck bulging, your hands ready to whip the old lad in and zip up so fast the risk of your foreskin getting caught in the teeth seems worth the gamble, anything to get out of the bog before you have to breath once more…

Eventually you have to breath just as you about to open the door and escape, but when you do. Have you experienced a hellish toilet trip?

If you were an 80's pub bopper enjoying the days of Spandau Ballet and Wham being repeatedly played on juke boxes in every local pub, you where young enough to be wearing pod's shoes, Brutus Gold jeans, Fred Perry polos and Harrington jackets.

We thought 80's pubs were cool, it was the beginning of strobe lights, bright colours, DJ's and alco-pops, but in reality, the pubs we were drinking in were cheap and nasty dumps, not really fit for what they were being used for!

Occasionally a great pub would appear following a big investment, but then every tosser and slag in the area descended and they just ruined that pub as they had every other pub before it!

People make the pub, or they used to, but at the same time greedy pub companies allow the punters to destroy a pub by reputation and physically. They won't spend enough money to keep it in tip-top shape and defend it from idiots, dickheads, teenage vandals and wear and tear! Tight bastards…

Pub companies allow their sites to disintegrate in front of their regular customers eyes. A pub will be going downhill for years and years because the bigger bosses refuse to spend a penny on repairs, then they blame the manager for losing the trade to the newly refurbished pub just down the road!

The revolving cycle of refurbishment, or sparkle as we call it when only a tiny amount is spent on just paint and nothing else, still goes on today. A pub has a certain amount of money spent on it, never enough I may add unless it is privately owned, to put right what has been poorly maintained for years. If the building, furniture, lighting, toilets were maintained properly by having repairs done instantly and to high standards there would be no need to completely refurbish a pub because it would never be destroyed in the first place.

Do you know about the broken window theory?

If an empty building is in good condition and not one single window is smashed it is not vandalised.

If a building suddenly has just one broken window that is viewed by the public, within days every window in the building will be smashed.

I really feel for tenanted pubs and the people that operate them. The landlord is normally barely scraping a living due to being totally screwed over by the landlord he or she rents the pub from.

The pub company owner who is the tenant's landlord will be charging the tenant eye-watering bonkers levels of rents for using one of their pub buildings to operate a private business from.

What makes a bad situation even worse is that the tenant also must buy the beer, wine, and soft drinks that they need to sell to us, the public, to scrabble together a living wage at the end of each week, at massively over inflated prices for every product.

It's the same wankers who are charging a crippling amount of rent that also have the tenant trapped in a "closed shop you must buy from us" system where the only winner is the pub company owner. The tenant is earning so little due to the pub companies polices they cannot afford to repair anything that is worn out, so the pub just sinks and sinks year by year.

It really doesn't need to be like this, but when we get onto finance later you will begin to see the link between nothing being spent and the root cause of this tight-arsed behaviour, the PLC.

I can remember visiting pubs in the "good old days" and being really surprised if it had actual toilet seats in place, cubical locks, and toilet paper!

Soap was rarely seen and the mirror, if not missing altogether, was always cracked! All too often there was not enough chairs to enable all the tables to be used, every pub had a broken chair pile.

Thread bare carpets, ripped wallpaper, foam poking out from sofa arms, and wooden surfaces that are so old and worn there is no trace of the varnish that once covered a long since shiny tabletop. Old tabletops were used to carve swear words around the fag burns that tell a story of heavy use, abuse and ageing in an uncared about way!

Modern pubs (can we really call them pubs?) are licensed retail shops that "perform" a service. Often unfriendly, bleak art-house vast spaces, they all appear to have the obligatory industrial pipework and ventilation spanning across the ceiling for some reason. Many years ago, this ducting was boxed in to hide it, but not anymore, I guess modern drinkers never look up.

Now let's talk about the highly professional robots serving you. When you visit a branded hostelry, every server will be saying exactly the same scripted lines written by a marketing department who have no sense of how customer service works in the real world. Interaction and spontaneous reaction with real people who can talk "off script" makes a genuine connection between people.

I bet you have sat in a branded pub or restaurant, and this will have happened.

You have had your food in front of you for around three or four minutes. Out of the corner of your eye you notice a team member in uniform heading towards your table. As they reach your table, they parrot speak the scripted line without breaking stride, turning their head towards you or even looking at you:

"Is everything ok with your food?"

This is the line I ban my teams from repeating like Parrots, good managers don't want robots, I can teach someone with a personality to do any job, but I cannot give someone a personality.

The reason why they don't engage? 99% of people don't complain, the just acknowledge that you have asked then if it's ok, they don't comment on the actual food itself. So, they may as well not stop as normally there is no reason to. Obvious once pointed out isn't it.

Most pub company marketing teams I have met over my many years personify the ability and personality equal to the awfulness and awkwardness of David Brent and his team from The Office!

Back to the BIG question I started with before wondering off in my own head:

Were what generation X call "the good old days of pubs" really that good?

I'll tell you what I would like to see.

All the modern legislation on air quality, no smoking, flashy well-made cocktails, fantastic tasting world foods, technology delivering great entertainment, plus the safety and hygiene we know and expect in 2022 but set in the old pubs we loved so much, where the people were the stars, the chat was vibrant, and the flirting was dangerous.

I don't want to sit in a pub where everyone is looking down at a 6" screen held in their hand without speaking a single word.

The fact that 80's and 90's pubs were often no more than piss soaked, blood stained, smoky boxes full of ash, sweat and B.O simply passes us by because we only remember the fun, the laughs, the shared happiness, and the people who made a certain pub your second home from home.

The pubs of the past were very different to what we have now.

40 years ago, the majority were dumps, very much as I have described above, there were a few good ones, but clean pubs with good quality drinks and stink free air were few and far between.

The expectation of pubs switched completely with the change of millennia from 1999 to 2000.

The process to turn every pub into a branded pub chain had begun.

Big money had to be spent so that pub companies could build exactly the same pub in every town and city across the land. Branded pubs where being rolled out across the country, the new city investors wanted to turn our local pubs into money making machines.

This story about our boozers has been unfolding for 40 years, everywhere you look it's the same boring pub. They may have different names, colours and be all sorts of shapes and sizers, but they are all basically the same pub selling the same "on trend" overpriced beer and crap food created on a warehouse production line ready to be pinged in a microwave.

A few of the old pubs of the Good Old Days are still around, but they are now rare, back street boozers in very small numbers. They have a dedicated group of regulars keeping them going, until one by one, the Bills of this world pass away to enjoy the taproom in the sky.

When too many Bills are lost, Bill's local pub will be no more…

Luckily, we do still have a healthy amount of fantastic, non-branded, independent pubs all over the UK.

They are out there waiting for the people who won't settle for second best, ready meals, mass produced lager and boxed wine.

If you don't want a meal from a plastic bag, beer poured by an 18-year-old with no known bar skills, and a youthful licensee carrying a clipboard around while managing a group of underpaid robots, seek out the independents, it is well worth the effort.

If you have a great non-branded pub near to you, use it, respect it and makes sure to contribute to its long-term survival.

If we don't use these fantastic independent pubs, they will become extinct faster than a closed pub is turned into, yet another dual carriageway located curry restaurant.

Remember, a truly great pub follows real life's ups and downs for twelve months a year, not just one months with a fake tree, twinkling lights and seasonal jumper themed Christmas and New Year's Eve parties.

Chapter 3
Cash Cow

Pubs take CASH *(or they did before Covid 19)* and CASH was king absolutely everywhere before the copper wire and fibre optics changed everything.

No matter how hard you try you cannot stuff bank notes into a WIFI router and make them spew out somewhere else.

Covid has made almost everything contactless in the world of licensed retail, we have all seen the signs stuck to tills saying, *"contactless payments only from you dirty unclean infected bastards!"*

Ok, I may have added my own interpretation after the word "*only*", but you get my point.

Advances in the 80's and 90's brought in the plastic revolution, it's not that long ago that a 4-digit PIN and card reader ruled the world. In 2022 even using a pin number seems so old school, we pay using our face, fingerprint, double clicking buttons or just wafting a card or phone near a small white box that goes ping.

Years ago, money moved physically, hand to hand, stuffed into bags, in vans, lorries, trains, it moved much more clumsily and slowly than it does in the digital days we now live in.

I can remember taking cash to London to buy an RS1600i where a man counted it on a table. The last car I bought was another X5 a couple of years ago and I just transferred the money electronically using my phone and a code that came through on text.

Money has become far too easy to spend…

Physical cash is not small, or light for that matter. If you have £20,000 in £10.00 notes that's a fairly big lump stuffed under your coat on the way to the bank from the pub. If you have been targeted by bad guys, then would know you are carrying cash because you are wearing a coat in 35° boiling hot weather!

Wearing a coat on a hot day scream's:

HE HAS A CASH BAG INSIDE THE COAT

In the 80's we had four different value notes squeezed into wallets and purses, a green £1 note, blue £5 note, orangey £10 note, and if you were flush you maybe had one purple £20 note.

Let's not talk about £50 notes, very few people even new they existed back in the day!

Lots of coins right down to a 1/2 pence value coin, and the 50p coin was fucking massive!

£1 and £2 coins didn't exist, a £1.00 then was a dog-eared tatty paper note that often just disintegrated as you unfolded the faded green rectangle. Not long after being printed by the Bank of England these thin, easily torn and soon to be grubby bank notes featured the queen on one side, Isaac Newton on the other.

Plastic was for wealthy people, debit cards didn't yet exist, and credit cards were processed on a zip-zap manual card machine with multiple layered carbon copy sheets imprinting the card details onto each layer. Three copies were made with every credit card purchase, white, yellow, and pastel blue I think, but I cannot remember who got which colour copy?

Everything else was paid for by cheque or CASH.

Wages were paid in cash, sealed into little brown envelopes, no wonder much of it never reached home or became housekeeping money, stand outside any factory, transport firm or pit wages office and torn bits of brown envelope littered the floor.

The nearest pub and bookies would be full of cash rich workers within 5 minutes of being paid every Thursday.

Huge amounts of *cash* were driven through every housing estate, every village, town and city because businesses had the cash, they had taken in payments collected.

Banks moved money by truck and train, physical cash had not yet been digitalised or turned into flashing numbers on a screen, it was still being passed hand to hand as part of a transaction between two people for the sale of goods, making a bet or buying a service.

There was no such thing as clicking on a banking App to check your bank balance, you opened a cupboard to see the savings jar that lived next to the bag of 2-year-old plain flour and had a guess at how much was in it?

Money in the bank was accounted for in little books called "deposit record" where the latest balance was written, in or printed, every time you put money in or took it out of your account.

Yes, cash was king, TV shows like Only Fools and Horses and stand-up comic Harry Enfield performing his "Loads-a-Money" character focused on loot, dosh and moola routines because those paper notes were still the only way most people understood money.

It was physical, foldable, spendable, cash was the daddy alright.

But cash can also be stolen, nicked, fiddled, hidden, lost and destroyed…

He's a thought, in the yuppie 80's if we saw someone whip out a huge wad of cash and peeled a few bills off the top, then toss the notes onto a table to pay for a meal we heard a voice in our heads saying "WOW, LUCKY RICH BASTARD."

If we see someone pull out a fat roll of cash in 2022 that same voice in our heads says, "DRUG DEALING BASTARD!"

How times have changed.

Then the world of money changed forever, debit cards arrived in 1987 nothing would be the same again. Barclays issued the first debit card closely followed by all the other banks a year later.

Just like that we could flash the "plastic" to pay for anything we wanted if the shop had one of the new electronic payment points.

I can remember going into the Army Surplus Store to buy some Doc-Martins and walking out empty handed because the salesman wanted to put my card onto a Zip-Zap card copying machine!

There was not a chance on earth I would ever allow my brand-new plastic piece of opulence to be run over with a manual wheel that could risk my precious Switch Card.

Get with the times grandad.

Out of nowhere people were able to spend their own money held in a bank branch by using a new super cool Switch card instead of having to travel to a bank, queue up and wait in turn to ask a person behind a glass screen for their own cash.

That actually sounds so stupid and made me laugh because I remember standing like a naughty schoolboy in line to see a cashier, then I had to prove who I was just to get £20 out for a night out!

ATMs were now becoming a feature on every high street, but the early versions were not that reliable, and the majority of people didn't trust a metal box to dispense money accurately. It was the ATM role out that led to the debit card revolution. When ATMs first arrived on the scene banks issued account holders an ATM card that allowed them to extract an amount of cash by using the card in the ATM and confirming it was the card owner with a 4-digit PIN code. That amount of cash taken out was automatically deducted from the customers balance the next working day.

The next step was pretty obvious, to make spending money even faster and drive consumerism to epidemic levels, take the ATM out of the process and take away the need for cash altogether.

What a genius business model, the banks would need to make a small charge for using the electronic payment system, that's only fair, it is their equipment and process after all. This payment to the bank will work by charging the shop that is using the banks card payment process a small percentage of the total sales.

KERCHING – Profits for banks have just become turbo-charged!

If you think all these changes to make money cashless was to make your life more convenient, you are a very naive and possibly think the earth is flat. The changes were made to make *MONEY*.

Money moved around on the analogue phone lines of the time, and it moved slowly compared to modern digital systems. But it was a hell of a lot faster than going to the bank branch in the town centre. In just a few seconds money was assigned by the payment process to be withdrawn from your bank account to pay for an item at the checkout. It didn't matter where you were spending your money, 50, 100, even 1,000 miles away from where your account was held, the money would appear in the account of the seller the next day.

Yes, generation Z and Millennial's, it wasn't instant like it is today, the payment was deposited into the receiving account the next "working" day.

What do I mean by "working day"? No money moved in or out of banking systems over the weekend, Monday to Friday was the "working" days for bank accounts.

In 2022 money moves in seconds 24/7 365.

The Switch card was a truly amazing break though, put it into an ATM machine, enter a PIN and get actual cash out, or use it with a PIN number to pay instantly. By the end of the 80's the digital revolution was well and truly under way.

Why am I talking about old ways to move money you may ask?

I have a couple of reasons as to why we need to understand how little cash physical moves around in these modern times, and when it is used, where cash gathers in bulk amounts.

The first reason is this, the only places still taking large amounts of cash (legally) in 2020 was pubs and betting offices, or it was until Covid 19 came along. Even with a global pandemic running rampant in every corner of the world, many old school pub goers still want to use cash as payment for a pint! Its tradition, the way it has always been done.

But paying by cash is vanishing year on year relentlessly.

With an ever-ageing older pub population moving into that grand tap room in the sky the demand to pay by cash will continue to shrink until anyone buying a pint in the near future will know just one way left to purchase a lovely cold beer, tap and go.

Digital payment will continue to grow year on year because Bill is no longer here demanding to pay with cash, but his grand kids are spending his house sales inheritance money using their phones and watches to pay using effortless contactless.

I'm well into my 50's, it's summer 2022, I have not had any notes of a monetary value in my wallet for at least a month. Have you?

Contactless payment was first introduced to the UK in 2008.

I bet many of you remember when many businesses wouldn't let you buy using a card unless the value exceeded £5.00.

Not anymore, any price £0.10p up to £100.00, it's just a waft.

Cards and phones have become the dominant means of payment, even more so with Covid, but cash was, and is, still the main way to pay over the bar in a proper drinker's boozer, for the time being.

The second reason I'm going on about money is because of modern ways of registering and recording a payment.

Smart tills, CCTV, fibre optics and the internet have created hellhole working environment for bar staff and managers due to constant and never-ending monitoring by the bigger bosses.

This process of performance managing people in a "LIVE" environment has become normalised over the last 10-20 years.

It enables business leaders to check everyone is giving 110% every second they are at work, and if not, you will be replaced!

In my day it was just called sales, money going in the till and the sale recorded on a paper till roll, how things have changed.

More of this later.

Crooks, thieves, robbers, whatever you want to call criminals that steal either due to opportunity, using brute force or detailed planning, they all want every bit of cash in the pub.

It's difficult to trace, find, identify if found and spent without record of who was handing it over when paying for something.

Betting Shops have fantastic security systems, bullet proof screens, cash boxes under the counter where notes are dropped into a purpose-built vessel that cannot be attacked because any armed robber cannot get behind the counter. Bookies are built in a way that there is no way past the screens and armoured doors that protect their money stash.

Bookie staff can sit behind the screens calling the empty handed poorly prepared robber a prick. I can see it now, staff with two fingers in the air laughing in the face a numpty with a home-made balaclava their nan knitted. If you are laughing at a dick holding a claw hammer it is because you are safe and protected by bullet proof screens.

The money is safe from all the bad guys, with the exception of the professional, experienced, and dedicated criminal.

Serious career thief's have access to high explosives, weapons grade tools and guns, but to be honest, I doubt many of them are willing to risk liberty, dropping their soap in the showers, or missing family for 10-15 years for a local bookie's takings on a cold winter's day.

It's the amateurs, desperate TV crime show educated criminal yobs who watch glorified heists in films like Oceans 11, who make it look easy, they will have a go at a pub thinking it's a soft touch. Wannabe gangsters mesmerised by listening to rap lyrics by Snoop Dogg and Eminem are the type I have known attack pubs and bookies. They go is acting hard and think they will just walk out with pockets full of cash for fucks sake!

I have seen many an East End London based flick on Netflix that is glamourising so called gangsters, but come-on, it's a fucking film. Now the Brinks-Mat robbery, a real weapons grade heists is very rare anywhere in the world, and rarer still in the UK due to our though and necessary gun laws.

Pubs are a much softer target than betting shops, it's a completely different mind-set from the overprotective approach of the betting industry. Pub companies want their pub teams to be super customer friendly, open, welcoming, let's get face to face with the donor, sorry, I mean customer, because it helps loosen their purse strings. The bigger bosses insist on face-to-face service that encourages the customer spend way more than they actually intended to. Hospitality has been removing all barriers between guest and staff for decades, it has been a huge change from the mentality of 20 years ago when you always kept that 3-foot-thick chuck of wood that was the bar top between you and the customer. The bar counter kept you outside punching distance.

Anyway, where was I, oh yeah, getting close.

You know what I'm talking about, you have all experienced it, and been a victim of, the money grab that is no different from Robin Hood getting close to take the wealthy traveller's money and redistribute it to the poor. But in pubs the noble quest has been spun 180°, these days he is taking money from the working class and giving it to the banks.

It's called *"The Up-Sell" or "Sell On"* …

Back to crime and money. What is the problem with the face to face and human contact in the hospitality business?

RISK

If someone pulls out a shotgun, knife, baseball bat or hammer in the pub and demands money from the till, it is *YOU*, not the building, not the reputation, not the area manager or the bigger bosses, *YOU* are in terrifying and serious danger of being hurt!

You are not behind a bullet proof screen sticking your tongue out like the staff at the bookies can, you are reachable, touchable, and hittable because you are probably out from behind the bar using the till on the service station right in the middle of the customer area. Remember the policy, *it breaks down barriers between guests and staff* as suggested by the bigger bosses who noticed in their private golf clubs that tills in the members areas and the staff using them are not attacked.

Of course not, it's a private golf club with a £3,000 per year membership fee and a fucking massive two-mile-long drive through the forest to get there by car only, plus private security guards!

Even if you are behind the bar when the robbing bastards comes in, like most pubs, the bar flap is permanently open, so the very scary man holding a 1970's 4 foot long sharply pointed fire poker in his hand and with one leg of his wife's unwashed tights pulled over his head to disguise his face, can get at you, hit you, badly hurt you, meme you, and even kill you!

There is nowhere to hide behind a bar counter, the bandit can easily lean over the bar to find you ducking down, step through the bar flap to see you lying on the floor, let's be honest, you are venerable to attack, being whacked, stabbed or shot and your body is soft, it bleeds, it breaks easy, and you only have one life.

Just hand the cash and whatever they want as quickly as possible:

IF YOU CAN?

I will admit, if I had a knife or gun pointing at my face, my nuts, anywhere to be honest, and someone holding the weapon was demanding money, I would be so polite and even offer to count it.

Pub companies don't like money being stolen, especially the area managers and Op's managers, it will be recorded as a loss against their PandL performance and so can reduce *THEIR* personal bonus because any loss is taken into account against bonus calculations!

Many modern things are done to stop the cash from being nicked by robbers, thieves, con-artists and even staff.

Sometimes there is a slot in a till area, it is often a cut into the bar counter itself, and hidden from view, somewhere the bar team are instructed to post all £20.00 and £10.00 notes into a hidden safe box that cannot be accessed, or even found by, a robber, thief or horse-riding highwayman.

These cash boxes have very limited access and Mr Robbery cannot get into it even if he can find it!

But he will automatically think *YOU CAN* get in it with an override code, because as Hollywood has taught us, the manager always has the code!

The pub company want to stop money being stolen at any cost, but that cost could be much higher than you are prepared pay.

The cost could be *YOU* if you are on duty and the bad men robbers want *CASH NOW. Bandits* don't give a toss who is in charge, about your health or physical safety, you are a means to an end.

More on not accessing the cash shortly…

As card payments started to become more popular with everyday spending, retail pubs became one of the only places where robbers knew cash would still be available. It also didn't take the bad guys long to understand when the largest amounts of cash would be swimming about in the safe.

Sunday evening became the prime target for the classic smash and grab robbery using a baseball bat and a Swiss Army knife! Saturday and Sunday's cash, in most pubs the two busiest days of the week, is in the safe ready to be banked on Monday morning.

It's been a long day; imagine you are duty manager on Sunday from 12pm till 11pm and it been a really busy weekend. Someone's uncle knob-head has been in giving staff grief about the Carling not tasting right, and you know this dick claiming his beer tastes off is eating a Fisherman's Friend super strong lozenge. There was, as usual, a daily knob-head moaning! This one ordered a well-done steak and then complained it was not pink in the middle for fucks sake. And don't forget the slag who was being fingered in the men's toilets, was caught by a team member, she then started gobbing off that it's her basic human right to do whatever she wants in the bogs without being kicked out.

You just want to go home to a large glass of red and jim-jams.

The manager finished at 4pm so it's you, paid just 50p above the minimum wage rate, and two team members on the lowest wages legally permissible, looking after the pub, closing it at 11pm and responsible for all that lovely cash in the safe. It's even worse if it's been a bank holiday weekend, it's become a ROBBERY BONUS EDITION, a bank holiday Monday late night smash and grab gang can swipe the bank holiday Monday takings as well as Saturday and Sunday's.

So, it's you and two teenagers working on the bar who are closing tonight at 11pm, this will be easy, you have done it a hundred times before.

To a smash and grab gang, risking prison is ok for 2 days' worth of cash, but if there is a 3rd days pile of cash to be swiped and we can rob it on Monday night instead of Sunday, that an even better risk vs reward.

In the 1990's the number of cash robberies was soaring throughout the UK, the gap between the rich and poor was becoming wider and wider. Nothing any government was doing put money back into working class pockets, the industrial jobs were disappearing as fast as Jimmy Savile's reputation.

We had left the 80's behind and with technology advancing faster than ever before lots of new toys were flooding the marketplace. Everyone wanted a computer, a big TV, DVD player and eventually a mobile phone, but you needed cash to buy them! Even if you did have a debit card, you still needed cash in the bank to buy, cash was still hanging onto it crown as top dog.

Even a thief's wants his Mrs to have a designer handbag.

Have you ever bought a twating designer hand-back, I thought I was going to have to sell a fucking kidney!

Theft of cash had become a growing and lucrative business, but where to steal money from in a worthwhile volume was becoming a much smaller pool of options!

Pubs DID still have lots of CASH locked away in the safe after the weekend.

Maintaining a low-cost model is critical to pub companies, every penny spent has to be understood analysed and reviewed, but they will spend the spondulies pretty quickly if there is a chance to save even more money or reduce their risk to financial loss.

Put simply, protect the dosh…

I once worked for a company who became concerned about losing money through robbery. I won't mention the company name, but anyone reading this tail who was also working for that brewer will know…

Robbery costs a lot of money, time, and energy for the victim to put everything right and move on from the incident itself. The cash loss, damage, repairs, and possibly short time closure all adds up to be a big fat cost to a pub company. Sometimes it also adds cost to recruitment because managers and staff involved in any type of attack won't return to the business.

So, our caring and considerate *Bigger Bosses* decided that they needed to act and protect the money. Insurance against cash loss was going through the roof! Rumour in our company was that the cash wasn't insured anymore, and something had to be done to protect the company assets.

I'll let you decide for yourself if you think the company was choosing to reduce the risk to its employees, or the risk of cash loss that affects the balance sheet, but you can only choose one.

We know by now that pub companies are cheap, thrifty spenders who watch the pennies, or rather, this is what they had become by the 90's! Most pubs had a fairly cheap safe in an easily accessible office. There was always far too many safe keys or way too many people knew the combination lock code! No one bothered collected safe or building keys from leavers or changed the safe's combination lock codes, and I know for a fact after conducting many investigations into cash losses, around 50% of robberies were always based on inside information supplied by disgruntled ex-employees.

Sceptic's will shout "CCTV will save us with cameras everywhere!"

Bollocks, it won't and read on to find out why it didn't.

These big pub companies employ people smart enough to demand a camera is installed in the office looking directly at the safe.

That's it, no one dare rob a pub safe if they are filmed in HD quality and clearly displayed in full colour on a big monitor, problem solved, happy days.

I said pub companies employed people smart enough to install a camera to look at the safe 24/7 just a few lines ago.

What I don't explain is that these same people are total dumb-ass stupid morons who have not noticed the multiple flaws in their so-called brilliant plan to monitoring the safe.

If a camera is looking at the safe door it is also looking at the back of the thief's head! He will be wearing a cap and have on some kind of covid mask that makes identifying him as easy a platting fog!

What else could a pub company property manager and area manager do to make identifying an armed robber even harder, or practically impossible?

It is not possible for me to describe just how stupid this is but read on and have a laugh at their expense.

They install a safe into an office, an obvious place to put a safe! Then they install cameras to watch that safe 24/7 and the camera angle allows sight of the thief's face, well done, we are almost there, you have a secure office with a CCTV protected safe.

Well done, give yourself a slap on the back.

There is only one last tiny job to do, just one thing that will turn this pub company area manager from being a rabid dog anal gland excretion most of them are, into a very slightly, and I really do mean teeny-tiny, respected boss because just for once they have done something right.

But *NO*, at the moment of success they go and fuck it up every time.

Because this bellend is so dumb, definitely displays the intelligence of a person with no more than a 2-digit IQ count, or they are trying so hard to save money in a way that will probably COST them more money in the long run, they order something to be installed in a place that defies any reasoned logic because they are too stupid to think it through!

Area manager:

"Let's fit the CCTV recorder in the same office near the safe"

WHAT, WAIT, SERIOUSLY, this dumb fucker thinks that no professional armed blagger wouldn't think about taking away the only evidence that could see them convicted?

Any thief who is 'on the ball' will obviously take the CCTV recorder with them, just tuck it under their arm as they leave the office.

Nicking the CCTV recorder as part of the robbery prevents the crime being watched by the cops. This is the best way to get away with the crime, no evidence, no suspect, and no conviction.

Sometimes Mr Robber doesn't even bother wearing a hat or mask, after being told where the CCTV recorder is located, why would he care about being IDed, the recorder is going in his swag bag before he even starts thinking about grabbing the cash.

Who was committing these crimes, how do they end up raiding a local pub and how did they do it?

Type 1

Much of the time it was local people who were pulling the mask over their face before trying something so risky on their own doorstep. They have been in the pub on a weekend and noticed all the readies being passed over the bar count and shoved into an overflowing till. A large number of these life wasters have either worked in the pub they want to rob or one of their mates still does work there.

That is where the inside information comes from meaning this bandit raid will be swift and neat because they know the building and inside out.

£5,000 robbery, fuck, what a result…

Type 2

Wannabe gangsters. You have seen the type I'm on about in films like Adulthood, Blue Story, and ill Manors. Watch Harry Brown and take note of the little bastards kicking the old man to death in the underpass. Tracksuit and hoodie wearing tossers who spend their time in the shadows, don't work, and talk in accents they picked up from watching too much Jeremy Kyle. Crime *IS* their profession, and they are, and I don't know why, always involved with drugs.

These are the opportunists who need cash and will use extreme threats of violence, shouting, screaming, and pushing their victims into submission and obedience.

Smash and Grab twats who damage things for fun, they will wound a person with hesitation because it gives them *respect-on-da-street*.

Landing a £5,000 earner, good nights work, keep them in coke and weed for a couple of weeks, then more action.

Type 3

Professionals. Not too many of these would hit pubs because in the days before the huge super-pubs because the amount of cash to steal was just worth the risk. These type of criminal does 1 or 2 big jobs years with lots of planning, and contingencies in place.

Stealing £5,000 from a pub on a Sunday night would not be a successful heist for these skilled engineers of theft.

Let's use our Type 2 as an example.

What do they do?

Hidden in the dark and dressed head to toe in cellulose triacetate and polyester track suits, scallies would be watching as the last customer or staff member leave through the exit door. Just before you lock yourself in to finish off the office work, they rush the door, barge their way in, grab you, hold a weapon to your neck and say "*OFFICE NOW*."

The Smash and Grab has started.

I'll go back to that question I asked much earlier, is it *YOU* or the *MONEY* that is the valued asset of the pub company?

Cash was being stolen, safes were being opened quickly by terrified managers and assistants, losses were growing, so the pub companies need a better way to protect the cash, sorry, I mean you you you, of course I meant you, honest.

I remember early in the 90's, while in an area meeting, about the rollout of new anti-theft timer delay safes.

As managers we all jumped for joy… *no, wait, hang on, something does not site right about this.*

These new safes were yellow and black combination safes, about half these sizes of an under-counter fridge! The clever bit, it had a drop slot so that newly sealed £1,000 packs of £10:00 and £20:00 notes could be placed into the protected empty belly of the safe without even opening the door!

I can clearly remember all the rehearsed spiel being spewed into our ears as we were being told how these new combination safes would make us, the managers, and our teams, much safer because no one robs a safe with a delay build in!

There was an addition that goes with the safe to make us the last choice pub to rob on any blagger's hitlist, we got a sticker for a window telling the naughty criminals that we have a delayed timer safe.

I felt immediately safer, wouldn't you?

What utter bollocks.

If a robber sees a sticker saying "money is protected with a 'delayed safe locking system'" they just bring a flask of tea and a packet of biscuits to dunk while they wait, relaxed knowing the safe will open soon.

Eureka the pub company cries, "our money is safe, making robbers wait for ages to open a safe will definitely **STOP** every badman from even trying to nick the companies cash assets from our new yellow and black super safes!"

I'm pretty sure that this new delay time-lock safe policy wasn't really thought through, and one thing is for sure, no one asked the pub managers or carried out a risk assessment that included the danger to people who work in pubs.

If I was to wear my cynical hat, was this policy actually thoroughly thought through in detail and the risk to people ignored?

Let's look at two types of robbery:

The Company Have **Not** Thought This Policy Through, What Happens in A **Smash and Grab**!

Most robberies in pubs are committed by the local scallies, wannabe gangsters, desperate drug addicts or ex-staff! As a member of the management team, you have probably crossed swords with them before, so they really don't like this targeted pub leadership because you have stopped them dealing drugs, smoking a joint, or just being a prick in the past.

This spells trouble for you, a chance for payback! Not one of these idiots will know, or care, that there is a new time-delay combination safe waiting for them, so they are coming in any way! After all, to these scroats, nicking anything from till floats to charity boxes, money is money even if they cannot get into the main cash safe!

In and out, Smash and Grab, the short version, safe not opened, the money asset is still safely locked away. But due to the scally's frustration with this new safe the assistant manager has a black eye, burst lip, and a twisted arm. This type of thief won't hang around, once they hit a barrier that prevents them getting what they want, they panic and want to be away into the dark of the night as fast as the huge steams of adrenaline will power their trembling legs.

But the journey to the office and the safe is executed with venom and hate as one of the scallies drags the assistant manager by her hair towards the office, they appear to know where the office is? The young manager is bumped into every door frame, her head dragged along the rough, uneven walls scraping the skin on her face. Then they see the safe, she cries softly explaining she cannot open it because it has a delay system built into the lock. Scallies are now really pissed, 'that's it, let's get the fuck out of here' and the tension now switchers to anger and one of these wankers punchers the female manager square in her left eye and she crumples to the ground, the second robbing cunt kicks her in the face as she rushers past her to exit the office and flee the scene crabbing anything containing cash such as the staffs tips jar and any charity boxes.

Never again will they work in a pub again because she is now too scared of "the" next time.

The Company **Have** Thoroughly Thought Through And Know Exactly What Could Happen In A **Planned Robbery**.

We have explored how scallies react when coming across the unknown, they find a safe that cannot be opened immediately, it's a result for the pub company, but not the team member.

Now let's take a look at Mr Pro Safe thief. He does not care if the pub has a time-delay safe or not, he will be getting into it and the young under paid manager **WILL** be helping him.

The pub company the assistant is working for has knowingly risked their employee in their desire to protect the cash: YES/NO?

Before I continue, I want you to answer a question.

How would you feel with a nasty and deliberate thieving bastard standing over you with a claw-hammer threatening to fuck-up your fingers one by one?

Regardless of who is committing the crime, what is really important to that poor team member and does Mr Badass Thieving cunt believe that they really don't know how to open the safe and bypass the time-delay?

Err I somehow doubt a sobbing young manager will be believed, a little persuasion may loosen your lips.

They may be telling the truth, but an evil committed thief will double check to be sure.

I now need to explain the mind-set of a nasty uncaring and determined robber, they want a result. Intentionally they don't know this pub, they have never been in it, they know not a single person who drinks or works there.

That is on purpose because they need to detach themselves from the job at hand and what they may have to do to make it all worth their time and energy. They switch into work mode where people are just a means-to-a-end and will be exploited a person without fear, concern, or conscience.

How should Mr Nasty Violent Robber fill his time waiting for the safe to open, what tactics could he use to encourage you to open the safe sooner, or right now?

How about a few threats with a knife to see if you do know how to open it without waiting, running the dull side of the knife across a young person's throat, or acting out the famous scene in Reservoir Dogs where he slices the hostages ear off?

Those threats didn't work, the employee is still insisting they cannot open the safe without the delay system kicking in, so how about a couple of slaps to loosen their tongue, after all a broken tooth or nose will definitely get those gums flapping, wont it?

Slaps didn't work, the blagger needs to up the game. What about testing the assistant managers resolve by breaking a finger?

Not the whole finger, well not yet, let's start with just smashing the nail part flat, that should do it!

Where is that ball-knacker hammer I put in my bag?

Think how far this violence could go? Trying to coerce information by inflicting pain on another human being is sickening, but professional thieves don't tend to be overly friendly, they don't tend to become their victims pen pal after pushing a corkscrew through their cheek is the pursuit of extracting hidden secrets.

Nasty Bastards are there for one reason and one reason only, the money and it's too often that pub company team members have to pay a much bigger price than the cost in lost cash and shrunken bank balance!

If anyone gets in the way, they could be hurt, and no, they cannot override the time-lock, but Mr Robber will not believe that is true.

So now I'm ask the same question one last time, which asset is the company protecting, is it the cash or is it you?

Back to the days of cash being the undisputed king in pubs…

In the late 70's local boozers ticked over with a happy bunch of regular's meeting up over and over again in *their* local pub. Nothing was fancy, imagine a world of Donkey Jackets and hats like your gran used to where when she went to church. If the pub had a TV, it was still black and white and there was no background music, it was just people's voices talking face to face everywhere you looked.

The man would be served at the bar by Doreen and Elsie while Ray (landlord) played cards with his mates in the Tap Room.

The couples were in the lounge, the husband with his pint of bitter, the wife with her port and lemon, or maybe a glass of house white wine that tastes had started to turn into vinegar, but no working class knew the difference between good and bad wine because no decent wine was available to the working class in those days…

This is what pubs once were, a building with a beating heart, a front room for a very large unrelated family spread over the entire housing estate. Things were affordable, the landlord/lady scrapped a decent living, they owned an off cream coloured Austin Maxi and earned enough for a well-deserved two-week holiday self-catering in Bournemouth once a year, plus four or five race day bus trips through the flat season. And don't forget the day trips to Skegness, Blackpool, or Margate where she could wear her latest summer MandS cardigan made in the Bairnswear factory.

Groups of punters went to the pub at least 5 nights a week, everyone knew everyone else and looked out for each other, it really was an extended family in the parlour drinking together.

Where did all the customers disappear to and when did estate pubs begin to die, and why?

A "pub regular" was a strange mixture of so many types of people. The majority of pub users were beer swigging men out on their own with the other men on weekday, but on Saturdays these men would be with the wife, on their arm as a treat, but in reality, she was no more than an accessory.

Next, we have handful of older men sitting in one corner hiding away from the new world of young people demanding to a juke box so they can listen to loud music by The Rolling Stones, Gary Glitter and David Bowie. If these old sippers who had been warming the same seats for 25 years thought the late 70's was too much to cope with and the changes to pubs was shocking, just wait till the 1980's hits full speed ahead and they are surrounded by lasagne, Tikka Masala, J2O's and expensive Sparkling Water while listening to Wham, Adam Ant and scratching their heads because someone has come into the pub dressed similar to Boy George or Phil Oakey.

Pubs were opening their customer demographic to a much wider potential customer base. Sales were creeping up as the years ticked by one by one, and the speed in revenue growth was about to be slipped an acid tab making the blood pumping though the pubs veins faster than ever before.

For the first time ever, every local pub had sales driving and greed firmly on the agenda.

Ok, let's get back to the subject…

Money has always been manipulated in pub's, clubs, and restaurants. At one time cash was moving about under the radar for many reasons. Inside job petty theft, the con-artist, pan-handlers, illegal betting, cheap cigarette sales or flogging stolen goods in the car park. Most illegal activities have stopped around pubs these days, the odd weed or coke dealing wanker pop up now and again, until they are chased away. The naughty stuff around pubs is done BY THE PUB'S, or the pub companies to be more accurate, in these much more modern times.

I'll explain more later.

I can remember the days long ago when tills only had a few push buttons. There were the numbers "0-9", and the words "total, clear, void and sale" printed on the big, heavy keys.

All the bar team knew the price of everything in their heads, they knew a GandT cost £1.10 because they only had one type of gin and one type of tonic to sell. Add 80p for gin, 30p for tonic, easy peasy.

These days bar staff need a PHD in chemical engineering and a diploma in juggling before even trying to choose which poshly named Orchid flavoured premium tonic enhancers well the taste of a high-priced artisan gin that has been exclusively filtered through Unicorn eyelash hair and blended perfectly with Mermaid tears.

"Would you like the extra cold Evian Mineral ice cubes that are carved into 3cm diameter ice squares using only ethical sourced shell fragments from antique Emperor Penguin eggs for only an extra £5.00?"

Oh, course I'm fucking joking of course, but you get my point! G and T in the 80's. You put 2 cubes of ice into a glass, added 25mm of basic mother's ruin, insert a wafer-thin slice of lemon, flipped the lid off the baby Schweppes or Britvic tonic and place both the glass and bottle on the bar, "that's £1:20p please", simple.

If you currently work in a bar, whatever you do, ignore the stupid twats in the marketing and training departments. They preach this ridiculous insistence of pouring the whole bottle of tonic into the glass before you give it to the customer.

What you will hear in a local pub will be something like *"you have drowned it"* as they stare at you with their evil gaze, *"how dare you ruin my drink, you better add another shot of gin"* …

And then they refuse to pay for it!

If it's one of these new-fangled gold-fish bowls that takes a full kilo of ice and a visit to Lidl's fruit section to fill it, just ask the customer "shall I pour it all in."

Knob-Off marketing tossers, you don't know every customer and not every customer, or pub, is the same.

In the old days we didn't even ask if you wanted diet or normal tonic. Anyone ordering a diet tonic was looked at with suspicion, diet tonic, who are they trying to impress, what are they up to, why diet?

"Hmmmmmmm… keep your eye on her, she's up to no good, probably having an affair… she on diet!"

Go into a modern "bar" and you can choose from 150 gins, 10 different types of tonics, 8 fruits, some of which I've never heard of it is such a big deal these days to ask for a bloody GandT.

Into the bar with my date and off to the bar I go. Firstly, I order my pint of premium lager and it better come out in the tallest glass possible.

Next, I ask for 2 packets of cheese and onion crisps only to told "we don't sell crisps, but you can have these artisan Salt Chicken Fry-Bites or Jalapeño Philly-Steak flavour Chorizo slices?" I order one of each.

Finally, I ask for a GandT, and so starts the theatre, it's show time and I'm now the star guest in a crazy pantomime!

After asking me 27 questions about gins, size, mixers and ice quality, I have returned to my date 4 times with questions about what she wants in and with her drink, I thought I was going to be getting a different type of exercise later, not 500 steps in the bloody bar just to buy a gin!

The bar "artist" finally presents me with a giant glass goblet standing 12 inches high and 6 inches wide! It is filled with specialist ice sauced from a glacier near the Swedish/Russian boarder and imported into the UK in ex-70° Covid Freezers that are now redundant!

The actual liquid of the GandT is lost under the kilo of super priced ice and the artistically placed fruit salad bouquet featuring petals from edible flowers gently protrude from the papaya, dragon and physalis fruit centre piece that has been woven together with pixie hair gathered in the Tibetan Himalayas.

The only way to reach the liquid GandT is by using a limp paper straw, you have no chance of getting your lips anywhere near the rim of the oversized goldfish bowl without stabbing your nose on the many types of skewers used to shape the exotic fruit crown.

"That will be £27:00 please" I just wanted a GandT ffs!

Pint of German pilsner £6, fancy alternatives to crisps are £3 each and means I have paid £15.00 for a double GandT.

WHAT THE FUCK!

It wasn't only staff who skimmed the basic tills because they were easy to fiddle, theft was happening in many forms, and it was often the managers themselves who were taking the lion's share of missing cash and stock.

These days every press on the modern till touch screen, or 'point of sale' as tills are now known, tells the pub company which item was sold, its size, the precise amount and the exact value in every possible detail. The pub company audit team know exactly how much lime cordial the pub should have on stock, right now, this very minute, in every pub they own, right down to 1 single 25mm measure.

Now let's talk about CCTV.

CCTV you say, but isn't that there to protect customers?

Don't be so naive, big pub company have very high-quality CCTV systems that record in HD quality, often 60 frames per-second and above.

These very expensive systems are often well over the top for just capturing some knob-heads face who spat at a doorman on Saturday night.

High resolution equipment is there to protect the asset, the cash itself, and is very often able to read every till screen in crystal clear imagery in the pub from 15-20 feet away. Every cash note, every coin and every input, including card transactions, can be watched live, watch later on and compared to till reports, of saved to file for later use.

Modern pub companies monitor tills, every press of every button is logged.

Algorithms constantly monitor till use and alert auditors of any suspicious activity. If anything dodgy is picked but the audit "SWAT TEAM" spring into action, clips boards are set to stun, four pens are loaded into a white shirt pocket and an overly complicated calculator is at the ready.

Let's go and do AUDIT.

They turn up at the pub, show their ID, leave any resemblance of humanity at the door, and like the dementors from a Harry Potter film, they invade the business, swooping into every corner, scanning with their soulless eyes for any hint of naughtiness.

But it's when they reach the CCTV when the heat really turns up.

The auditors will watch recordings of staff and managers using the tills for any reason, zooming in to see the actual till screen and compare every key pressed visually with the till logs on the office computer. They will watch for hours and hours, focusing on every transaction as a potential theft, "did the staff sell that glass of wine as a 125ml size but give the customer a 175ml?"

"No not this time, but I'm sure I will catch someone soon."

A customer has bought a pint of lager and lime, tasted it after paying for it and asks the staff member for a little bit more lime.

The staff member adds a splash of lime to the customers drink, the customer offers no payment and walks away happy.

It's just a splash of lime, no problem.

The auditor has seen this, witnessed the crime, has the evidence, THAT STAFF MEMBER GAVE AWAY OUR GOODS FOR FREE. The auditor springs into action, gesticulating wildly to the manager, they demand the manager watch the crime on CCTV.

The manager watchers the heinous crime, shrugs his shoulders and is laughing when he says "*so what, great customer service.*"

The auditor is perplexed, shocked, stunned at the lack of contemplation, this capital crime cannot go unpunished!

Someone must pay, they are all in it together, EVERYONE.

To the auditor it is obvious, this manager is corrupt, a thief, and has no place in our morally superior organisation. "I will work tirelessly to catch this manager doing something, or even make something up, anything to remove him save our cordial stocks of the future."

How dare a manager put customer service ahead of our cordial stock integrity, just image if every manager gave away a dash of lime cordial, it could cause our shareholders to lose a whole 0.00001% of their dividend!

You may be thinking that I am exaggerating about auditors, I am not, they are robots. It's not their fault, it's what they are encouraged to do and how they are expected to behave, no clemency, no compassion, the only think that computes is the value, everything is just black and white to a financial auditor.

The above is a true story that I experienced, just the product has been changed. In the real-world pub staff and managers have to offer tiny freebies in the name of service and reputation, a splash of cordial, replace a spilled bottle of OJ and the operations team will normally support this as the customers service 'image' of the big pub company is the public face. But when audit become involved, customer service is reduced to a worthless concept, it is all about the real cost value, volume and control, customer service gets in the way, it really is that bad for staff and managers who must justify nice gestures and great customer service against a 40p loss.

Auditors suspect everyone, and often they were right, there is always someone on the rob in the pub…

In the "good old days" with really basic tills, dipping staff would use a system to track how much money has been left in the till, for now, but it will be taken at the end of their shift.

It works like this:

Customer approaches the bar, asks for 2 pints of beer.

Staff member pours 2 pints, each pint cost £1.00.

Staff member asks customer for £2.00

Customer hands £2.00 over and off he goes.

Staff member rings in a sale of just 1 pint totalling £1.00 but puts the full £2.00 into the till and closes the cash draw.

The stealing arse staff member then needs a way to keep track of how many £1.00's they have scammed to make sure they only take the correct amount of cash that has been skimmed out of the till without raising suspicion. If the skim £5.00, they must only take £5.00, or alarm bells will ring if the till doesn't balance. So many ways to do this but let me tell you about one of the oldest.

Take a match box on the back bar, turn the match box 90 degrees to the right with the first £1:00 skimmed. Continue to turn the box 90 degrees for every £1.00 you scam. Once you complete the 5th skim, turn the match box over and start the process again.

Very soon you are able to take £5.00 at the end of the night, but the till still balances.

No one would ever suspect Margaret; she has been working here for donkey's years…

Stealing cash was just the normal practice in pubs, huge amount of notes was just vanishing into everyone's pockets, staff, managers, tenants, even area managers were bent, using pubs to pay for lavish lifestyles. One area manager from the East Midlands was in cahoots with a couple of the managers who worked for him, they all had villas in Spain, big houses, and cash to burn…

Everyone knew what was going on, but until we got EPOS (electronic point of sale tills) no one could prove anything.

For the first few years of EPOS, the expectation did not meet the reality. They were not fit for purpose, but it was the start of till development into what we know them to be in 2020's.

The very first tills were programable and there were still cons to be performed to skim cash.

The first tills I remember was the Data-Checker till, it was loud, clunky and rubbish because it was easy to trick.

These Data-Checker were installed on mass throughout the country to help control cash, stock and monitor sales in detail.

But a mistake was made…

These new tills were still not wired into a modern internet, the data was very limited travelling down an old dial up phone line and information on sales and volumes was very limited.

And then there was the **P** key…

This was the Holy Grail, if you had access to a **P** key the world was your Oyster.

The **P** key was the program key for the Datachecker tills, Unscrupulous managers could program their tills to increase prices for customers without the pub companies knowing because the till still recorded the sale at the original price!

This was industrial level stealing, imagine adding 25p to every drink on a mega busy night in a venue that holds 2'000 people!

Each person has 3 drinks on average, many will have more!

25p X 6'000 transactions = £1'500.00 skimmed from the tills by the manager, but the tills balance as far as audit know.

Sometimes the area manager knew all about this cash fiddle and they always got their cut!

The problem the company had with detecting these tricks was, when the auditor went in to examine the cash income vs the stock volume the amount of money always matched the amount of drinks served, no issue found!

The Datachecker tills lasted about 10 years before being replaced with new smarter EPOS tills (electronic point of sale) that were by now connecting permanently to dedicated phone lines. Then came along the internet, the money was no longer being skimmed, lots of managers started to retire, I wonder why? The pub company profits shot up because for the first time they were receiving almost the full value of the sales and the full profits from the total turnover.

In the mid 90's EPOS tills become the industry standard, they were delivering better reporting to audit departments, the net was closing in on the people with light fingers and any hands dipping into the tills would soon be identified.

At the same time food suddenly become a big deal in pubs, it was no longer just Beefeater, Bernie, and Toby pub/restaurants.

Almost all pubs with a kitchen began focusing on food. This was mainly targeted towards families and food was taking over from the wet trade to be the main driving force behind growth and sales!

As usual, big pub companies don't like to miss out and are even faster at taking advantage of a sales opportunity. Pub kitchens were being installed and improved everywhere across the UK.

With big food pubs opening on mass, EPOS tills were embedded into the sales and reporting systems, margins could be managed better, losses prevented, this new, previously untapped huge amount of cash being passed across busy bar counters and stuffed into tills without a penny being skimmed made financial whizz kids in the city drool with envy, they now wanted a piece of the hospitality action.

Pub Company and Brewery profits were growing, fast.

The financial city was taking notice.

Financial heavyweights are sharks, they circle and find opportunities where there were none before, then they exploit regardless of the effect on society or individuals. Investment fund managers, venture capitalists and the city big wigs had been taking an interest in the changing face of UK hospitality now was the to start queuing up to invest massively into licensed retail, it was fast becoming the newest CASH COW.

Pub companies were now firmly in the crosshairs of the city, new spending money was being generated by changes in society and the city wanted a slice.

In the 70's most wives stayed at home to bring up the kids.

A few "other-half's" held down a part time job, working just a few hours per week so that she had her own money to spend how she wanted to, on herself, treat the kids or save it for a rainy day.

The husband passed on the weekly housekeeping to his lady, but no decent wife would ever spend a penny on herself, cash handed to the wife by the bread winner was spent on the family and house.

The 80's onwards saw the most dramatic change, from nowhere huge numbers of spouses suddenly had full time jobs, sometimes doubling the household income. Millions of young women were choosing a job over marrying young, and once they had a job, they were not giving up their independence, not a chance in hell. Eventually marriage happens, but instead of being a housewife, she continues to work driving up living standards and helping to flood hospitality with new money due to the new phenomenon, dual-household-income.

The second wage began driving an explosion in eating out, entertainment, family attractions and 1'000's of licensed venues where parents could completely ignore their children while they themselves slowly get pissed on lager and cider.

How many of you dumped your kids in a Wacky Warehouse and immediately ordered a double vodka on ice?

This is where generation X came from, we were left to look after ourselves once we hit double digit age. I was walking over two miles to comprehensive school at 11 years old. I would get home from a day "wagging it" and cook a Bachelors Pasta'n'Sauce for my tea because mum and dad were both at work.

Pub companies were becoming increasingly efficient, tightening the rules, introducing controls to ensure compliance, consistency, and by preventing the leaking of cash, increasing the profits like never seen before because nicking wonga had become almost impossible for the first time ever in pub history!

The other natural growth unit that pub companies have is property.

If a financial company buys a branded pub chain, that brand will have a value because brands attract customers to what they know. But when it buys a brand, it also owns the property the brands trade from, and as we all know, almost all property grows in value every year. Owning lots and lots of property gives a financial institution easy access to borrow money to buy even MORE branded pubs, so it now owns even more property, and so on and on…

The pub companies *LOVE* electronic management.

Skimming the tills has just about stopped, the bottom-line profits have jumped to new heights, here was an opportunity for city slickers to make piles new money for themselves and those with even larger mountains of old money, the city investors!

Venture capitalists realised the public, the little people who use leisure (pubs) were an untapped revenue stream and could help create the huge financial institutions we started to see publicly for the first time in the early 2000's. These financial monsters had been hidden away from an unknowing public gaze for a lifetime, but with the emergence of the World Wide Web, greed could no longer sneak around in the shadows.

Profit was pouring like rain into investors pockets, it was nothing short of a revelation, but there is no amount of money that will ever satisfy a financial investor.

Yeah, the balance sheet and stock value grows every month, but what they now want is added speed to the revenue stream.

Imagine the investment fund Chief Executive sitting behind a desk talking to advisors

"What tools can we use to further unlock this wealth tsunami, we need the sales to come in faster, bigger and just MORE MORE MORE?"

What they came up with is:

Super Pubs, the bigger the better, target children because pester power is the most irresistible force in the universe.

Families, Dad, the wife, the kids, and oh yeah, the grandparents, they don't need old Bill sipping in the tap room, drinking his three pints of bitter for £6.00 in two hours, we want 6 or 7 family members spending £55.00 on food with a few drinks in 90 minutes.

The new philosophy of these new Bigger and Financially led Pub Companies simply became this:

5. Fuck Off old Bill, you are the past and not financially viable to us with your small pension and limited spending power.
6. Welcome Mr and Mrs Smith complete with extended family and a 7-seater Renault Espace. You are about to be tempted, tricked and

unknowingly forced to hand over every penny you have using tricks in our vast armoury of profit-making skulduggery.

Did you have a favourite pub, a preferred drink, and certain beer that turned you into a genuine loyal and regular customer of a local brewer?

The vast majority of 70's pub goes did, Stones drinkers drank only Stones Bitter in Bass pubs, and Trophy Bitter was a Whitbread pub stalwart. Old school regulars picked, and stuck with, only one side of the taste test for the majority of their drinking life span.

Local beer breweries, and there were 100's of independent brewers throughout the UK, brewed beers for their local area. A certain taste enjoyed in Carlisle may not sell at all in Essex, that was the power behind a local brewer, they knew what local people wanted and connected with their regional population.

I can name dozens of brewers who no longer exist due to nothing more that the greed of even bigger brewers wanting to be the biggest. These bigger brewers are all run by city connected CEO's who are on a single mission. They want to increase the company share price and in doing so, growth their own wealth and ego.

Boddingtons comes to mind, a local beer brewed in Manchester at Strangeways brewery next to the prison. The brewer had been around for many decades, but this particular beer was first produced in 1971 for a local Mancunian market by Boddingtons and Co.

The beer became known as The Cream of Manchester and it became very popular, so popular that it was even selling while beyond the Manchester region. Boddingtons became so successful it was being exported to 40 countries around the world in the 1990's at the hight of its enjoyment.

Whitbread had bought a share of the brewer in the 1960's, and then in 1989 took full control of the brewery, removing any independence or family involvement. Whitbread expanded the brand, took it huge, marketing campaigns that were simply brilliant, the beer became a national and international success story.

Who remember the "Cream of Manchester" adverts, funny, eye catching and like nothing before, male or female, everyone wanted to try Boddingtons at least once!

Then Whitbread ruined things for the Boddingtons brand through one simple act of greed, they sold their brewing business to Interbrew, a Belgian company known as InBev so that Whitbread could become a retail pub company focusing on food, coffee and hotel rooms.

The Boddingtons brand, that had started life as a small local brewer just outside Manchester city centre and had lived at an address everyone over 20 years old has heard of, Strangeways, was eventually absorbed into Whitbread, one of the UK largest brewers and pub owners. The Cream of Manchester was now lost in a soulless nationwide public limited company, a tiddler in the fishpond. Next blow for Boddies, Whitbread sold its heart and life blood, the part of the business where it all started, the brewery side of the business. This was done to return huge share dividends to investors that would in turn trigger even bigger investment to grow its hotel and coffee brands.

After a while InBev moved production of Boddingtons Beer away from its Manchester home, the city where it was truly loved by the locals. Boddies was connected to Manchester by history, the place it was created, it had carved out a hard-won reputation for being a good price, unique taste and fantastic looking a catchy branding.

The news broke that brewing of Boddingtons was to be moved away from Strangeways brewery to Magor in South Wales.

Just the perception in Boddies drinkers' minds that the taste will no longer be the same because its brewed somewhere else was enough to see the evisceration of the Boddingtons brand, sales volume fell by 75% and it never recovered. Boddies, as it was affectionately known in Manchester, had a history, heritage, and a historical home. When a big international brewer takes over a brand that people care passionately about, the executives in the boardroom have no understanding about how much that brand, that product, that name and its history means to the people who have lived side by side with that brand throughout their lives.

What InBev did by taking Boddies away from its home was a catastrophic mistake, they took a product that symbolised Strangeways Brewery, forcefully removed it from its ancestral home, and just to add insult to injury, then they sold the brewery land to developers.

Boddingtons drinkers felt betrayed, cheated, and hurt, how dare some foreign crap lager brewery now own "their very own manc beer"?

That is the story of just one local brewery in Manchester, this story has been repeated over and over again nationwide across the UK, there was very few independent brewers left in the UK by 2020.

Why were local breweries so important?

When any business of any type is launched, it is created to fill a need that is not being filled.

In the old days before radio, telephones, TV and the World Wide Web, the only entertainment around was a local hanging, stoning a blasphemer to death throwing cabbages at people in the stocks as a punishment for stealing a turnip! If you were lucky a few people with talent would put on drama shows in the village hall.

All a bit tongue in cheek, I may have wandered a bit too far back with my metaphors, what I am saying it, people normally had no-where to go and be entertained unless they lived with wealth.

Social spaces are somewhere people gather together, after all, humans need company, people attract people and there was a gap in the market for somewhere where this mixing closely could happen. These spaces eventually became hostelries, Inn's, and eventually the very early form of what we now know as pubs.

People like beer, all kinds of beer, and beer needs a brewery to be produced. A brewery needs workers, a brewery creates employment, and also invests in the local area and community.

Many family brewers became wealthy and used their money to build better communities, traders and farms all benefitted from the local brewer, it was a win-win for the village, soon to be a town.

A brewer opening pubs to sell its own beer was genius, he pays your workers to brew the beer, distribute it.

Next, he pays farmers to grow the crops, and also millers to prepare the wheat and barley. Lastly you create and build a place where the brewery workforce and traders will spend the wages and revenue you pay them on a product you brew using their ingredients and skills.

The closed shop tied house brewery and pub business was formed and the same model is still in existence to this day.

WIN WIN WIN

The UK's biggest pub operator still owns its own brewery, rare in modern pub companies, most of the big players sold their breweries to overseas vast beer brewers like Heineken, InBev and Coors.

But not Greene King, that little local brewery in Bury St Edmunds is still brewing in the town where the interesting story of Greene King started.

A story that has become very interesting indeed over the last 20 years of super expansion.

Greene King owns over 3000 pubs, restaurants, hotels, and bars all over the UK. You have all seen the brand names they own, such as Hungry Horse, Chef and Brewer, Flaming Grill and Farmhouse, you are never far from a Greene King pub in the UK, they are absolutely everywhere.

Are pubs still pubs, no, I don't see branded retail pubs as pubs anymore. They are actually licensed retail shops.

But most of the time when you are using a pub you don't know you are in a very clever revenue generating shop that we still call a pub out of old habits.

Greene King PLC is a huge corporation, it probably happens to own your local pub or one not too far away.

As the UK's biggest pub company, it is really happy when you think you are in a small privately owned independent pub, or a small gastro pub chain where the food is freshly made! You wish!

Let's go back to the 70's again and examine Greene King from when it was still a local brewer concentrating on Cambridge and the surrounding area. They were doing really well for a local business started by Mr Greene and Mr King in 1799.

Is Greene King, our biggest pub operator, really defending our traditional pub way of life?

Or is it helping destroy pub life as we once knew it in the name of profits for shareholders?

I have already told you the story of Boddingtons and its very sad demise, but surely a house-hold name like Greene King, a local brewer, wouldn't be guilty of treating any other local brewers the same way Whitbread and InBev treated Boddingtons, would they?

First of all, who actually owns Greene King plc?

Any idea, step away from Google and guess, is it still family owned?

Surely being such a wholesome locally owned brewery, it is run by family members and local people from the local area.

Or is it shareholder owned in the UK?

Before I reveal the answer, let's go through a bit of Greene King's long and interesting history.

Greene King started up as a new brewery in 1799, created a local market and became successful in Suffolk and the surrounding area. It has been stable, reliable, and part of the community for a very long time. From its humble beginnings to the 1960's Greene King brewed beer in Bury St Edmunds and sold it in its brewery owned, and other, local pubs to town residents and travellers alike.

The Good Old Days.

But something changed, in1996 a different mind-set had entered the board room, to the old-time traditionalist's is would have felt like the Devil itself had crashed through the fortress doors to cast the very soul of the business into darkness and pits of fire.

Suddenly much bigger wants, needs, desires were the focus of those in charge, financial backing from the city was sniffing around.

Allegedly, the financial backers ready to invest in expansion needed a different type of leadership if they are to supply funding. They wanted a cold hearted financially driven egotistical monster to drive the future growth that makes investing worth it. This person must be cold hearted, an elite who knows nothing of the little people's plights, they need cutthroat and calculating business magician to guarantee the elusive Eternal Growth!

Would the right person or people be found, eventually?

When Greene King purchased Rayments Brewery it appeared to be a one off in 1931. Did Rayments come begging to GK to buy?

It was an unusual take over as the Lake family were left to run the company until the 1960's when GK finally took over the running of the Rayments Brewery and their 30+ tied pubs completely.

This demonstrates that GK was not a ruthless brewery, did they take over Rayments in 1931 just to help them out financially? Maybe that is why the Lake family was left in control for so long?

I cannot answer that question because I just don't know why Rayments ended up being fully owned and managed by GK, but have you ever heard of Rayments

Brewery or the brands of beer they brewed up until the 60's that are now owned by GK PLC?

I bet the answer is NO.

To be honest that one take-over is irrelevant to this tale, our real story of money, shares and greed really begins when further acquisitions were made a full 35 years later.

What changed in Greene King to suddenly make them predators? They were not snapping up other breweries until the mid-1990s, it would appear something had changed, was it new leadership I described a couple of paragraphs earlier because the expectations had changed from local needs, to The City of London demands?

It was 1996 when Greene King decided to start swooping in on weaker, smaller, breweries and snapped them at bargain prices.

The gloves were off, Greene King PLC, financially backed by billions in investment, was on the war path and splashing the cash.

This is the list of breweries bought and CLOSED by Greene King PLC, the friendly local brewer.

- Bought Rayments Brewery in 1931
- Bought Magic Pub Company in 1996
- Bought Hungry Horse in 1996
- Bought Moreland Brewery in 1999
- Bought Old English Inns in 2001
- Bought Morrells in 2002
- Bought a large part of Laurel Pub Co in 2004 (this was the old Whitbread locals' estate)
- Bought Ridleys brewery in 2005
- Bought Belhaven Brewery in 2005
- Bought Hardy and Hansons Brewery and pubs in 2006
- Bought Loch Fyne restaurant chain in 2007
- Bought Cloverleaf 2011
- Bought Realpubs 2011
- Bought Capital Pub Company 2011
- Acquisition of Spirit Pub Company 2015

As you can see from the list of breweries and pub companies acquired aggressively by Greene King PLC over around 20 years, this local, friendly and lovely small brewer was not really supporting regional brewing as they would like you to think.

Do a quick on-line search to see if any of these bought up breweries are still brewing their original beers in the original brewery and still financially supporting their local communities?

You won't find any!

Almost all of these famous local beers, produced by the once famous, great and revered local breweries, have been moved to a huge beer factory to be brewed under license by a mass producer. That is not even the worse thing, often the recipe is changed, such as having the alcohol % reduced, to save money on duty and VAT taxes?

Questioning what I'm telling you?

Just check out Old Speckled Hen to see the truth. Greene King reduced this historical, famous, and enormously loved Cask Ale from 5.2% to 4.5%.

I don't want to sound cynical or call Greene King a money grabbing deceitful company, it could just be a coincidence that they pay less duty tax if the alcohol percentage is reduced, but regardless of what they say, it DID change the taste and feel in the mouth, drinkers could sense the difference in strength.

Old Speckled Hen was ruined in 2006.

Back to my question about ownership?

I asked you "who actually owns Greene King PLC?"

We are talking about Greene King plc, the local friendly brewer who owns your local pub, fills supermarket shelves with cans and bottles of its local beers, and calls almost all its nationwide branded pubs "you're local" is owned by:

CK Assets in Hong Kong

they bought Greene King for nearly 3 billion pounds in 2019.

Who the hell are CK Assets I hear you ask?

They are a property developer registered in the Cayman Islands for tax reasons and has its head office in Hong Kong.

The company is listed on stock exchanges and is an investment company that pays its shareholders dividends when its investments are successful and very profitable.

What that basically means to us in the UK is:

- it will only spend money when there is an almost <u>guaranteed</u> return on the money they invest.
- The chances of the staff being paid anymore that minimum wage is ZERO because shareholders want their money first.
- Cayman Islands are considered a Tax Haven, make of that what you will.
- The destruction of communities. In the past local brewers invested in their local communities, but the new Greene King PLC of today and the future, close breweries, destroy jobs and the money vanishers quickly offshore.
- GK is a supersized company with huge purchasing power that drives down the price paid to producers and so caps wages and investment by their suppliers.
- Greene King customers are not customers! They are financial assets to be sweated at every opportunity.
- The Pandemic is almost over as we sit early in 2022, hospitality is fully open, but more money saving tricks than ever before are being used to claw back shareholder losses, shareholder required results… or they take their money out.
- The only people who will pay for the Covid lockdowns in the pub companies are the pub teams, the minimum wages earners.

Not such a local brewer after all…

This story is not just about Greene King and their victims, it is about how we, the public are being fooled, conned, and used to fill shareholder pockets by financial companies who invest as little as possible in the staff and pub mangers who work at the sharp end, and the people who pass the money over the bar, the customers who buy the expensive trendy drinks, often with reduced alcohol, and a microwave re-heated sausage and mash…

Customers and workers deserve better, much much better…

Chapter 4

Men in Hoodies and Flip-Flops

I'm old, there, I said it, a dinosaur, on the scrap heap, an old and decrepit fool at the ripe age of 56! Or so I am told by the new youthful bosses…

Call me a sentimentalist, traditionalist, old fashioned, out of touch and outdated, am I holding onto the past when I should just move with the times?

Not if moving with the times is the wrong move.

I don't really care what others of a more modern persuasion think, as a person who started working decades ago when the boss wore a tie, I still respect a role of authority, a position of seniority, my line manager, male or female, any gender they want to be in the new fluid world, I don't care, just act and look like the boss and I will welcome you as a happy subordinate and look forward to any guidance and instruction from my line manager.

I'm all for casual dress, feeling comfortable, I'm down with that, who wants to be overly "managerial" in the pub, the customers like a little bit of informality, the modern manager type landlord or landlady should be one of the people.

But if I'm sitting down with team members dealing with a serious HR issue, I will be wearing a formal shirt, shoes and I'm clean shaven so that the person I am sitting across from knows I am treating them with the greatest of respect. It is so important that a team member knows I am taking the matter seriously and I am the one they can trust, will not twist the truth, or deny the facts, to behave without reproach and deliver the correct result.

There is a time and a place for flip flops, I myself have worn brightly coloured foam Jesus sandals when on my holidays enjoying the sun, I have even been known to wear crocs like the sad old git I am.

But I wouldn't go to court in a striped cape and mask and surely no one would turn up at a christening dressed as a 7-foot bright pink rubber cock and balls complete with prince Albert, you get my drift.

There is a time and a place…

One day my new area manager, or BDM as they are now called, turned up to a formal business meeting wearing a hoodie and flip flops. I looked at him, my professional soul sank, my respect withered, the journey I had enjoyed with what was once a fantastic company that that had standards, expectations on personal presentation, was obviously now aimed in a very different direction.

How can I take someone seriously when they are dressed exactly the same as the dope smoker, I kicked out the night before?

This to me was the beginning of the end, not only for me with this company, but also for the company's reputation and standards.

How could anyone take someone seriously if this is the first thing, they say to you on the first visit to you in place of work…

And looking like a back-packer for fucks sake…

Area manager:

"Hi brooooo, greeaat to meet you, we will be spectacular together, you managing the engine, Moi steering the rudder while delivering brand projection to ergonomically grow the business as a family team, me you and the staff, all and sharing our minds and success"

Me:

Kill Me, Kill Me Now… (said inside my head)

I just smiled, a professional response eluding from my face.

This guy, who I actually met, is now telling me we are to be family!

FUCK OFF, if were related I would change my name and deny his existence because he is an absolute prized wanker of the highest order!

He is talking a language that I just don't understand, you may have suffered yourself having to sit across from a nose pieced bearded poncho wearing prat who is now your BDM regurgitating the new bible: MANAGEMENT SPEAK…

If you are unsure if you have even been a victim of this bizarre form of communication, it is vitally important that you cleanse yourself immediately just in case you have been infected with this dreadful university spread virus party created by watching the sycophantic American rom-com TV series called Friends.

To apply the antidote and build future resistance levels high enough to repel further verbal bullshit attacks try watching any Guy Ritchie films, Brassic, The Full Monty and reading the Sun newspaper.

How do you recognise if you have been a past victim of this verbal projectile vomiting crime?

What are the clues that tell you a toxic exposure has occurred in a conversation, that you have been unlucky to be subjected to a load of bollocks by a new age modern BDM?

Quickly, think back to the conversations you had had with the very youthful and inexperienced leaders of the company you currently work for, have you ever heard any of these phrases?

WARNING, MANAGEMENT SPEAK MAY COURSE ANGER

"That part of the project is net-new"; *"let's take this off-line"*; *"feel free to ping me"*; *"after careful consideration we have decided to pivot"*; *"bucketize"*; *"synergise"*; *"core competencies"*; *"idea shower"*; *"the strategic staircase"*; *"square the circle"*; *"cross pollinate"* and my personal favourite from a recent conversation *"mission critical"*.

Over the last few decades pubs have evolved from being managed by a landlord / landlady, with skill and experience, knowledge and foresight, into licensed retail outlets led by diversity focused gender erasing woke non-threatening green environmentalist marketing interns who control a new generation of managers like puppets on a string.

Unfortunately, the area managers, sorry, I mean BDMs, like the one I'm talking about above is not alone, there are hundreds and thousands of these pricks, every gender, every skin tone, every size.

The problems start when you have to talk to any of them.

If you end up with speaking to a prat similar to the one I met with, it means you will have to swallow more bollocks than Debbie Does Dallas ever did (Google it).

Many of the new BDM area managers come across as dope smoking, obnoxious, arrogant, unshaven university leaving entitled wankers with no business experience, very little useful skill set or connection to the working classes. Worst of all, I will be forced to listen their bullshit and obey supercilious instruction for years to come if I want to hang onto my job as an ageing licensee.

Fuck That… In my time with that company, you would not believe the number of hours I spent trying to tune out the hyperbole bouncing around a meeting room. Instead of being with our teams and customers driving business through genuinely connecting with people we were being forced into listening to these pricks and cunts self-flagellating.

I will never get the lost forever looooooong, extremely dull and deeply unpleasant hours of time taken away from my life back.

Unless you have been in a one-way meeting with an overly excited BDM who is showing the composure of a puppy watching it's owner fill the food bowl, you will never know the pain inflicted by listening to a rattling on dick-head talk about attracting diversified demographics and ultimately enabling a "retargeted data led" price increase that will pick the low hanging fruit and place it into the basket of the bottom line.

It was fucking painful. I'm sure my ears have bled a few times!

For those last few years in pub management, I did everything possible to avoid talking to any "new" area managers. I'd would rather spend my time licking and nibbling the sores on the faces of lepers living in a colony on a remote island with no power or plumbing than spend a single minute within the company of my new Boss-Dumb-Moron.

Feel free to insert your name of choice to replace the term of. Boss-Dumb-Moron, you will probably want to replace it with the name of your new area manager, or BDM, because you probably feel the same way as I did if you have been forced to sit in a meeting with these clowns with the make-up or big feet.

This description will resonate if you have ever been required to report to one of these "blue sky thinkers" as your boss at any time you have managed, assisted or been a worker in pubs in the last 10 years.

I'll stick with the old ones who deserved the effort we put into running our pubs because they were inspirational. We enjoyed spending time with and working for great bosses.

Glenn C, Nicky B, Hugh M, Ben A, Chris C, Pete W, Old fashioned John from Liverpool who has, a number of years ago, sadly died, you should all feel proud in the knowledge that the teams reporting to you felt valued, cared for, trusted, supported and importantly, treated like friends.

But not this new lot, they really do not care about you!

Area managers are called something different depending on which company they are working for.

BDM is one I am familiar with; it is the abbreviation of Business Development Manager, but I like to change the words for a much more suitable description such as Bully-Dumb-Moron.

Then there is RBM, this one is short for Retail Business Manager, but I have changed it to Retard-Bellend-Motherfucker.

I could easily carry on with this renaming acronym, but I should get back to writing.

And just because you now know the "alternative" words you can use, promise me that you would never be so cruel as to describe a person you respect so much in such a way.

The quality of area managers, or BDM's as I will use to refer to all area managers from now just to keep things simple, who are working for most pub companies these days are utterly useless, self-centred and to be honest, embarrassing compared to the generation before.

I once had to listen to a modern BDM moaning and groaning about sexism in my pub because my doormen upset his girlfriend by holding open a door for her in heavy rain because they thought the right thing to do was to be nice, but it turns out they were being fascists…

How dare my doormen be so passively aggressive by forcing this man's life partner into a gender box that stereotypes a birth-giving human as a woman!

Who knew we should only be chivalrous to ladies who are over 35 years old, or didn't attend university in the last 10 years, it's a brave new world!

My opinion of this idiot BDM? Tosser of the highest order.

My new BDM had ended his Uni life around 2 years before he stood in front of me talking absolute bollocks!

He was probably a representative for diversity at the metro-elite London student union and this is where he has learned is echo chamber management skills, "the only opinion that matters are my own reflected in my echo chamber back to myself."

Having completed a six-month internship at a global soft drink brand, in the south, he now believes he is totally suited for a multi-site management role based around South Yorkshire, a traditional blue-collar area with working class roots and values…

In his perfectly preened designer stubble empty head he thinks Doncaster could be twinned with Brighton!

This is not going to end well…

The modern BDM are very difficult to understand or take seriously. As a licensee I spent 30 years keeping knob-heads, pill-heads, dope-heads, and big-heads out of my pubs, but now in some strange and bewildering twist of fate I now have someone with all those tosspot characteristics and qualities, plus bad dress sense and a degree in management speak, as my boss for fucks sake!

How many working class people, in any trade, not just pubs, reading this will recognise the following continually repeated scenario?

A new BDM is appointed to be in charge of 15 pubs, almost all of which are pubs in working class areas and have been delivering reasonably well for the last 5 years under the recently moved on BDM who is now in his early 50's.

Surely no modern pub company would move a successful BDM just because of age, would they?

These 15 pub managers have worked hard for the old BDM and been collectively very successful. They don't understand why they have lost their boss and he has been replaced by a BDM that no one has heard of and is in his early 20's?

The whole area of 15 pubs and their managers has a collective pub management experience of 125 years between them, experience that is learned, proven, tested, and understood.

These managers, along with the old BDM, have served their time, worked well together, shared their success, and had widespread mutual respect.

New BDMs are a little different! What these up-starts do have is a degree from the London Metropolitan University (LMU) that once was a run-down bottom-feeder tech college (ranked the worst Uni in London many times), his only job prior to his new senior position was to be a rep for a major soft drink company, he has absolutely no experience running a licensed retail operation!

Oh, hang on, I'll have to take it all back!

Turns out he once worked as a 16-year-old waiter in a Toby Carvery over the summer before he went on to 6th form college to undertake 2 years of media studies, so apparently, he knows the pub trade inside out, doesn't he?

He has spent three years at LMC where he spent most of his time in the pub, or because he has the gift of the gab and can fool any person under the influence of alcohol and drugs to remove their clothes, in the sexually transmitted disease clinic.

After his years of "studying" he leaves with a 2.2 in creative writing and gender studies! This guy, armed with the knowledge of which penicillin clears up knob-rot fastest, is on the verge of starting his well-deserved and appropriate career as a checkout operator job at Pound-World.

But NO, at the last second, he is saved, after all, his education in gender, media and creative writing will serve him perfectly as a BDM in a national pub company, this is just the leadership that 15 seasoned pub managers are looking for, a 22-year-old with itchy balls!

Did I forget to mention that he is the Op's director godson?

That fact alone appears to make him fully qualified and the perfect candidate to lead, inspire and manage the financial performance of 15 pub managers and teams who turned over in excess of 22 million in sales last year.

In his deluded wet dreams of future BDM success, award ceremonies and a 60k per year salary, surely, he is the pick of all those available to lead 15 experienced managers into a new era of super-success? Can you imagine the enthusiasm of 15 working class area pub managers as they look forward to meeting their new "leader of the pack" and him telling them how to run their pubs, manager their teams and deliver what he thinks their long-term customers will want from their local from now on?

This appointment of a new, and untested, BDM to manage an established area of successful pubs is about as strategically smart as it would have been appointing Black Adder's Baldric as PM instead of Churchill in May 1940!

I sat in the first area meeting with this smiling, bouncing, almost giddy little boy spouting management speak as his first language and I won't repeat the licensees' comments after the meeting, far far too rude even for my writing…

Most long in the tooth managers like myself would agree that thinking no longer matters, compliance is the new master!

Do as you are told, do not deviate, do not question, do not engage brain, you will follow the brief absolutely as instructed.

Now tick this box to accept and agree with the instruction regardless of how daft it is, or you will forfeit your job, your home, your pension and your life!

Ok that may sound a little over the top, no company is that ruthless and you may be right. But the nasty career hungry new BDM's will use any missing compliance tick-box as a good enough reason to attack you if you are not showing total obedience and capitulation. Everyone working for a big pub company will have had the "tick-box" of compliance pop up on a screen in the recent past, heavy handed forceful top-down management, so maybe my line about losing your job, or at least deeply affecting your life, is not so far-fetched after all!

A modern BDM will happily scrap your career, make you homeless and ruin your life for years to come in a nano second if they are not obeyed, saluted, even loved, without question.

The modern landscape the lower classes have to negotiate in pub companies is treacherous to say least. It has become about worshiping your line manager without daring to question right and wrong. Being thankful and kissing the arse of the new boss is the main survival tool for a pub manager new and old.

The all-powerful trendy BDM of today must be honoured, petals thrown under their feet as they walk for allowing you to exist in their universe and you MUST be increasing their bonus and status at every opportunity. YOU MUST NOT CRITICISE, EVER.

The really unlucky pub managers end up opening their hotel room doors on a drunken area night out to a sex pest BDM, yes it does happen more now than ever before.

These modern area managers don't actually know how utterly useless they are at the job because they never worked alongside their old times counterparts.

Modern BDMs predecessors have been side-lined because they know a degree in Hand Embroidery is NOT more useful than someone without a degree but does have 5 years' experience as a deputy manager in an actual pub, learning from an expert licensee and manager. In the modern world of pub companies experience and knowledge has been downgraded and eventually I think it will be removed completely.

Taking away the value of experience means that there is no one left to challenge these new BDMs with their bad attitudes, bad ideas and poor skill set.

Why does a pub company remove its front-line customer care people with real experience from its pubs?

COST

I will talk about costs later on, for now just accept that costs increase steadily over the years with sustained success.

But that very same success becomes a key reason that a successful manager is dumped through the exit door.

Just for your information, if you do fancy taking a 3-year course to achieve a BA (Hons) in Hand Embroidery you can sign up at the University of Creative Arts (UCA).

Apparently, it is the perfect grounding and knowledge base to enter the hospitality industry in a senior position.

Why knew!

Warning

Are you an entrepreneurial highly trained pub manager who wants to run a great pub for local people, but also work with the financial protection a large pub company because you don't want to risk all your savings by taking on a tenancy?

So, you decide to apply for a job in a big pub company and attend the interviews where you describe yourself as a creative and positive sales driver. You tell the panel that you feel you set yourself apart by the crazy and fun promotions that will make the pub you are managing better that the rest of the BDM's area pubs, given a chance you will become a superstar in the company and help deliver sales and profit. You are confident, need very little supervision and build close family type teams who stay with you for many years.

This stability will create a strong, long term customer favourite pub that will be a model that other sites can copy.

The panel will listen carefully, they will tell you that you are a "perfect prospect, suit the culture, and we need to find the right fit within our portfolio." That is what you heard…

What they are actually saying is:

GET OUT YOU TROUBLE CAUSING REBLE, HOW DARE YOU USE YOUR OWN MIND?

WE WANT NOBOBY WHO DARES TO THINK FOR THEMSELVES TO DO OUR BIDDING.

THE MARKETING DEPARTMENT GODS MUST NEVER BE DISOBEYED AND NEVER QUESTIONED, EVER—IT IS THE LAW.

THE COMPLIANCE TEAM INSIST THAT YOU MUST AGREE TO BECOME A PUB COMPANY ZOMBIE AND FOLLOW ALL INSTRUCTION WITHOUT THINKING FOR YOURSELF.

WHO DOES THIS REBEL THINK THEY ARE?

LITTLE SUPERVISION, WE DON'T THINK SO.

YOU WILL BE MICRO-MANAGED BY YOUR BDM TO THE POINT OF HARASSMENT AND YOU WILL SHUT YOUR MOUTH AND EAT SHIT WHILE WE CONTROL EVERYTHING YOU DO, SAY, THINK.

The mistake you made was telling the interviewing panel that you are a very experienced entrepreneurial pub manager.

They don't want that anywhere near the business, can you imagine the chaos if a free-thinking manager influenced the other drones on the area, the BDM's and head-office prats could be found out for what they really are, useless. Compliance is the only accepted business model in financial market owned pub companies.

The modern BDM cannot cope with anyone in their team having their own ideas because that will uncover an appalling lack in their own ability. They bully to keep control, use fear of losing your job as a weapon to disable the minds of those reporting to them.

Over exaggerating, am I?

Pick a company and do a web search on employee satisfaction, makes some very interesting reading.

This brings forward an interesting question about BDMs and pub companies wanting success?

Why not employ a manager full of ideas, drive, creativity, and a history of huge long term profitable delivery?

They only want corporate success, NOT individual success.

Big pub companies did once celebrate success with lavish balls, big ceremonies with stylish awards, great food, free flowing booze and dancing until the early hours.

Individuals were celebrated for their work, ideas, and performance.

Pub managers were praised and cheered by the bigger bosses and their fellow pub managers; we had some very big nights.

I had a good run in the last pub company I worked for, 9 years with consecutive awards including the biggest one they give out, but it all ended with a change in high level leadership that ultimately filters down to the bigger bosses' positions.

I guess the high-level leadership focus changes from person to person and maybe the new financial people right at the top didn't find the bigger bosses ruthless enough?

The only thing celebrated these days seems to compliance, audit results and wages savings.

Sometimes the different regions of the company will put together low-key get-togethers to pat people on the back, but it's not at the topflight level it was before with black tie, ball gowns and champagne.

Dress suits and feather boas have been replaced with chinos, leggings, and sparkling wine.

Modern branded retail pubs are a collective entity, there can be no winners or losers because there are not individuals.

Just like little kids on sports day in Surrey, everyone is a winner in 2022, everyone gets a trophy.

Groups of branded pubs are judged on the brand integrity and total dominance; sorry I mean compliance.

As long as every unit, every pub, and each individual within that brand does exactly the same thing, even if it means doing something BADLY, this is seen as success, a result, brand growth…

Brand specification delivery is what really matters to brand managers and the city. because branded pub groups can carry a value far higher than the pubs as individual stand-alone units.

Performing badly is not a terrible thing as long as it is consistent across the brand, it is dressed up as a public success story.

Why? Because brands attract investment from shareholders.

Brands are the brainchild of marketing executives, people who went to Uni and landed a 2.2 degree in hospitality at Hull University.

These marketing plebs and their teams spend leisure time in Pret a Manger, All Bar One and The Botanist consuming Sweet Potato Fries, Char-latte and are slowly working through the extensive list of cocktails one by one.

They are not found local pubs with local people, even the ones owned by the company they work for, so how the hell do they know what should be offered, due to branding, in your local pub?

Even harder to understand, marketing teams talk to pathetic modern BDMs about pubs they have never visited and what the BDM does not understand, and they decide between themselves what brand to drop a local pub into.

It is fucking madness when you break it down…

They live in Cambridge, the local they are branding is in Scunthorpe and the brand is based on a metro-elite pub in Knotting Hill.

I'll will return to brand power later on.

The following is an example of the type of conversation that takes place daily within modern branded pubs everywhere in the UK:

Experienced pub manager:

"But boss, my customers don't like posh hand cooked crisps, they just want a bag of walkers ready salted or cheese and onion."

BDM / marketing manager:

"We are a brand, your customers will like what we tell them to like, you people in the North think you are different and special! As your bosses we always know better and what is best for your customers. Eventually they will realise that my our is the only way and that we will be telling them what they SHOULD LIKE and WILL LIKE from now on.

"And you, Mr manager, it is your job to impose our will and convince your customers that they are all wrong!

"It is the marketing department and ourselves who understands more about what the public want, your regulars and locals just need to get on with it because their opinion does not matter, the posh crisps are superior and sell well in on Chelsea high street!"

Experienced pub manager:

"But boss, these hand cooked crisps cost twice as much, and the bag is only half the size, we are losing sales as people nip to the pub across the road to buy what they actually want…"

BDM / brand manager:

"If your sales volumes shrink, that's ok as we make a better margin for selling less, this is good, this is modern thinking.

It means we are doing a great job and the marketing director will send me an email telling us we have done well.

But if the profit falls on crisps and snacks because you don't sell enough, that Mr manager, will be your fault, you will be displaying weakness, you will have not convinced your customers that we are right and in failing to do so you have let the marketing team, and myself down, shame on you!

This failure will trigger a personal performance review of yourself that could lead to disciplinary action."

So according to your BDM and an idiot marketing manager all you had to do was prove that our commercial and marketing people are gods and are never wrong.

They told you what to sell, but if YOU fail you are in big trouble.

Long live the Gods in Head Office, the all-knowing bringers of BDM and bigger bosses bonus payments.

People from a pub background recognise at least one BDM from what I have described, the young, thrusting, power hungry gobbledygook talking male, female or gender-neutral BDM!

But there is another type, a far more sinister and dangerous BDM, the one who climbs the slippery pole by leaving their hotel door open, reliving his or her bigger bosses' tension after a long car journey.

"How friendly is she/he, offering the Op's manager a place to stay so he/she is much closer to their first meeting in the morning, less driving will help him perform and do on excellent job."

Yeah, I bet it will, nudge nudge wink wink…

If you didn't know, some greasy poles come complete with G-Strings, KY Jelly, batteries, and butt plugs…

I have come across some of the smartest people I have ever met working in pubs, more women than men if I'm honest, I think women make better pub managers, better BDMs and better senior managers.

They are not led by their dicks and ego.

Saying that, many men and women in pub companies have some of the highest levels of integrity I have even known.

But not all. I once had the pleasure to work with a BDM in the East Midlands who was a breath of fresh air. She understood the high street and realised that the days of 1970's steak houses well and truly over.

And then there is the ones who will stop at nothing to achieve personal success, pole climbing to become the queen of BDM's, the shining star without any evidence or ability, the golden-haired centre piece of every meeting, but sadly, she is just a trophy to look at and relax with but is a little too dim to realise that is all she is.

Just how desperate is it for a female BDM to need everyone to fawn over her, desire her, the reach her goal by using her body to advance because her mind on its own would never be enough to climb the stairs of power?

You know the type; some people call it sucking (up to) the boss!

I always thought losing lots of weight, dying your hair platinum blonde and wearing dresses and skirts so short that no one will never need to ask the question "are you fully waxed or do you have a Brazilian?" Just like so many others, you have seen the evidence.

I though looking after yourself carefully, managing diet, teeth whitening and endless hours in the gym was all about presenting yourself with confidence and self-empowerment, not just being popular?

I was wrong…

As an area we were once out in West Yorkshire on a night out with our new BDM. Yet another dickhead with an intolerable ego and very little ability. He has not yet learned how to control his still rampant teenage hormones, it can only be his own childish, silly behaviour and immaturity that is stopping his teenage hormones from changing into the adult versions!

At one point he started a fight with one of the young male pub managers who was working for him! That is how brittle his ego was, using violence to force his dominance as the boss. All that young manager had done was "motor-boat" a rather large breasted female manager for a laugh, and when he did it, we all fell about laughing uncontrollably, even has playful victim was giggling and laughing along because it was very funny. Unfortunately, her boyfriend found out, he was not happy, and she changed he tune from enjoying and laughing about the incident to being abused. The boyfriend complained to our child-like BDM, and he reacted with anger and venom ending in a scuffle with the young male manager.

Our infant BDM now has his dander up, teenage like levels of testosterone are now running un-checked through his body, he has had a couple of drinks and now cannot stop himself pelvis thrusting towards young female managers.

Later on, he was trying to drunkenly kiss some of the young female manages until he eventually finds his target, the one who flirts back a little, the one he now knows will go that little bit further for a great, polished and bonus boosting quarterly appraisal. She wants a career boost that her ability as a pub manager has sadly failed to deliver because she is just mediocre at best and overlooked for a career boosting big pub appointment.

She knows deep down that she will never be good enough to win the top posts, the best pubs or even land any promotion she craves so much.

It is time to play dirty, really really deep down dirty to get ahead…

I wonder how many of you recognise anything, behaviour, or actions of others, or yourself, from this chapter?

Do these stories sound real?

Shamefully these stories are based on real events, this is the underlying culture in some pub companies. I have talked about bigger pub companies using city finance to snap up smaller brewers and pub companies. At times a decent PLC would buy what was known as the dregs of the pub industry because it was so cheap to buy it was not possible to say no.

Buying a company that has within it some of the nastiest and slimy people you could ever meet is always going to be a challenge, how do you stop these snapped up for pennies wankers poisoning the clean waters of the purchasing company?

I will get to some of these people later…

As someone who has journeyed with these changing times of hospitality it can be difficult to look back and see those great days of pubs slipping away for good. There was so much promise, fun, satisfaction and success.

The megalomaniacs were not involved, it wasn't about money, shares, egos, it was just about getting together, having a pint and a laugh with friends.

I hope that anyone reading this book will get some ideas of why and how it all went wrong, financial market owned pub companies have become the enemy and humble drinkers and traditional pubs.

So where are our great British pubs heading?

It can be difficult to see the wood for the trees or allow me to explain what is going on in a much more representative way of modern pub company middle management structure.

It is fucking impossible to see any positive future for pubs because the ever-thickening forest of bosses with stupid job titles coming through the doors spoils the fucking view.

How many bosses do I need?

Many years ago, we had an area manager, the pub managers boss, and an Op's manager who is the area managers' boss.

That was it, you would see your area manager about once a fortnight, your Op's manager once every 3 months, there was lots of other people at head office, but I didn't meet them, and they didn't affect my day-to-day job.

Every 90 days or so an auditor called in for the day, where I was based, it was normally Malcolm or Stuart, and they counted everything, balanced the books and stocks and off they went.

Working in pubs in modern times means you get a never-ending shit stream of "bosses without portfolio" that come through the door and think they are important and in charge of us and our pub. You will be amazed how many "made up new jobs" have been created by supposedly slick and efficient business process aimed at reducing paperwork and time away from the customers.

Every single one of these "new ways of working" actually increases the time needed to complete paperwork, ticking boxes, taking time away from the paying guests.

What does the never-ending list of bosses visiting look like?

Enjoy the list:

Op's Director; Op's Manager; BDM; Audit Manager; Auditor; Area Audit Leader; Regional HR Director; Regional HR Manager; HR Business Partner; Area HR Liaison; Compliance Manager; Brand Manager; Head of Learning; Regional Food Development Chef Manager; Area Chef; Gaming Machine Manager; Security and Risk Manager; Licensing Manager; In-House Financial Auditor; Sport and Communication Manager; EPOS Manager.

Yes, it's a big list, and it's not nearly complete, these are just the ones I can be bothered to remember. Many companies have different names for the roles, but this is the ridiculous number of prats demanding your precious time you could get, numerous times throughout the year, calling in to do nothing but speak down to you, inspect something or perform a fucking pointless audit.

Worst part, if you are on a well-deserved mid-week day off because you worked the whole weekend, the wanker who has just called in unannounced will call your idiot child of a BDM and report you for not being at work or available to kiss their arse.

You will then get a call from said BDM asking you where you are, have you taken the appropriate time off that fits with the sales trends and insisting that you email your rota explaining exactly when you will be at working this week, and the prick is demanding you do this on your DAY OFF for fucks sake.

In modern branded pubs the manager spends so much time dealing with "company people" that their week ends up being extended to 70+ hours working time because the manager still needs to put the hours in to keep the wages down!

If an auditor come in, the manager is required to go around the pub with the auditor as they count everything, check the paperwork, the office number and balance the cash.

This may take 6, 7 or 8 hours, hours and you were supposedly working on the bar or in the kitchen for all those hours.

When an auditor comes unannounced as normal, you have to ask a staff member to cover you while you stay with them for most the day.

This will increase the staffing hours by that same amount that you need to cover yourself while you accompany the auditor.

This extra number of hours is extra to those agreed with the prat BDM last week, what he is allowing you to use this week.

Even though you are a general manager of a multi-million-pound turnover business you are NOT allowed to increase the hours used for staffing even if the reason is valid!

If you do increase the number of hours you use in any week above what the BDM has allowed you will receive a disciplinary notice from the BDM, even though you were taking the correct and appropriate action in your pub.

Even though you may have 30 years' experience you no longer have the ability or authority to make decisions that may affect the BDM's reputation and future employment with their line manager, the Op's manager.

For modern pub managers it never ends! You are expected to work 40 hours on the bar just to maintain low labour costs, but the BDM will call you and say, "why have you not responded to my critical email yet?" Simple really, the office is in the cellar, and you are the only person working the bar, but that means you are being argumentative and not compliant!

The constant barrage of emails, the video clips, the printed brief, the pop-up message on the tills, the phone calls, what exactly do they want from managers with just two hands?

From the experienced manager perspective, we can either serve guests with perfect customer service and a great smile as their friendly landlord, or we can be our own secretary attending to priority emails, phones calls and face to face un-planned meetings?

We cannot do both…

Some of the modern BDM's and their bosses have enabled the new trend of dressing down for work. I just cannot understand why some people in positions of authority think it's ok to go to a meeting with someone they expect to respect them wearing the clothes worn at yesterday's boozy family and friends informal BBQ?

As professional pub managers we must accept as our line manager may turn up to a business meeting in a hoody, track suit jackets, scruffy jeans, shorts, scruffy trainers and even flip-flops.

To all the older pub managers, let's be honest and say it out loud, how can we take these people seriously?

10 years ago, we were stopping these coke snorting, dope stinking wannabe uber cool dickheads from coming into our pubs.

Anyone dressed in a tracksuit or chav-pants was viewed with deep suspicion, professional pub managers don't allow these so-called followers of leisure fashion, or stupid wankers as I call them, coming into our pubs, ruining our reputation, and driving away the nice people that we want sat in our seats.

How things have changed, now these wannabe gangster look-a-likes come into our pubs, act the big man, and talk loudly to show who is boss while telling the smartly dressed pub manager what they want us to do with this pub on "their" area.

The world has gone barking mad...

What was wrong with a boss making an effort and dressing for work? Dressing for a skateboard park outing with teenage mates is an odd look for a boss, dressed in a way that indicates smoke you weed all day, is in my opinion, not a great look for a for a business and people manager, especially when alcohol is involved.

If you are a manager from the old days, you will be made obsolete soon, you cost too much, it's not your fault you received a pay rise every year and are now seen as too costly for a high-income low-cost business model and young BDM's really don't like old time manager salaries suppressing potential bonuses.

As a long-term older manager, you will be slowly coerced into believing you are past it and useless, you don't deserve the money you are earning because you no longer deliver a vision for the future, how could you possibly have vision age your age?

You will all be replaced as quickly as HR allows by young exciting, vibrant and programable people who have not yet realised that in a few years' time they themselves will be replaced with vending machines that can receive phone payment directly by Bluetooth while simultaneously checking your ID and age.

What are your thoughts on all people having a chip implanted?

You may not like the idea of it, but I think it's coming…

A chip would confirm you are legally allowed to consume alcohol as you enter the pub, next use you phone or watch to order a drink, a signal containing your drink desire informs the vending machine what you want, and the drink is dispensed.

Don't believe me?

Check out the latest cruise ships that already have robot bar tenders making perfect cocktails on YouTube. They are simply amazing, efficient, and precise every time, plus they don't expect a tip.

Many millions of people have loved working in the pub business, they were there to serve all types of customers, talk to them, befriend them, serve them again, and at the end of the session it was those friendly staff who would send the customers' home. Never forget the good old days and history of the UK pubs.

When I started glass collecting in The Ship in the early 80's I knew there was a big business somewhere in the background, but as far as your employment went it was the contract between the landlord of the pub and yourself, nothing else was ever said and to be honest, why would a 17-year-old glass collector care?

When and why did that change, and people became nothing more than number?

I am hoping that by the time you finish this angry rant of a book you will have a far better understanding about how, and why, pubs have evolved over the last 40 years and how they have changed into what is almost completely opposite of what pubs were created for in the first place, Society has radically shifted in almost every aspect in the UK over the last four decades, 1980's British consumer base is almost unrecognisable by anyone looking back from 2022 and there is just one, a single main reason behind all this dramatic change.

Everything I have written about and described up to this point is part of an ever-changing plan intended to mixed-up, complicate and induce chaos intentionally into a business framework. Changes in how business is done by use financial market power, and who is targeted to provide the cash-flow, has had a profound impact on society and the population in ways beyond imagination or description in back in 1984.

That one thing in my humble opinion: GREED It is because of the way society has changed and the fact that we are all just mass consumers of an ever-increasing option list filled with desired goods and services, a pub sitting in the heart of the community has become less and less important.

The local pub is no longer needed as the social hub it was, the centre of the village, the place future mums and dads met on a Friday night and then again on Sunday to share their first romantic drink together at 7pm.

We no longer meet potential lovers in pubs, we use dating and hook-up apps to meet someone we swiped right for a walk in the park on a get to know harmless date. Listen to how boring that sounds, how can an ice cream and a chat while walking past a duck pond ever compare to noticing a perfect female ass in a tight leather skirt and heels, or a mans chiselled jaw and blue eyes, while under the influence of four bottles of Mad-Dog 20/20 and your own imagination of just how far could you stick your tongue into her their ear while undoing buttons on the way to second base.

If people are no longer meeting is pubs to satisfy raging hormones and sexual desire, the aim of a pub had to change and choose a different target market.

Families

We can agree that times have changed, fashions have moved on, in the last 50 years the UK is almost unrecognisable from what it was in 1980.

Just think about this very clearly and shocking fact:

1980 is closer to WWII that it is close to 2022.

Let that sink in for a moment…

Even though times have changed, society is split more unevenly than even since the Edwardian times, some simple things still remain with us, but and not exactly the same!

Two types of Pubs:

Type 1, The Independent

Whether it is on the high street, village or countryside location, there are still lots of great pubs out there waiting for you.

Walk in without a booking, buy a drink at the bar, sit with friends, and enjoy the time together.

Type 2, Branded Pubs

We don't visit this type of pub go because we love the banter, the staff, or the location.

We are certainly not visiting because our extended family will be there with a welcome smile and a seat waiting with your name written on it.

NO, we go because we can get a pizza with a deep crust and cheese filled edge at the same time as a sizzling plate of baby ribs, sirloin steak or prawns layered onto Seabass.

Family Feeding Time

Sunday roast can be eaten on a Wednesday, and you can leave with a big slice of cake to eat at home.

The cocktails are poured from a pre-mixed bottle, shaken just for effect, and poured into a glass with a paper straw with minimal garnish.

Modern food pubs, no one's really goes in for the conversation or the banter, they go for food or to distract the kids so the parents can have a bevvy or three.

Food pubs are not a community hub anymore, they are nothing more than a family service feeding station for the modern nuclear family, the type of people who have forgotten what society was supposed to be and just accept the brave new world.

How far have we moved away from the original local pub?

Only the general public can answer that question, but they won't ask each other, they will probably ask Alexa while sitting across from another human being because AI is everyone's best friend.

So, I ask you, is the new version of area managers (BDM) as good as the old ones?

In my opinion no, not even close, but still, they are what we have to guide our pubs into a modern future! God help us…

This new version of area managers, or BDMs to call them their modern name, don't care or think about the history, quality, or the experience they could learn from by understanding the hospitality of 40 years ago delivered by big personalities, to them it is all about looking forward to the exciting new automated personality void world!

They are idiots…

Chapter 5

Bonus Skulduggery and Wankers Mugging Your Workforce

Pub companies generally pay pub staff and managers as little as they can get away with! Almost everyone who is under the level of BDM will be paid the very basic and slave labour hourly rates the government sets as national minimum wage.

Watch out if you are not on foodbank feeding the family wage levels, especially if are a very long service manager who has delivered fantastic results for many years.

You WILL become a target…

Success over many years of service has seen your pay slowly creep up to 40, 50, even 60k, this is what your modern BDM sees as obscene for "just a manager", a newly employed BDM with no pub experience has no idea what you do and what you have been through, the sacrifices you have made, to earn your healthy and well-deserved high salary.

In the opinion of this prick BDM, pub managers just do what they are told, they are easily replaceable with better, cheaper puppets whose strings can be tugged make them dance to the BDM's tune.

As an older expensive general manager, you are soon to be toast because your salary is seen by an idiot BDM as a potential future cost saving, a quick way to boost the bottom line and make themselves that bonus they were teased with at the interview.

And so, the game begins, the witch-hunt is underway as the BDM starts investigating every tiny action you perform in the workplace.

You swore in the kitchen out of frustration and the chef heard it. Can that be used against you? You accepted a delivery of barrels into the cellar without wearing steel toecaps on your feet. Surely it can be proved that you have put the company's reputation at risk. You removed a pissed-up prat who has wet himself sat on a sofa and sent him home. He has complained that you made him leave, you are now under investigation!

Does this sound far-fetched?

It is NOT far-fetched; these are the real types of witch-hunts that happen…

This new BDM will use any excuse they can muster up to dump your ass on the scrap heap as cheaply as a fly-tipped mattress down a country lane.

In the eyes of this child-like boss that has been inflicted on you, old managers are just out-of-date old farts, a nuisance and replacing you with someone half your age, half the salary will be a big win for them. Unfortunately, a young inexperienced manager being placed in a massive volume pub has none of the hard taught knowledge needed to manager a big turnover very lively capacity trading pub. But because it is beyond the modern BDM's ability to comprehend the type of manager that is NEEDED for a very busy venue, they will appoint a new, young general manager with only half the ability to generate all that cash and profit that drove up the previous general managers salary in the first place.

What this dumb, young BDM does not appreciate is, replacing a great manager who has learned every trick in the book to make a pub a great and safe place to be with friends and family with a youthful general manager with less than half the ability and mental strength will actually cap their own BDM bonus because the income and profit will collapse within months.

Less income leads to much less bonus…

Removing an expensive, but high performing manager never works as a cost saving measure, it does exactly the opposite!

The standards and the community in and around the pub fall dramatically and the team begins the churn increasing problems with customer service.

The commitment to quality by the team is lost because the company had no loyalty towards old high achieving GM's.

It all breaks down…

Every good GM (General Manager) has a long list of problem people and unwanted customers who have been asked every so politely to leave and come the fucking return.

The word spreads far and wide, that old cunt of a manager has fucked off, so they are coming back with the same attitude and unwillingness to stay on the right side of legal, but this time there is no one to kick 'em out!

The pub will start to spiral down, eventually ending up with around half the sales and even less profit.

Every penny the BDM saved on the GM salary by swapping out the old life-lived GM for the youthful cool assistant who "thinks" they are a GM, say £28,000 per year, and probably much more, will be lost as profits shrink and this idiot, who appointed the new GM as a cost saving plan, has no idea how to put things right because they are completely out of their depth.

All that fake drama, secret planning, sneaky goings on, spying and hounding out the old GM with lies, tricks, and skulduggery, was it worth it?

In the end it everything done to the old GM that finally removed him from his beloved pub and community brought no benefit at all did it, a great manager was scrapped, demoralised, and broken and a customer base damaged because the child manager that has taken over will never live up to the guests' expectations due to a lack of ability and poor leadership by the useless BDM.

But this is not the worst thing this dickhead of a BDM will do.

They also ruin a highly effective winning team, spoiling a fantastic business that will turn it into a poorly managed and unfriendly boozer for weed smoking scroats and nylon wearing tossers.

After the BDM has made the changes, a little time passes before the bigger bosses begin to notice that the jewel in the crown pub is no longer the top performer, something has gone badly wrong?

The idiot tosser modern BDM has ruined a great pub that no longer generates the massive income and profits it once did, but who do you thinks will get the blame?

The BDM will throw the new inexperienced manager under the bus.

Who helps manage a pub, I don't care who you are, all GM's need great help to manage a successful hospitality business?

Let's examine the role of a supervisor in a big busy pub with lots of food trade from 11:30am to 10pm.

I want to run through the job list they have on their plate, so let's look at what they do when left in charge?

Supervisors are effectively standing in for the GM for one of two reasons:

1: the GM is having some well-deserved time off, this genuine hard-working manager, who covers all the hours to keep the wages in check.

2: or they are a lazy twat who does as little as possible and somehow gets away with it because they always have.

Bad pub managers survive in poor taking pubs because that is what their boss has come to expect, nothing from them, ever.

As long as they are fairly low paid, they stay under the radar because there is no saving to be made by removing them. They are not daft, being successful can bring nothing but trouble for this type of manager if they deliver once they may be expected to deliver again.

Best not give a success it go; we are alright where we are.

This overworked supervisor holds the keys to every door, all the secure areas, the cellar and the safe. They have the responsibility of counting the takings at the end of the night and declaring it on the PC to the company.

Watching out for everyone's health and safety while they are under the influence of an immense amount booze, they have consumed in the last 7 hours is stressful and problematic at best.

Supervisors head up the customer service, handles the idiots and tosspots who somehow emerge from the bodies of normal looking humans after being filled with alcohol as the night moves along. There is also looking after the cellar, overseeing the kitchen, delivering food to tables, washing pots in the kitchen, a supervisor needs speed and ability.

Plus, in-between doing everything else they also have to manage the sound and vision for tonight's premier league match kicking off at 8:00pm for a hostile crowd who thing that the poor signal is the pubs fault.

Eventually it is 2am and it's time to lock up, make sure everything is secure, everyone goes home safely, the building is secure, and the money is tucked up safely in the alarmed heavy steel box in the office.

If you think about the number of duties that a supervisor performs in a working day, half the time they don't even have time to have a break because the customer service quality so much important to them they put the guests and the team before their own needs without complaint, without fuss and often without being appreciated.

Even though these supervisors and assistant managers are overworked, overlooked and treated no better than objects by so many horrid and nasty customers, many senior team members managing big pubs on the GM's days off are paid just 50p per hour above the basic minimum age-related wage!

I am not kidding; this is taking advantage of people in my eyes.

Is there any other industry that could get away with passing on so much responsibility and personal risk onto a 20-year-old and pay them just £7.33 per hour in 2022?

I very much doubt it...

Did you know that the young 16-year-old waiter who delivers your food, or is collecting your glasses until 11pm, is only being paid £4.81 in 2022? It's a fucking scandal.

Back in the days when I was a pub manager, I paid all of my team the over 21 rate which was the highest rate I could pay per hour (there wasn't an over 23 rates in those days) because even if they were only 17, 18 or 19 years old those kids worked just as hard as anyone else in our team regardless of age.

Or at least I did pay them the higher rate until I was stopped by a new bigger boss who was suddenly working as our reginal leader even though he was one of the architects of the dramatic failure and cheap sell off that embarrassingly poor quality and ruined company he had helped run into the ground.

One of the main reasons that company failed and was bought for pennies by a much bigger pub company, was because of their cheap bastard pay policies and cruel treatment of their pub staff and managers.

People only worked for them if there was nowhere else left to go.

I can remember when I first met a senior manager from this finished pub company, my initial thought was "what a prick, what an ignorant arrogant prick!" His white shirt was too tight, he had the resting bitch face of a miserable twat and was as engaging and warm hearted as two-day old roadkill.

He spoke in a soft, but very passive aggressive way, all the BDM's working under him feared him because he was widely known as a serial bully, managing his region by fear and threats, using carefully worded emails to push his personal agenda, and was generally a fucking tosser!

This imaginary cunt needs a name, let's call him Donald Knobbush shall we, suits him to be honest.

And my initial impression was, yeah, I was right, WHAT A PRICK!

Quick question:

If a company has failed very badly in every possible way, financial markets, reputation and was best known for it's really poor customer service and quality, why would the company that bought this poorly managed, led by donkeys group of branded pubs calling itself a pub company, keep on the people, even promote them to loftier positions in their new employer tier of endless management, when they had led their old employer to collapse and ruin?

Not only were these wankers kept on as part of the deal to buy, but many were also put in charge of areas as BDM's, some of these donkey's where actually given senior positions above the very successful managers of the company that just bought the bad one for peanuts, fucking madness.

We had good area managers, BDM's who understood a culture of quality and fairness, then overnight, we were handed complete and utterly useless wankers who knew nothing about the way things were done before they arrived, so they did what they had done before and slowly started to fuck their new employer's company up as well.

Anyway, back to Donald Knobbush

This is the type of man I think he would be:

The financial week has not been going as well as he has budgeted for and there is a senior management concern that his region will not hit its labour cost plan.

Labour, manpower, whatever you call it, is by far the most expensive continuous cost in all types of hospitality, it can be a business killer if not controlled carefully.

Donald Knobbush will be in charge of 7 or 8 areas with a BDM managing each area and reporting directly back to him.

With just 3 days remaining until the end of a financial period and Knobbush is looking at the numbers, just Friday, Saturday and Sunday are left before closing this current financial month.

There is a slight risk that his region will not make its budgeted profit expectation. If that happens and he misses has budgeted target it will *NOT* trigger his bonus.

This will not do, he cannot fail, inside his swollen big head he is a god amongst the mere mortals who worship him, await his commands, fawn for his praise.

What can he do to guarantee the profit line for the month end, there is only three days left, but he must not upset the plans he has made for a perfect weekend away with his family?

It's simple for an evil bastard with no conscience or empathy, he just makes one conference call to all the BDM's who report to him, he will be laying out his orders of how to drive up the profit line while delivering veiled threats for non-compliance.

So how can Knobbush pluck an extra £10,000 profit out of thin air by the close of business on Sunday from the 120 pubs on his patch?

Firstly, lets divide £10,000 by 120 pubs.

That equals £84.00 needed from each pub.

£84.00 divided by the average hourly wage paid in those pubs to hard working skilled staff, including holiday pay and NI contributions is about £10 per hour as most of them are over 23 years old and cost the highest rate minimum wage, £9:50 per hour, and for ease of understanding and because I don't have a calculator with me, I am rounding the number up and down.

The £85 saving means each pub will need to cut just over 10 hours of staff hours from the rota before they close on Sunday, but also, they must not lose a single sale, or they will have to cut even more hours to match the fall in sales.

It's a vicious circle that starts the spiral of decline for a customer service led business.

Sales haven't been going well this week, if we don't match our sales predictions the budget still won't come in, Knobbush needs insurance in place guaranteeing his numbers will come in.

So he decides he needs a bit of wiggle room, let's increase the cost saving per pub from £85.00 to around £125.00 each just to be on the safe side.

Now we know how much each pub needs to save in wage costs across his region to ensure the month end numbers will work in his favour. Knobbush calls the BDM's all at once and tell them to instruct every pub in their area to save at least 12.5 hours from the team's current rotas between 5pm Friday and Sunday close of business.

As all the BDMs are shit scared of this pompous uncaring arse, most of them talk behind his back about him being "void of any feelings and a bully", the BDM's now have no choice but to use unethical management practice and underhandedly threaten the managers that report to them to comply with the labour reduction before the close of business on Sunday or their will be consequences.

These consequences are never explained, of course not, this way the threat casts much more fear, sneaky bastards eh…

How can a reduction in labour cost by slashing staff hours this late in the week be done you may ask?

The manager calls Tom, a bar worker, on Friday night and cancels his shift for 4 hours on Sunday. Poor Tom, he was relying on that money to make the final payment for his driving test.

He will have to cancel it now and may lose what he has already paid as a deposit.

Next, he catchers Tina as she is coming in for her Friday night bar shift and cuts her 4 hours shift on Saturday night.

Shit, she needed that money to pay for the babysitter she is using tonight (Friday) while her husband drives his taxi. Her husband doesn't work and is home on a Saturday night so she wouldn't need a babysitter on a Saturday, this is so unfair!

She thinks to herself *"my manager is so heartless, if my Friday shift was cancelled instead of my Saturday shift, I wouldn't need the babysitter for tonight, I fucking hate this company."*

Karl is the kitchen pot washer Saturday daytimes, his 4-hour shift is cancelled. Karl normally works 16 hours per week as agreed when he applied for the job, but now he is down to only 12 hours this week so he won't qualify for his universal credit payment!

How will he pay his council tax if he cannot claim tax credits by working 16 hours, this is so unfair, they know my position, fucking wankers.

And guess what Mr manager, the hours you cut from your teams' members because you were told to do so under the threat of "consequences" will have to be covered by **YOU.**

It was your turn to have a Saturday night off, tickets for the cinema bought and table booked at Miller and Carter ffs…

You have just added at least 8 to 12 hours to your own working week, if you don't work to cover the slashed hours on Saturday night the bar teams' job will be so much harder and it will reduce takings on the bar because they would be short one member because you cancelled their shift.

Turns out it is not only the team who are pissed off with this tin-pot dictatorship company, *"they ruin my time off most fucking weeks, I'm going to start browsing the job centre web-page, twats!"*

But what is really important in this balls-up panic-stations ordering management cuts bullshit is, everything is ok for Donald Knobbush, he is out in a fancy restaurant with his wife and kids enjoying suburb service and lush well-made cocktails.

You will never find Donald Knobbush eating in a pub in the region he operationally directs on the weekend, the service is never good enough for him and his family It's Monday morning, why was Knobbush worried, everything has worked itself out. The numbers are in, the cuts to staff hours in all our pubs saved the financial month and I will get my bonus.

Donald Knobbush rejoices while sending out an email to the whole region quoting:

we are all in it together...

So now you how some of the savings are made, this is not made up, that is exactly how last-minute savings are made, by inflicting cruel and inhuman instructions to front line workers and they're long-suffering managers.

Let's look at just how retarded Knobbush and this instruction to cut the wages for the weekend actually is?

Mr Knobbush wants to save on staff wages to make his numbers work. By achieving the targets set the bigger bosses thinks he is good at what he does, and don't forget his other motive, as I said earlier, bonus bonus bonus bonus.

What is dickhead is doing is actually <u>reducing</u> sales instead of driving them. What a fucking burke he is...

What Mr Knobbush doesn't understand is, because he is not really that bright, most bullies aren't very smart I think we can agree that is why they are bully's in the first place, is that by reducing staff hours by 12 hours per pub totalling 1,440 hours slashed the teams in 120 pubs on the 3 keys trading days/nights sessions is in fact driving down sales because there is not enough hands to serve thirsty customers fast enough. If service does not meet the customer expectation, the customers does not buy another pint in the same pub, they move on to the next one just down the road where they don't have to wait so long to be served.

There is still worse to come, next week the customer and his 5 friends, who last week moved on from the slow service pub, will now miss out that pub altogether and start from the pub where they received better and faster service.

It's not fucking rocket science is it, but the Kidult BDMs and dozy narcissist Op's Director just cannot accept that 2+2=4, not 3.

Even if the hours lost by slashing the rota are partly replaced because the manager takes up the slack and works extra hours, as many do, the loss available hands to perform the task of serving is still big enough to affect the whole regions sales performance, but not just for that weekend, every weekend that follows because dozy Knobbush's action do have an actual consequence.

Let's run a few numbers shall we:

Let's say you are the manager of a pub overseen by Knobbush.

Reducing staffing levels makes 6 customers walk away, and they would almost defiantly of had another round of drinks in your pub if they could only get served.

That round of drinks is a lost sale, let's say a couple of soft drinks are included, let's call it £25.00 per round of 6 drinks.

Out of the 120 pubs that had their hours cut at 5pm on Friday we can estimate that just under 20% of those pubs also lost customers for the same reason, poor and slow service.

To keep it simple, I'm calling just under 20% of the full 120 pubs a nice even and easy to work with 20 pubs.

That's £25.00 X 20 pubs = £500.00 SALES LOSS

If the 6 customers who left these 20 pubs, an action that caused the pubs to lose the £25.00 on the night, decide to no longer include the slow service pub for the next year, it begins to really add up.

The same group of 6 go out drinking just 26 times over the next 12 months. But now they buy their 1st round at their "new" starting pub every time they go out, missing out the slow service pub, your pub, every time.

20 pubs, 6 customer each, the loss of just 1 group of 6 per 20 pubs over the next year would totals £13,000.00 SALES LOSS. WOW.

Now try to imagine the effect if just a few more customers changed their habits because the service was slow?

12 customers leaving now totals £26,000.00 SALES LOSS.

24 customers move on, and that total grows to £52,000.00 LOSS.

This total will continue to grow as more and more customers desert these slow service pubs, but this dozy Op's manager, Mr Knobbush just keeps making the same mistake over and over again, cut staff hours to save the numbers, this is when the spiral of decline kicks into overdrive because every time this last minutes hours-slash happens the spiral speeds up getting faster and faster until the pub becomes a broken shell of what it once was.

And what makes this dozy wanker Knobbush even worse, when the sales loss begins to be noticed by the bigger bosses and they now want answers to the questions about losses and failure, Knobbush instinctively blames the pub managers and the BDMs to save his own ass, before moving on to another company to start the whole process again.

Dangling huge bonuses will create evil greedy monsters, in the city, major corporations, civil servants, and mid-level bosses, greed will always hurt those at the bottom of the food chain.

As an employer, the leisure industry grows bigger every year, it diversifies, changes and invents to fill need and market gaps.

The bigger the player greater desire to increase its revenue, the slice of the market, their share. Seeking out new avenues for sales, revenue streams, better customer facilities, bigger premises and trying new directions to endlessly drive up the amount of money rolling in to prop up the corporate business model.

Here is an example of adding revenue streams, I visited a frozen food shop last week and while I was there, I bought a pack of loo-roll and a can opener, and nothing I bought was actually frozen?

What you may find surprising is, the cost of paying an employee an hourly rate versus the growing total in company turnover actually shrinks year on year. Put very simply, the more money a company takes in sales the less money they spend per head on their employees.

I'm not talking about ALL employees of course, in pub companies the lowering levels of hourly pay versus growing income only hits those who work in the pubs and perform the sales and service. Anyone above being a bottom feeder that losers nothing, BDM's and above, they just get more and more perks, better company cars, salary increases, bonuses, the works!

The people who work in leisure retail of any type, pubs, restaurants, fast food and even hotels, are a soft target for profit hungry financial company owned leisure businesses who need to reduce costs by more every so they can to deliver ever bigger dividends to shareholders year on year.

How is it possible reduce total yearly wage costs I hear; you think workers' rights at the lowest positions are protected by the law?

I'm here to clear the smog that hides many truths.

Discounting is the biggest key to grow in retail these days. Licensed retail is just the same, and everyone loves a bargain.

Have you ever wandered into a supermarket just wanting a pint of milk?

But when you leave you have a salmon fillet, 2 scotch eggs and 2 litres of milk in a bag that you have also paid for?

Who doesn't enjoy yellow label shopping, it has basically become a sport, people milling around MandS and Waitrose waiting for whole chicken to be reduced by 30%, only the fastest on their feet with a keen eye will eat cheaply tonight…

Hitting the supermarkets at just the right time is pure luck, if you are at the perfect spot and at that exact moment the shop assistant places the SECOND yellow label on an item because the shop closes in 60 minutes, BINGO.

You have innocently entered a retailing shooting gallery and excitement takes full control of your sense and reasoning just because you find a Tuna Steak reduced from £7:50 to £3:00, winner winner…

I once went into MandS just after the first Christmas in lock-down. MandS would have ordered its stock for its Christmas shelves at least 6 months earlier, if not more. Lock-down created a down-turn in large party food because no one was allowed to meet up with family or friends. I found myself wandering around MandS and I come across an end isle display fridge full of Gammon Joints priced with yellow labels. Original price £9.99, yellow label price just 90p, just one last thing to check, are they freezable? YES, YES, YES.

I bought 5, but no saw my smile behind my mask.

Everywhere offers yellow labels these days, ASDA, Tesco and even Waitrose sell yellow label items, but it's always a gamble.

Go into Tesco at lunchtime and you see yellow label cartons of 12 eggs that pass their sell by date at midnight. Currently they are reduced by 25% from £2.00 down to £1.50.

A saving to be had. But wait!

This is where modern day food-shop-gambling begins, a game of risk vs reward.

Are you ready? If you come back at 9pm tonight and there are still yellow labelled eggs available, they will now be down to just 25p, that is just 2p per egg! Now that is a REAL saving.

The risk? They may be all gone for the original 50p reduction.

Can you remember when was the last time you yourself yellow label shopped?

Don't lie, unless you are a Cheshire housewife, Pimlico pensioner or a footballer's fancy bit, everyone enjoys a bit of yellow label.

Long gone are the simple January Sales, the Autumn Spectacular and Black Friday.

And here the fuck did Black Friday come from?

Sales are now 24/7/365 every year, and this is especially the case in so called pubs that only care about selling food.

All the big pub Co's have branded food led pubs, doesn't matter if it is called Hungry Horse, Sizzler, Two for One or Brewers Fayre, they all do the exactly the same thing.

The menu makes you believe there is a bargain to be had, you are winning the battle, you are so smart you think you are outwitting the pub and getting more for your money than the pub company wants you to have.

You are sure the pub company is losing out, it makes you feel powerful, charged, you have finally got one over on a pub, your deal and buying prowess is greater than the retail marketing department, you are finally achieving "better than value for money." Or so you think!

The pub companies are really good at tempting potential customers in with an unbeatable bargain, the vast majority of the public are tricked daily by bright, colourful, and smartly worded billboards and posters showing these amazing imagers of food, but it never really looks like the poster image in real life, does it?

I have eaten an American burger brand's "Big Burger" twice in my life, both times I regretted it. The reason why I tried it both times was because of the advertising board on the exterior advertised, with a photo, this amazing, plump, generous and fresh-looking burger available to purchase from within the outlet.

First time was in Luton, it was late 90's and I was staying in a pub with rooms in Luton Town centre because I had a meeting in the same pub the following morning. I didn't want a lot to eat, just a bite before bed. So off to branded burger I go, buy a "Big Burger", walk outside and open the little box.

What a sad sight, a flat, dull, and lifeless burger that tasted as bad as it looked! I held it up and compared it to the image outside, the only comparison I can make is from the Film Twins starring Danny DeVito and Arnold Schwarzenegger.

Guess which one of these two film stars I compared the burger in my hand to? Next time I was lucky enough to be NYC and I was walking out the rear corner doors of Bloomingdales when I saw the same branded burger joint as I tried in Luton just across the road, so I thought to myself, let's have a "Big Burger" in the home of the "Big Burger", the USA.

In I go up to the counter and order my "Big Burger".

What a miserable twat serving, no smile, totally robotic, communicates by grunts, but that was not the worst thing about this retail purchase I was enduring.

Once outside I opened the box, had I order the wrong thing?

Had I accidentally ordered "a burger from last week's leftovers" instead of a "Big Burger"?

It was small, limp and very sad looking, just lying there occupying the bottom of that brightly coloured box. The comparison between to quality of the branded well-made packaging versus the actual pathetic, poorly prepared and presented food that called itself a burger was immeasurable.

I decided to take a look inside the actual burger, I opened it with a gentile pull of the bun top! What I saw looked like a second-hand lettuce leaf with large brown spots under a slimy slice of Gherkin with some form of orange shiny plastic looking cheese poking out at four points from under a patty of meat that looked more like broiled flood damaged flotex carpet.

Now I compared this "Big Burger", limply sitting in this coloured box held in my hand, to the huge back-lit poster outside displaying the version of a "Big Burger" I was expecting. There was no comparison in any way shape or form, they didn't even contain the same fucking ingredients. The poster version had red onion, tomato, and mayo, the one in my hand did not!

I didn't even taste it, straight into the trash-can, what Americans call bins, in it went and I have never bought a fast-food burger since.

Every branded big pub chain has discounted food to drive footfall.

We see them everywhere, Two for One, 2 for £9.99, Buy One Get One Free, they are dotted around the country, and always near any mass of humans living a large conurbation.

These brands are experts at dipping their hand into the pockets of unsuspecting victims, sorry I mean customers…

UK branded food pubs follow their USA counterparts when it comes to marketing values, just whack a brilliant image of a perfect plate of food onto a poster and add an unbelievably cheap price.

Add the words Meal Deal, Two for One or 2 for £9.99 and now the public start to take notice.

Ever heard someone say, "I couldn't make it for that price?"

Yeah, you could if you make it on an industrial scale, volumes wed cannot comprehend, use the cheapest possible sauced ingredients available and paid the workers the base minimum wage in whatever country is producing that ready meal.

The marketing goes up, brightly lit from behind and the food available look top-nosh quality.

The food on this newly erected billboard looks just like the food that is being served at the Ivy by some of the best chefs in the UK.

Just looking at that steam rising from the food photo is making the saliva slosh around your mouth.

Then you see the price, it's £9.99, but wait, this is a buy one get one FREE offer.

How can anyone possibly refuse a deal like that...

Now, I can see the appeal of an amazing money saving deal, we have all fallen for the bargain that is too good to be true, we all love to feel smug because we are savvy enough to buy one get one free.

But let's be honest with ourselves, if a deal is too good to be true, someone somewhere is paying the price for you exploiting this amazing deal.

Pub companies don't lose when offering deals, so who does?

Well let's look into who pays the price for all the cheap deals in every branded food pub, fast food and take out everywhere across the UK.

Let's take a business that sells one meal and gives you a second meal for free, it is always cheapest of the 2 that is free.

Before I explain 2 for 1, how do we pay for food priced individually?

Like this, if the one meal costs £9.99 and a 2nd meal also costs £9.99, that would be a total spend of £19.98 at retail sales price, the amount you pay for the 2 meals as you order at the bar. Simple and easy.

Almost all leisure business and pub companies work out the labour (wage) cost to produce a meal and get it to the guest.

Wages budgets are worked for a pub from the expected sales over a week. A percentage of the total sales in a week minus the 20% VAT (NET sales) is used to calculate the amount to spend on wages.

So how much money is available to pay the staff to cook those 2 meals you have just paid £19.98 for?

Let's round it up to a simple £20.00 to make it easy to follow.

£20.00 minus VAT at 20% = £16.00 net.

(We take off the 20% because that's not our money, that is the government's money in tax).

126

Wage cost is calculated as a percentage of the net sales, so if the pub is lucky enough to have an 18% wage budget that will give the pub a total of £2.88 to spend on staff wages to cook the 2 meals bought for £19.98.

£2.88 wages to prepare the 2 meals equals 18% of the £16.00 that is left from the £20.00 sale after VAT is deducted.

The £2.88 is not only going to the kitchen team to cook your food, but also towards the cleaners, the bar staff, the waiter, the pot washers, the glass collector, the supervisor, the assistant manager, and the managers wages. It also pays everyone in head office, marketing, HR team, bigger bosses, it is very thinly spread, the thinnest bit going to pub staff.

Now let's look at buying meals when you receive 2 meals for the price of 1.

When you buy meals that are part of the fantastic deal that is a customer's favourite, the amazing 2 for 1 meal deal, the wages are calculate exactly the same way as paying full price for 2 meals.

So even though you have bought food **worth** £20.00, or £16.00 net, the wage percentage allowed to cook this food is worked out from what actually goes into the till minus the VAT.

The amount of money gone in the till is only £10.00 for 2 meals, take VAT off and the value is now only £8.00 net.

The 18% wage allowance to cook these 2 meals is no longer £2.88, is in now only £1.44.

I know, its fucking madness, how can this be possible?

The wages cost for preparing the food is only applied to the actual sales price after discount, not before, so wage spending is now down to just £1.44 to be spent on staff wages to produce £20.00 worth of retail food sales with VAT still included.

This means that the ACTUAL wage cost has been cut in half from the original budget of 18% of net sales down to just 9% of net sales, a 50% staff wages allowance CUT.

The company will claim the pub has an 18% wage budget, but in reality, it does NOT, it has 9% as you can clearly see from this example.

Think about it, now you understand the con, while you let this cruel discerption sink in, I'll run through it one more time in really simple terms.

The team in the pub are still making the full 2 dishes ordered by the customer, but the pub company is only charging for 1 meal.

Then the pub company applies the wages allowance to make both meals from just the 1 meal sale price.

Wages to make two meals is cut to the level allowing just one meal to be made but the volume of food to actually be prepared and served is still 2 meals.

The customer gets 2 for 1, the staff are paid 2 for 1, do you get it?

This practice generates huge cost savings for pub companies, it is sneaky, it is a despicable practice that should be condemned, it is unfair on the workforce, it is virtually slave labour, doubling the pub teams work rate for no extra pay!

It's already bad enough on pub staff who are just trying to get by on minimum wages while paying a mortgage, but these meal deals are just too much, the workload becomes too much and staff members and managers crumble under the pressure of hitting impossible wage targets that are set by greedy bigger bosses.

Let me try to explain just how bad the working conditions is in some of these food pubs, it is either double the work for single pay, or it is half the pay for the same work, it means the same however you want to say it.

This treatment of pub staff is sometimes the equivalent to making them work in modern "work-house" conditions and the team and managers delivering the food at crazy discounted prices to the customers, we are moving pushed secretly back to Victorian standards of employment!

The media waffle on about the poor treatment of nurses, police and teachers from their employers, the UK government.

But not one of these professions comes anywhere near as bad as the way pub team members are often treated by the pub companies that use and abuse them daily for minimum wage rates, in poor environments and horrible anti-social hours.

Pub staff don't get public sector pensions either!

Let look at this as an actual sales scenario:

A pub restaurant business sells 400 steak meals at £15.99 retail price, £13.33 net price, in a week.

That is £5,330.00 in total net sales, the 20% VAT equalling a tasty tax lump of £1,066.00 belongs to the government.

If that pub has an 18% wages allowance of net sales, this pub should have £959.40 to spend on wages.

From this total amount of wages, they have to order, prep, cook, plate, maintain safety, deliver the food to table, wash the pots, remove the waste, and of course, it is a pub, serve the drinks etc.

But because it is a Buy One Get One Free pub, in reality the wages are reduced by 50%. The actual amount they have to spend is on staff and management wages is only £479.70 to produce an amount of food valued as £6,396 at full sales price, the amount paid over the bar counter!

NO wage allowance is given to making these second free meals, preparing, safety, waste and serving the food to table.

Just £2.99 in staff wages to deliver 2 steak dinners with a value of £31.98: This is only 9% of the sales value being spent on staff wages, not the 18% the pub company tell us and everyone else they spend on their staff.

UK pub companies are about as nice to work for as criminal prostitution gangs, but at least in criminal prostitution you don't have to accept 2 punters for the price one 1, well I hope not! Who is the lowest paid and most exploited workers in the UK? It is either pub company minimum wage team members, or prostitutes trafficked by Eastern European gangs? (it's the prostitutes of course, I'm just making a point).

You go out with your husband, your wife, significant other and you pay £15.99 for two steak dinners that is advertised as being worth £31,98, you found yourself a bargain, well done.

In reality, you would expect the kitchen team to be paid a lot more than just £2.99 between everyone who is involved with perfectly grilling the meat, seasoning the hand cut chips, blanching the veg and stirring the sauce that makes up your expensive sirloin steak meals!

If you knew a kitchen team were being paid just £2.99 to prepare and cook your 2 steak dinners, would you really go there?

I will leave you with one final question in this chapter:

When you go out for something to eat will you still be seeking out cheap meal-deals from this point on?

Now you know how it fills the bosses' pockets with bonus cash, ruins the working life of every team member preparing these bargain bucket deals, could you look that waitress in the eye now you know she is paid such a pittance for working so hard?

Go out, enjoy, eat great food, but please pay full prices for all of it.

Let's stop the pub teams, and managers, being exploited by greedy money led institutions without soul or conscience.

Chapter 6

The Biggest Pub Companies Are Pickpockets...

By now you may be aware that I'm no fan of the big pub Co's because of their contempt for customers and employees.

I'm now going to let you in on more underhanded tricks that pub managers are forced to use by nasty little modern BDM bosses. These twats don't give a toss about succeeding in hitting the pubs wage budget, they insist on driving down staff costs every chance they get because they have a deluded belief that this action will increase the bottom line.

Seriously, they will push in every way possible to cut labour costs, it comes across as an obsession.

If you are working for a pub company and you are paid through their payroll system/provider, you will be paying Class 1 National Insurance contributions.

But only if you are paid above the base threshold.

You will only pay a NI contribution from your wages if you earn over £120.00 per week.

You can earn up to £9'568 in a tax year, April-March, before you pay NI.

This flaw in the NI system allows wankers like a nasty BDM or an arse like Knobbush will use YOUR NI relationship with HMRC to cut the overall wages costs of their area or region. So how is it done?

1: Bad bosses want rid of as many employees who are earning enough in any week that triggers payments of NI by removing all full-time staff from the business. The trick is to replace one full time team member with three-part timers.

2: They want rid of as many employees over 20 years old as possible.

2022 national minimum wage for someone 23 years old and over is £9.50 per hour.

2022 national minimum wage for some old enough to serve on a bar, 18 years old, but is still under 21 years old is paid just the pathetic sum of £6.83 per hour. That is a £2.67 saving for every hour used in wages.

By keeping the number of hours each team member is given to work every week below certain level stops the requirement of a NI contribution being triggered.

But how does this benefit the company if someone is paying NI from their own wages? This is the genius bit that only heartless bastards would ever use.

If an employee IS paying a NI contribution the company must also pay an NI contribution for that employee. By keeping the total wages cost below £175.00 per week the paying NI threshold forcing the employer to pay a contribution to NI is not triggered!

If the NI contribution is not triggered by the employee's low wage, the company also does NOT need to pay their share of the employees NI, so it's an instant saving on the overall wage costs line for the company.

Can you imagine if a company removed their share of NI contributions for 10,000 staff?

Massive savings every week for monsters in charge…

Now let's look at how many hours someone on differing pay rates can work without triggering a NI contribution?

I'm not working with exact figures; these are just example showing you the way it works.

If you earn £9.50 X 12.5 hours = £118.75

If you earn £6.83 X 17.5 hours = £119.52

The LOWER wage rate means an extra 5 hours on the rota for every staff member because they are paid so much less per hour.

Work it out, let's swap 10 staff who are all over 23 years old for 10 staff who are all over 18 years old but under 21 years.

THAT COULD ADD AN EXTRA 50 HOURS TO A TEAM ROTA

without increasing the wage cost by a single penny.

Back to NI now We have already discovered that if you pay NI on your wages, the company ALSO has to pay NI employer contributions on your wages, 13.5% to the wage value known as Class 1A.

So, if a nasty twat or a senior manager bully, sorry I mean BDM or Op's manager orders a pub manager to reduce almost all their team to each work no more than 17 hours per week, this is saving a of 13.5% off the total wage costs just because the company does not have to pay its share of NI.

Kerching…

The savings made by reducing the teams age, plus reducing each team members hours to save having to pay any NI contributions is a huge money spinner for every one of the bosses towering above pub manager level.

Now extrapolate that saving to an area of 15 pubs with an average of 20 team members in each pub!

Next, we can extrapolate again this to 8 BDM areas in the Op's managers region. These saving can be in the TENs of thousands, possibly even HUNDREDs of Thousands of £££££. And still there is more:

Many years ago, we had an amount of money to spend on wages that was generated by the number of sales taken by the pub.

A typical pub may have wage percentage around 18% of the pubs total net sales.

If the pub sold £19,000.00 in sales, the 18% wage allowance means it has £3,240.00 it can pay out in wages.

Some BDMs have changed the way wage allowance is calculated. A number of pub companies have also introduced AI wage scheduling systems that plan can plan manpower use for the team without the manager's input.

The manager is TOLD how and where every single staffing hour will be used.

Both the BDM's system and the scheduling systems both have the same aim, saving money on labour.

Let's go back to the ages of the team!

Remember, reducing staffs ages can save £2.67 every hour that the younger staff member works compared to the team member that is 23 and over.

I've already told you how this hourly pay cut by using younger staff can be used to increase the maximum hours for each team member from 12.5 hours to 17.5 hours for the same cost.

How does this work?

7. 250 staff hours at £9.50 per hour = £2,375
8. 347 staff hours at £6.83 per hour = £2,370

So, as you can see, employing the young staff equals an extra 97 staff hours being available for almost the same cost.

But the BDM and the scheduling systems don't let you add the extra 97 hour available to deliver fantastic service, oh no.

This 97-man hours you SHOULD be able to use is "banked", the money saved by NOT using the 97 hours is not spent on extra staffing, it is plumping out the bottom-line profit.

As a GM you have followed the orders about lowering staff hours, so no one earns over £120.00 per week.

You lied, hidden the truth and found excuses to lose all the full-time staff as instructed to do, and now have a very inexperienced team all aged under 21 years old, I wonder if customer service will suffer?

The actions you have forced to go through with means most of you team are now costing £2.67 per for every hour worked.

In a pub that uses 475 staff hours per week this hour wage cut is saving the pub company approximately £1,268.25 in staffing wages every week.

This amount of wage saving equates to 180 staff hours and these hours should have been made available to the GM so that an investment was made into increasing customer service levels, easing pressure at busy times, making the GM's life a little easier, but no, it is used to build bonuses for BDM's, Op's Managers, Directors and dividends to share-holders.

How do all these changes lowering staff age and NI cuts affect the pub team and the GM?

They get royally fucked over by being made to work even harder because with less experienced colleagues who are still learning their roles.

Any pub being put through this crazy process is always going to deliver poor service to customers. Utter Fucking Madness.

In day's long past into history pub managers and teams didn't have the stress levels that the customer now witnesses daily, short staffed, panic speed serving, rushing about with a face like a slapped arse on a daily basis. The pub was always a relaxed place to visit, somewhere time slipped by effortlessly while sipping an after-work pint.

These days in these modern food pubs you see stressed faces, anger, attitude and unhappy people with worried expressions.

You don't see pub managers without drooped shoulders, furrowed brow and with an angry stare into the distance as they are trying to deliver service to customers with impossibly low levels of company support and unrealistic low numbers of staff to help!

No longer do we see a cheery landlord enjoying pub life.

Funny thing is, as a customer you feel the tense atmosphere, you wait far too long to be severed, you don't witness for long if you are lucky because you buy a drink just once, and then move on!

Financial targets are sometimes changed hourly, orders from up high by bigger bosses about cutting wage costs, there is never any consideration of the people working, service quality or impact on customers, apparently this is now "how we do business."

Modern BDM led pub businesses are about as far from the customer experience journey as is humanly possible.

Most of the team members working in these branded food pubs are actually ashamed of how low the standards have fallen.

Poor quality and slow service, the flippant and robotic staff paid less that £7.00 per hour, pub companies have created their own crisis by putting the shareholder above customers and staff.

Current branded food pub staff are forced to deliver sub-standard service, microwave food and pre-mixed poor-quality cocktails.

This is a really cheap business model, in a single word: GRIM.

Bad and slow service creates frustrated humans, annoyed, angry at the people trying their best.

The companies' policies dump the manager and their team with having to deal with pissed off customers who will always blame the hard-pressed managers and they're loyal, worn out, tired and demotivated teams for the really poor service they have received.

But the professional and hardworking manager and their teams never let the cat out the bag about the wage cuts, the 3 days to save 12 hours, the hidden threats about losing jobs, the customer will always blame the manager, and head office desk jockeys get off blame free.

This IS the real cost of reducing wages, everyone pays in their own way.

Managers working for modern pub companies are paid as little as the company can get away with, really poor pay rates when you compare the hours put in to make the business work.

Modern BDM's and Operations Managers have never run pubs, they have no idea what a pub manager, chef, cleaner or bar staff actually do for a living and couldn't help if they wanted to because they don't know how.

How do you become a modern branded food pub manager?

After browsing the isles of the job centre web site you spot a job vacancy for a pub manager on Indeed.com, Having watched Eastenders for the last 15 years, it looks pretty easy:

48 hours per week over 5 days nattering with my mates and being paid for it, I'll have some of that…

48 HOURS, OH REALLY…

FUCK THE FUCK OFF, FUCK YOU THEN FUCK OFF AGAIN!

Let's delve a little into this 48-hour pub manager working week.

Every real pub manager knows, claiming you will work a 48-hour week is even bigger than any lie a politician would spout out to cover their own ass…

Shall we take a look at the working life of a big pub company branded local food operation and the part the pub manager plays in the weekly workings making sure everyone has no reason to complain, what do they really do?

Yeah, that's right, the main thing that flashers through the mind of a hard-working GM is "how do I not get a bad review or complaint", it is a permanent fear, when it should be about genuine hospitality.

At the interview for the GM position, you are told:

9.6 hours per x 5 days = 48 hours

Salary £28,000 = £11.21 per hour

You take the job as a pub manager, the GM, in a typical food pub with sales of around £14,000 per week (net), but will you really be working just 48 hours per week over 5 days?

This need looking into, what does the typical young manager do on one of the quietest days of the week?

Monday: A typical working day…

Up early, 7am and into the office to make sure the assistant who locked up last night balanced the books, counted the cash, and entered all the information onto the company PC.

Time to end the financial week and declare all activity for the last seven days to the company account team, so it's time to fire up the PC and start filling in number after number after number into the company spreadsheets advising everything from detailed sales, receipt values, banking details and amusement machine income.

Next, it's the teams' weekly wages, so you fill in the electronic timesheet while, at the same time, you are desperately trying to think of a water-tight excuse why you have overspent the amount of wage hours you were allowed to spend? This wage hours budget was created out of thin air by the "oh so fucking smart *AI algorithm*" that tells the managers how many hours they "should be using."

Speaking of algorithm led labour planning *AI* systems, some of the pub companies I have been associated with are suspected of "fixing" the algorithm itself so it always delivers less hours for use with manpower planning than it should do.

It just takes a tech-smart savvy system controller a few minutes to switch a couple of numbers around within the algorithm and boom, everything changes. With these adjustments made the system will automatically spit out a smaller number of budgeted hours than it would before the crooked number juggling.

This is yet another nasty and hidden money saving trick that impacts the staff, the GM's and eventually the guests, but it does deliver bonuses and dividends to everyone BDM level and above.

Now it's on to the stock taking, counting everything in the pub down to the smallest thimble of lime cordial. GMs are expected to deliver over 100% yield on drink sales.

I'll come back to this later on.

By now it's 10.30am and you finally finish the office work.

You still need to wash the vomit off the rear steps, unclog a urinal and change 2 bulbs before you set up the bar with drip trays, nozzles, fruit and put the till floats in place.

And don't forget the cellar, empties to be pulled out, full barrels rolled into position, cask barrels needing to be racked, and the bottles skips require emptying or they won't be any available for later today.

5 mins before opening at 11am the phone rings, it's the 24-year-old BDM wanker demanding to know why you didn't hit your wages cost line and you also have 3 pints of Carling missing according to the stock monitoring systems.

Also, Trip Advisor has flashed up a warning on the BDMs monitoring page, your pub has received a 4-star review over the weekend, not a 5!

What the hell are you going to do about it?

Mr prick BDM now tells you that a serious chat is needed tomorrow at 10am (on your day off) so you better get some answers ready.

11am and you unlock the door, in walks Charlie and Ben for the start of their Universal Credit funded 10 hours of slipping beer.

This is their "full time job" provided by the state, their job includes where they share their knowledge of how to run this pub much better and why the Stella isn't as good as it is in Wetherspoons?

You pull 2 pints of Carling, neither Charlie or Ben would ever pay for Stella even though they know so much about it, and you hear the side door opens with a loud creek.

It's the local police, "can we see your CCTV please, you have a camera facing the road and we are tracking a suspect?"

Now the shit has hit the fan, you still have the kitchen to set up because you cannot afford to have any staff in before 12pm, the team wage budgeting algorithm system that tells you how many hours you can use within each individual hour of every day, it is of course always right and must not be questioned, says the BDM.

Time for fast action, slow things down, Mr policeman, "would you like a cup of coffee while I just turn on the kitchen?"

"Yes please."

So now you are stuck doing something unnecessarily stupid and extremely time wasting, you have to make the policeman a barista style coffee in the traditional "froth the milk" way because the company you work for are so hung up with perceived style and image, you are stuck with a traditional coffee barista machine with a separate grinder, steamer arm and metal jug.

What your pub company employer has not yet worked out is that most of your customers are much more like Charlie and Ben, just sipping their Carling all day, rather than like anyone who picks up a Starbucks on their way to work.

A pint of Carling takes 30 seconds to pour, a medium latte takes 4 minutes, or 6 minutes by the time you have retrieved the milk from the pub's kitchen. The reason for not modernising.

The regional Op's director enjoys barista coffee and would never consider changing to a simple, efficient, easy to use, cost effective one button automated machine that expertly and consistently creates a quality latte with freshly ground beans in under 60 seconds.

After all, faster coffee pouring would NEVER work in a pub!

It's now 11:07am, you rush into the kitchen, turn everything on in a panic, oh no, the oil needs changing in the fryer, fuck it, one more day will have to do, hopefully darker chips won't matter, it's only Monday, or hurt our reputation with the public.

Down to the office in the cellar followed closely by the policeman to where the CCTV recorder is, and guess what, a pain every GM will have experienced, you are desperately trying to remember the recorder fucking password.

Whoever remembers the CCTV password?

The company policy handbook says "a non-employee must never be left unaccompanied in the office" but now it's 11:55am and you can hear Charlie shouting "anyone serving" so you rush up to the bar to serve Charlie with his second, pre midday, pint of Carling while leaving the copper to play with the CCTV on his own.

In walks 19-year-old Zack, our "never done a day's catering training in his life" chef, complete with a massive hangover and stinking of the 5 quickly smoked fags he has dragged on during his 20-minute walk to work.

The policeman is done and asks "can you burn me a copy" just as a lady comes to the bar asking about allergens.

It is now 12:08pm. The lady orders the gluten free bread to go with her hand battered fish and chips…

FFS, if she wants gluten free bread, she must be celiac.

Should I tell her about the batter… fuck it, you don't have the time to spare.

Back down to the office, DVD in, hit record, there you go, now on your way Mr policeman, I need you long gone.

"Anyone serving" shouts Ben.

On your way back to the bar you pop your head in the kitchen, "Zack, get a fish and the batter from the fridge, I'll be there in a minute", you reach the bar look up and realise there are four more people who all needing serving. Action stations, that means nine drinks to serve and nine meals being ordered, you crack on whizzing through the serving, cutting corners, who has the chance to "sell-up" when you are this busy?

Just one more customer to serve then you can get back to the kitchen…

"Hello, what can I get you today?"

"Can I get 2 x latte, a flat white and a hot chocolate with cream and marshmallows please?"

you die inside…

"I'm just nipping to get some more milk from the back" you say as an excuse to get back to the kitchen, you grab the 6oz cod tail (reduced from 8oz on the last menu change, but the price stayed the same), Zack has not got the flour out for the wet fish, where is Zack, you grab the flour with the other hand, rip it open and shake some on the surface you hope is clean, and prey that Zack has not sat his arse on while playing on his phone. You slap the fish onto the flour, each side is now sort of coated so into the batter it goes, then into the fryer.

"Zack, grab a portion of chips, open a can of mushy and get me a wedge of lemon. When the fish starts to float chuck the chips in the other fryer and microwave the peas for 60 seconds, I'll be back."

You rush back to the bar, time to lay the tables, shit, where were they sat?

Ah there they are, table 10, cutlery down, you realise the vinegar has dried tomato sauce smeared on one side, but it's too late, you have no staff with you to wipe it.

Back to the kitchen, where the fuck is he? Zack is outside having a fag AAARRGGGHHHHHH…

You get him back in, give him verbal instructions to get the next 9 meals started while you plate the slightly overcooked fish and chips.

Out you rush with the plate, "there you go, is everything ok for you?"

"Can I get some ketchup, mayo and BBQ sauce please?" *YES*

Back to the bar you go to make the coffee's that was ordered 10 minutes ago, inside your head you are screaming…

"BITCH BITCH BITCH, WHY THE FUCK NOT HAVE 4 J2O's."

It is now 12:30pm, you are alone at work in the public gaze with an imbecile you employ as a chef because your area manager and Op's manager think paying more than minimum wage for kitchen staff is a waste of money, how hard can cooking a bit of food really be?

This day goes on, you have mad hours where you are running about so fast you see yourself coming back from the other way, then you have quiet periods where you try to complete next week's rota and finalise the beer order for the up-coming Bank Holiday.

Finally, 5pm comes along, at last your shift is finished on the bar, whoopee, time for celebration as a single supervisor comes on to work the bar from 5pm till close and act as manager when closing up at the end of the day.

Then you remember, Zack is about to go home because you can only allow him to work a maximum of 5 hours today to ensure he does not go over 17 hours total for the week.

What is really critical is, we need to make sure we do not pay expensive company contribution national insurance payments.

Mr arse of a BDM and Mr Knobbush don't care if the publics NI contributions funds health, the NHS, social care and eventually Thomas's future pension, it will reduce their yearly bonus.

So now you move your working station from front of house and the bar into the kitchen where your next shift begins, 5pm till 10pm, on your own and by now wondering "what the hell am I are doing working this many hours in one day, and this is just Monday, the slowest day of the week?"

During the 5pm till 10pm kitchen session you thought you had just one job, cooking the food. But in reality, you have been called on to change 2 barrels, kick out some tosser stinking of weed, change the sport channel twice and remove 5 underage feral teenagers from the smoking area for pissing under a table and setting fire to the tabletop. It has been a good night though, you got off lucky when kicking them out, you only took only one light punch to the head from a 15-year-old, you can survive that.

At last, you finish cleaning the kitchen down at 10:55pm and it's out to the bar ready to call last orders. It is now it's your job to be the doorman and remove everyone by 11:30pm because the law insists that no member of the public is allowed to remain on licensed premises or on the pub properties licensed areas beyond 30 minutes after the bar closes.

Then you see it, the BIG problem, what you hoped would be long gone before you left the kitchen after your very long day…

it's Charlie, still in since opening, he has finished off 10 pints since 11am, including watching his beloved Man Utd play, and lose, he is pissed off, wankered and still has half a pint of his 11th pint of Carling left in his glass at 11:28pm. Fuck…

Some people are nice drunks, happy, they hug, they giggle, even easy if you know what I mean, they go with the flow.

Charlie is not a nice drunk, he is a total cunt nut job that becomes an angry twat, someone that users shouted swear words, spitting and his fists as way of dominating a simple discussion.

OMG what do I do with him this time?

Snatch his pint glass and run, tempt him outside with a fag, talk with him for an hour and get absolutely nowhere, or wait till HE himself wants to leave which won't be till about 12:30am knowing Charlie!

You would be surprised how often this scenario plays out in many different ways at the end of night, and it's a pain you any licensees fucking arse…

It's 11:50pm and Charlie is finally out by bribing him with a free shot of Jameson's, the pub is locked up, time to count the tills and declare the takings to the company computer system.

Bloody hell, you only have 9 minutes left to declare to money before the companies auto-cut-off money declaration alert triggers a visit from a financial auditor tomorrow who will hold a formal investigation into why you didn't follow company policy and declare all income before midnight… ffs not again, third time this year and you will definitely end up with a written warning from that tosser BDM you have to report to!

Tills finally declared and the numbers entered onto the system, just 1 minute late, my boss and the audit git's will understand when I tell them about Charlie, won't they? If only they had once run a pub themselves…

Next comes double checking the site for security, then it's the lock up, alarm set and now a 20-minute drive home.

Home at last, into the shower, scrub the grease out of your hair, flick the tv on while I have a small glass of red…

wake up at 5pm on the sofa…

Monday is done…

That was just a nice slow Monday, an easy day compared to the rest of the week, you have completed a 19-hour shift and that means you only have 29 hours of you working week left.

Yeah, right lol. 48 hour per week with excellent work life balance, the words you read when signing on the dotted line to be a pub GM.

If you are a conscientious GM who cares about the public and the team you will never work less than 60 hour per week, and that just the volunteered hours you will labour. On top of these will be the ones added when a boss drops in the see you on your time off.

Yes, it will happen every week. Remember, you are being paid £28,000 per year, of £11.21 per hour for your 48 hours.

But you are working 60 hours per week and that means you are earning £8.97 per hour and that is 53p per hour BELOW the UK's NATIONAL MINIMUM WAGE.

As a poorly paid pub manager in a big PLC pub company, you will need to be super successful over many years to eventually earn really good money.

Oh yes, I was very successful, very indeed and my salary reflected my success, but there was a huge cost in achieving business and financially rewarding highs, the main one, you will have a never-ending list of doomed relationships because I was a horrible and really crap boyfriend.

Those who know, know… I am sorry. I always put the pub first over anyone, lady friend, family, nothing mattered, my job was my life, and it dominated my social life.

I lived to work instead of working to live.

Eventually I was earning really good money, 9 consecutive years of winning awards at the yearly big company bash added to the awards I had received in previous years. Success equals decent salary increases, my pay just went up and up, fantastic.

My success and high salary eventually created deep resentment and jealousy amongst some of my fellow managers, but especially with the people who perceived themselves to be my boss just because they worked within the head office gang of numpties.

My high salary became my eventual downfall.

New, first-time managers receive a rubbish salary, they are poorly treated and often abused by their young thrusting BDM.

This bullying, it happens daily, and it is done in a very quiet, but passive aggressive way.

It happens because the modern BDM is useless and normally overly promoted to a position beyond their intelligence, and they will always blame the pub managers for their own failings to ensure their area delivers.

So the BDM's own action are the reason their pubs end up with forever revolving doors, churning recruitment for new managers again and again that just causers even longer terms of unsettled teams that will only ever fail.

Pubs must have consistency; it is that simple piece in the puzzle that with deliver success.

Time to let you in on one of the biggest Hidden Tricks, using recruitment as a tool of manipulation.

An advert is produced and hits the recruitment agencies. WANTED, PUB MANAGER FOR THE DOG and DUCK.

live out, salary £22,000-£30,000 PA Plus OTE Uncapped Bonus, Health Care and 25 days paid holiday.

Eh? Will the pay be £22,000 or £30,000?

PA must mean per annum but the weekly difference between those two salary rates is really wide, one pays just £423.00 per week, the high one pays £576.00 per week?

That a difference of £153.00 per week, which one will be paid?

The pub company will tempt potential employees with the big number of £30,000, but in reality, the new employee will not see a £30,000 salary for many hard, tough, stressful and long years.

And what the hell is "Plus OTE Uncapped Bonus?"

Will a bonus be earned?

Does OTE mean overtime, but if thought salaried employees don't receive extra pay for overtime, or do they?

The way the job description is written is to win people over with dreams of money in the bank, a nice car, and one day you may be able to buy your own house.

This job is perfect for you, verbal promises of big pay packets, great life balance, chilled and relaxed fun with the punters.

But what the advert does *NOT* say is that the term "teamwork" actually means "you will be working on your own a hell of a lot of the time."

Yep, you are a one-person team…

The job advert will also include the line "excellent career progression".

It does not say, "but only if you are willing to suck the BDM's cock and eat their shit."

(Metaphorically speaking, but I have heard whispers that shenanigans between boss and GM does go on, quite often)

Unless a new GM has an exceptional ability to manage a pub delivering significant financial success, they will not be noticed by the bigger bosses, so the modern BDM will treat them as badly as every other mediocre manager, a worthless and replaceable employment number.

If your business does attract interest and it becomes a cash cow, just like that a "protected status" is cast over everything connected to the pub because it is delivering the wonga the bigger bosses need to drive up their huge bonus derived from your hard work and creativity.

What happens to the new GM who does well?

You are doing an amazing job for 2 years, you have received a small salary increase of 1.5% each year, but you are still on fairly crap money even though you are delivering fantastic sales growth and profit conversion.

Bigger Bosses are calling you "the manager with the Midas touch."

What you don't know yet, because you are not included in the conversation, you have been singled out and placed on the "manpower planner". This is where the bigger bosses pick out which is the best pub for you to maximise your ability to build their next bonus pot? You are a golden goose, wasted in that small pub, let's put you into a huge pub to work your magic on a bigger stage.

The day finally comes when your future will be revealed to you by selfish people deciding your future for "their" own needs.

The BDM and the Op's Manager are calling in to see you, a very rare occasion for the Op's Manager to visit, it must be something pretty important.

The three of you sit down in a quiet corner away from any team members or customers, they are talking about your fantastic performance, you are being nominated for an award at the yearly manager piss up after Christmas, at last all that graft is being recognised, you feel proud and valued.

You find yourself asking with the voice in your head "why do so many other managers on your area always moan about being treated so badly?"

You are sipping coffee and enjoying the compliments aimed squarely at you by the very people you were warned to fear by experienced GM's?

How wrong the other GMs were, you are with your supportive and trustworthy line managers, feeling content and relaxed, it doesn't get any better than this.

And here it comes, *"Have you thought about moving to a larger site, one with fantastic potential, somewhere that needs a manager like you to take it to the next level?"*

Next step, they start feeding your ego with words like "amazing, stunning, midis-touch and manager of the year."

Then the killer blow:

*"**WE WILL PAY YOU £30,000**"*, That's it, the magical number £30,000 is now swimming around your head...the promise has finally come true.

But there is something they are not telling you, and this is yet another *Hidden Money-Making / Saving Trick.*

The last GM who was running the pub that they now want you to take on and manage for a £30,000 salary, was earning £58,000 per year. The old GM was forced out because their high salary was seen as an opportunity to save in an instant £28,000 by replacing them with a much cheaper model.

You, who is the GM deceitfully being removed?

He was once just like you, a hero, the golden child, their star of the moment, the deliverer of piles of cash and was still innocently thankful for a rip-off low salary of the time.

The old GM was earning nearly double what you will be earning, but the bigger bosses know that you are still naive to their money grabbing actions, you will still do everything they say, and while ever you do you will stay comfortably in their good books.

You are not yet wise to the bigger bosses' sneaky manipulative tricks; you don't know that this is their chance to instantly boost their own bonus pots because saving on a GM salary creates a huge boost to the bottom line of any high turnover pub.

But that's not it, getting a one-off boost to the bottom line is not enough, there is more profit to be made.

After you have agreed to take on this new pub a couple of things will happen.

Suddenly the pub receives tweaks to the existing budget, but you are not told about these changes, my friends, the bigger bosses are looking after me. Sucker…

- The wages % will be cut by at least 1%
- The margin expectation will be increased by at least 1%
- The promotions budget will be cut by 10%
- The facilities monthly budget will drop by £100
- The prices of products will go up by a minimum of 10p each.

You may ask yourself "will these minor changes above make much difference?"

Let's crunch a few numbers shall we…

The pub they want you to move to takes an average of £25,000 net per week.

The annual sales turnover is £1,300,000 net.

The wage % has been budgeted at 21% of net turnover.

That equals £5,250 you have to pay staff every week, or £273,000 per year team wage bill.

Let's now reduce that wage budget by 1% shall we!

The new budget for wages drops too £5,000 per week, or to put it another way, you will now have £250 less to spend on staff wages every week than the old manager had.

This change to the wage budget of just 1% equals a cut of £13,000 per year for paying staff.

What this boils down to is this, you will now have to cut 25 hours off every week's staff rota leaving less staff to serve customers, cook, clean or whatever.

And guess who will have to pick up the extra work that the 25 hours cut leaves undone? YOU…

Your enthusiasm is exactly what the bigger bosses are relying on, your commitment to make sure the job gets done at any cost to yourself.

When you move to this new bigger pub with the bigger salary because it's much harder to manage, you will have around 1,300 less staffing hours per year to use than the old manager had.

Are you still feeling valued?

Now let's do the numbers on profit margins.

Your new pub takes 70% in drink sales and 30% in food.

So that is £17,500 every week in drink and £7,500 in food sales.

The drinks you sell make a margin (sales profit) of 70% overall and the food makes 60% overall margin.

£17,500 sales = 70% margin amounts to £12,250 sales profit.

£7,500 sales = 60% margin amounts to £4,500 sales profit.

The whole years sales margin generates £871,000 before expenses or wage cost being deducted over the year.

This is what is known as '**Total Margin**', or profit before costs being attributed.

Now let's add the extra 1% required margin added to the budget that you need to make. 1% more than the previous manager.

1% extra on drinks will generate an extra £175 margin every week.

1% extra on food will generate an extra £75 margin every week.

This new budget of 1% added margin will generate an extra £13,000 total margin every year (profit before expense and wage cost).

Now let's take away the costs of running the pub and any wage cost and include the new budgets.

These two costs to run the pub add up to approx. 50% of the extra £13,000 generated.

We are left with an extra £6,500 profit margin. Happy days.

All those changes to margins have increased top line profit.

Now let's move onto the promotions cut of 10%

In a week you spend £100 on the quiz, £125 on DJ's, £25 on social media, £25 on good will (free pint for a regular's birthday / cake for a member of staff etc) and an average of £50 per week on flyers, posters, and banners.

That is a total promotional spend of £325 per week, these promotions bring in 50% of the pub's overall sales revenue.

You have been ordered to reduce you promotional spend by 10%.

So, you have hired a cheaper, but lower quality DJ, or you reduce the prizes for the quiz, and there are no more treats for the team or regulars to save the required £32.50 cut every week.

You are trimming your promotional budget by £1,690 per year.

That is an extra £1,690.00 into the profit pot by cutting back.

More happy days, get in…

But is it really?

I mentioned that 50% of the pub's revenue was driven by marketing and entertainment.

Saving £1,690.00 WILL LOSE THE PUB FOOD AND DRINK SALES Facilities spending is a base cost for all businesses, including hospitality. But do you know what it is?

It is the toilet roles, the new pint pots and wine glasses, hoover bags, plates, washing up liquid, beer mats, window cleaner, straws, rubber gloves, it is everything you need to buy and pay for to make the business safe, legal, and able to deliver great service and standards.

Keeping everything running and enabling managers and teams to deliver drinks, food and services to customers is very expensive. Too many customers think pubs get glassware for free, they don't. Pub company pub have to buy them.

I have no doubt everyone reading this will have experienced toilets with no bog roll, no soap, being served a pint of Peroni a cheap Nordic style basic pint pot, dirty carpets, mixed crockery, really cheap tinny cutlery, and they are just the things you see!

What you don't see is the degreaser and sanitiser being watered down, kitchen cloth's so old, tatty and dirty they should not be anywhere near a kitchen, cutting boards beyond worn out and mop heads that are filthy, crust hardened twisted knotted balls of germs. The favourite cost saver is the dishwasher machine detergent and rinse-aid, they are always being watered down, so guess what is not being sanitised how it should be or to a standard you would expect?

These are the same plates and glasses you are about to eat and drink from.

I would spend £1,200 every month on consumables and facilities supporting my pub in South Yorkshire, a very special pub because we had one of the very few old-fashioned BDM's who supported us, encouraged success and accepted risks without ever being selfish himself, he let me spend the money to grow the customer base and we were rewarded with a record-breaking pub business.

They were fantastic years…

Most BDMs are greedy tossers, they will do anything to get themselves a bigger bonus or to climb the greasy ladder of promotion.

There was once a BDM in the Northwest who came across as an ok guy, he talked a good job, seemed to care about the people who reported to him, but when he left to take on an Op's Manager role for a hot drink company, he left behind a disaster zone that was about to implode with effects on everyone left behind.

He got out just in time, almost perfectly timed just before his actions ruined every single one of the whole area of pubs he left behind.

I had spent a few days with him before he moved on and I remember him telling me how successful he was. Turns out he was a cunt.

He had found ways to increase profits on his area of about 18 pubs far ahead of any other BDM ever in this large national pub company?

He had done it all to earn himself a bigger boss position and a bigger salary in a different company.

He also bragged that the bonuses he had received over 2 years achieving these huge profits had been very welcome indeed.

A couple of months after he had moved on, I was back in the Northwest and was visiting a few pubs that had been under the care of the recently departed BDM. Talking to the managers without the ex-BDM looking on anymore was very different to previous visits, they could speak freely and without fear. One manager I met told me it had been hell working for him.

His success had not come from driving sales, coaching, training, encouragement or fresh thinking like it should have done.

Oh no, the profits had come from cutting every expense possible, forcing wage cuts in every pub on his area just to increase profit. No more gardeners, window cleaners banned, reduced cleaning hours and people, and by cutting the facilities budgets by 50% he was piling on the bottom-line profit.

These pubs had almost nothing, they were short on crockery, cutlery, cleaning products, bulbs had not been replaced, broken hoovers had been ignored, uniforms were tatty and scruffy, optics missing from the back bar, toilet seats missing, patio heaters disconnected, the BDM had made everyone working in his area of pubs a misery while lining his own pockets and forwarding his own career.

By the time the sales drop started to bite, and the bigger bosses started to ask questions, this selfish money grabbing wanker of a BDM had already gone.

It can anything between 6 months to a year to ruin a great local pub and turn it into a hovel. His tactic was to lie, lie, and follow up with even more lies.

He was telling the GMs on his area that the bigger bosses were forcing these cuts through and he was doing all he could to protect his pub managers and their staff from the evil bigger bosses and their crippling cuts.

Absolute bollocks, it was all him.

What this cunt of a BDM was relying on was the loyalty of his passionate managers and team members.

They continued doing everything possible to keep their pub running as well as possible, even spending their own money on cleaning products and repairs.

Imagine the abuse those managers and teams were suffering because there was no bog role in the loo's again, heating was turned off on cold days, not enough salt, and pepper shakers to go round the grubby tables.

That BDM got what HE wanted at the expense of innocent GM's and pub teams who had trusted and believed him.

What A Twat

So back to the facilities cut, you are required to reduce your monthly spend by £100 to just £400 every four weeks.

Many companies divide their financial year into 13 x 4 weekly financial monthly periods instead of the more normal 12 calendar months periods with their varying weeks counts of either 4- or 5-week financial months.

13 periods of exactly 4 weeks each does make sense.

This monthly cut to facilities totals £1,300 for the whole year, a 20% budget reduction!

Another £1,300 into the profit pot.

Happy Happy days and finally, prices are going up 10p on every drink you sell. Let's works this out with a simple sum.

I will use an average price for all drinks to keep it simple, and I get to this price by taking £25,000 net sales at an average of £4,00 per drink (drinks range from £1.50 to £9.50 with 80% of drinks below £6.00)

£25,000 / £4.00 per drink = an average of 6,250 drinks per week.

Add 10p price increase to 6,250 = an extra £625.00 every week.

£625.00 x 52 weeks = is an extra £32,500 per year.

£32,500 extra sales at 71% margin = £23,075 extra total margin per year.

£23,075 with running costs and wages taken off at 50% = £11,538 extra profit.

Ok, lets add up what differences the 5 budget adjustments will make to the profitability of your potential new pub:

£13,000

£6,500

£1,690

£1,300

£11,538

£34,028

This is an EXTRA £34,028 extra profit that will be generated by your new pub with a couple of budget tweaks. But these extra profits depend on you working to these new budgets and delivering exactly as the bigger bosses want.

And you are expected to be grateful these people have put their trust in you to run this bigger pub!

THEY are not really being nice to you by asking you to move to a new pub, they are actually USING YOU.

And don't forget, you were never told that you are being paid £28,000 a year less than the last manager for being expected to deliver even more, this is fucking bonkers.

£28,000 salary saving + **£34,028** operational saving = **£62,028** extra profit in total for that one single pub.

And don't forget, you expected to "thank the bigger bosses" for paying you £30,000 per year, which is actually less than 50% of the extra profit they expect to be delivered by *YOU*.

Now imagine the bigger bosses in a very large national company with over 3,000 pubs doing the same trick over and over again in lots of pubs?

Imagine changing the manager to reduce salary costs and tweaking the budgets that make managing the pub even harder to just 50 of their pubs?

The company's bottom line profit would grow by an unbelievable lump of **3 MILLION** sterling, 3 MILLION by driving out older managers and fooling new ones.

And guess who gets the bigger bonus, yes that's right, it's the bigger bosses.

And this is a practice that *IS* used year on year.

In the words of the great Boomtown Rats:

It's a rat trap, and you've been caught!

This tail of trickery and deception is real, this is not a made-up fictional story, this is how the licensed retail game is really played.

Worse still, I'm only telling you about the tip of the iceberg! Read On…

Chapter 7

The Great British Employee Rip-Off

As a pub manager you start the financial year with the dream of triggering the well-deserved big bonus for all that graft you are committing to for the next 12 months.

But why does it seen to get harder and harder to achieve any type of bonus, no matter how much you work your finger to the bone? The financial year always starts with a sense of hope.

You have read 6 chapters up to this point, you know by now that this is a tail of cheating and skulduggery, by I have only just scratched the surface, please read on…

Starting a new job with a financial-fund-backed pub company plc, or just starting another new financial year, it's the potential bonus that is dangled in front of the eyes that fires up the GM's drive and energy more than anything else.

If you are an existing manager the company needs a big old hook to revitaliser's you, give you renewed energy to replace all that was sapped out of you over the last 12 months.

First time GM's, bonus as well as a GM salary, they are as excited as a puppy with a squeaky toy.

But as the year financial nears its end, long term or within the first year of being a GM, you will for the first time, or once again, succumb to the realisation that all the hard work was pointless, you added nothing to your yearly income, not a fucking bean.

Somehow in the last couple of months as the business approached its year end, it has all goes wrong and the bonus chest went from being bulging full to cobweb empty…

Where did it all go, an amazing bonus vanished, how and why?

I have already explained how the bigger bosses build their own bonuses through skulduggery, sneaky wheeler-dealer accountancy and many other tricks. The money saving schemes will eventually hurt the business, the team and customers, be they do grow the profit line and bonus pots.

But now it is time to tell you how the bigger bosses weaponize the bonus system against you to increase their own bonus paydays!

The big plc-based pub companies all offer some type of an uncapped bonus allowing an additional 100% of current salary, yes that's right, you can DOUBLE your yearly salary.

FUCKING YES, I'll have some of that you think when you see the yearly bonus scheme introduction letter that comes through your door printed on high quality headed paper.

It arrives like clockwork every year and is the thing bigger bosses pray will keep you pushing through the despair, the hurt, the worry, the hopelessness and the shame of treating your team so badly, even cruelly, just so you can hit the absurdly high budgeted numbers given to you buy those vet same bigger bosses.

The HR and operations team have listed all the rules and regulations you must not break or its auto-forfeit of any earned bonus without appeal. The list of sneaky ways and reasons to withhold a bonus payment grows longer each year as the HR department are now identifying as woke.

They will publish a few of the rules, the legal ones, but they don't tell you the hidden, nasty and underhanded ways that they will use as an excuse to refuse to pay you a bonus payment, even if you have really put the hours in to earn it.

Paying you a bonus could reduce their bottom-line profit and so limit their bonus. You see, bigger bosses and upwards trigger their bonuses from the profit left AFTER your bonus is paid, but let's remember a fact, these people do not care about you or your team.

Absolute arses and greedy wankers, most of them, but not all I will say just in case you have met a modern one who is not a bastard?

Let me take you back to the original £30,000 annual salary you will be earning if you take on that bigger pub you have been pushed into taking on.

You say to yourself "If I work really hard, do as well as they are telling me I can do, I have a chance of doubling my salary to £60,000":

Do you really believe you will be allowed to double your salary?

If you do believe that you are naiver than a lime green Telly Tubby behind a curtain in Spearmint Rhino wondering why two arse cheeks and an anally bleached butt hole are pressed hard against his face?

Sorry if that image stays with you for a while, I don't know where it came from myself? Anyway.

You will be given a large number of hoops to jump through, clown shoes to jump over, banana skins to avoid and BDM ever moving hidden Bear Traps to skip past in order to achieve this oh so tempting bonus.

Wage controls must be delivered under budget, stock results must be in surplus, Trip Advisor reports have can be no less than 4.5 stars, lower than company average staff turnover to showing a warm caring pub company, and you must beat every single financial target on the PandL.

There is no room for failure, you will need to be at the top of your game, push to new heights, drive the team even harder than last year, no compromise will get in the way, you can do it.

You are not concerned as you take over your new pub, you have been told that you are a fantastic manager, a one off, the best they have seen in decades, and you have been rewarded with the honour of managing a huge pub, but unknown to you, with reduced running costs.

You are convinced that you, the golden one with the Midas touch will be the manager who actually makes the 100% bonus and that juicy extra 30k will be all yours.

Just 12 months to go and you will be laughing all the way to the bank and no doubt, the award nights once again.

You are now the manager:

Let's look at what you will have to achieve to earn my bonus?

Wages:

You will need to keep the labour costs inside the wage percentage budget at any cost.

We have talked to death about the subject of wages, you know you will end up working 60, 70, even 80 hours per week, but you will do what you need to do to hit the labour budget for the day, the week, month, and full year.

You also need to keep your immediate boss, your BDM, happy and on your side because you think he is up for helping you keep your eye firmly on the big bonus prize.

Errrrrrr ok… I wonder if you will still be feeling the same when you have not had a day off for 18 weeks just to achieve the wage budget?

Stock Results:

To measure success or failure of stock control is really very simple.

If you have the correct amount of stock items on hand when physically checking the amount and that physical count of stock items equals what the sales record total is, stocks are good.

If, when you have physically counted the stock items, you have loss stock on hand than the sales report says you should have, you have a stock deficit, or put plainly, stock is missing, and you will be blamed for losing the stock and its value.

Stock control is that simple, and it should be if we were all smart-arse robots and have never spilled a pint, over poured a shot, or dropped a bottle in the cellar.

Stock, drink, or food, is lost because of so many reasons, it just takes one wanker who has just conned a team member out of a large glass of Cola because they reckon, even insist, a glass collector took their drink while they were taking a piss!

Staff bumping into each other while serving behind a cramped and badly laid out busy bar.

A customer asks for a vodka and lemonade, but no one ever asks for lemonade, it is always served with coke, and you have served thousands of them over the years.

Autopilot kicks in, after putting ice and fruit into the glass, next is adding the vodka over the ice while also replying to another team about changing barrels, you automatically press the cola button. For Fucks Sake…

That is a wasted double vodka and cola splash, WASTED.

There are so many ways to lose stock, drinks are spilled, miss-poured and spoiled by mistake every day and you keep your fingers crossed that the pub company auditors will recognise that people and humans, no one is infallible, and we all make mistakes.

But NOOOooooooooooo That is NOT how pub companies work.

Managing stock is precise, if you don't lose one single drop of wet stock will have achieved 100% stock, or in audit terms, 100% stock yield.

We already understand that drinks are spilled and wasted, this means that making 100% yield should be impossible because no week ever passes with a slip-up and a wasted drink.

And if you could achieve 100% stock yield that would mean it is a perfect stock result, yes?

Er **NO**… Your pub company budgets your pub to achieve 105% stock yield, that is your target.

How can fuck do you make 105% stock yield from a base of only 100%?

Where is this extra 5% and how do you add it to the 100% yield?

We are pub managers, not fucking magicians…

The next 12 months of stock control is now laid out for you, as a pub manager you will be obsessing about two finger deep heads on pints of beer, extra ice in every soft drink, wine poured into jigger measures before it goes into the glass.

Why don't you let the bar team use the line printed on the glass when pouring wine, isn't that what it is there for?

NO NO NO NO NEVER When pouring wine from a bottle into a glass you are normally looking downward towards the glass. Because of the angle you see the line on the glass from you will pour approximately 10ml extra than they are paying for what should be a 250ml measure.

It's only10ml extra, that's not a lot is it, who cares about a free 4% of liquid that a customer receives for nowt because you served them 260ml instead of 250ml by not being careful?

This is why is matters:

You need to care because your pub will sell around 300 bottles of wine per week, almost all by the measure of 175ml or 250ml.

A bottle of wine contains 4 x 175ml glasses of wine at and 3 glasses of wine using the 250ml measure.

Let say for the sake of it 150 of those bottles of wine are sold as 175ml glasses of wine and the other 150 bottles are sold as large 250ml glasses.

This equals 600 glasses of wine sold as a 175ml measure, and 450 glasses of wine sold as a 250ml measure.

Let add these two totals together and we now know that 1,050 glasses of wine have been bought by customers.

I want you to imagine that just 50% of the glasses of wine are sold without using a wine measure, and so each one will include the extra 10ml over-pour in each of the 525 glasses of wine.

The line on the glass is never in exactly in the right place when you look down at the glass from above, and that is a fact.

Using the numbers above to calculate volumes, how much wine has your pub "lost" by not using a wine measure for the 525 glasses of wine in just one week?

Your team have over-poured and given away a total of 7 full bottles of wine in "*not worth worrying about*" tiny 10ml amounts per glass.

If your team continue to give away 7 bottles of wine every week for a whole year they will give away, for free, a total of 364 bottles of the company's wine stock.

They will want to know where it is. Even if the wine is a cheap Pinot Grigio with a retail sales value of just £5.99, or £4.80 at net sales costs after the tax man nicks his bit, the total value of wine your team are giving away is £1,747.20p in just 1 YEAR!

Sales LOSS OVER the bar tops out with VAT included as £2,180.36 over a full financial year.

You won't be making your bonus like this will you?

You become a spy, watching any move every team member makes, "is that her dad?" Has she just slipped him a freebie?

Next you see someone order a whiskey and you find yourself watching closely just in case Lucy pours a double scotch but only chargers for a single for that man who "could" be her brother, but you have no idea... paranoia is taking over your mind. Are you losing your control?

I've still not answered where the magical 5% yield is conjured up from by using magical, secret, licensee powers...

Here we go, strap in, how do you turn 100% stock yield into a surplus of 105% stock yield even though drinks are spilled?

It's really simple, everyone serving the public is ripping them off by short pouring their drinks.

The most shocking part of this company sponsored theft, you as a GM are being forced, by a budget, through passively aggressive threatened actions, and the promise of a big bonus, to make the pubs "long term, trusted and loyal" team members steal from the regular customers, many who they know in their personal lives as friends or family.

Short pouring drinks is the main trick used to increase the number of pints or shots from a sealed barrel or bottle. It is used on guests who hand over their hard-earned money for a quality and legally measured drink, but they are oblivious to the game of growing stock yield by selling thin air.

Everything being done to rip off the customer is sanctioned by the pub company because they have budgeted you to reach 105% stock yield from what started out as physically just 100%.

The GM is expected to make an extra 5% from what is basically an invisible mixture of N_2, O_2 and CO_2 or they won't get their teased about bonus reward.

The pub company denies this of course, publicly they would never ask their managers to rob the customers and pull 5% out of a hat with a rabbit attached, noooooo, the 5% is just natural growth in volume through handling liquor stocks in the best way possible.

This is the public face and what they will tell you and everyone…

BOLLOCKS BOLLOCKS AND BOLLOCKS AGAIN

If you buy a can of beer, a bottle of wine or a fruit juice carton and handle it perfectly, store it at the idea temperature for the perfect length of time, it will **NOT** increase in volume by 5% when you open it.

Think about it, drinks don't grow in size or volume, so where does the extra 5% come from?

It is robbed, ripped off, nicked, stolen and swiped from YOU, and every other customer visiting the biggest PLC pub companies.

Hypothetically, if you have 3000 pubs and 2500 of them all hit their target stock yield of 105%, just imagine the amount of money the pub company is generating for NOTHING with this magic trick of creating 5% volume to sell THAT IS NOT REALLY THERE.

If a pub sales total £750,000.00 per year, that is 3/4 of a million in liquor sales transactions that will take 100% stock yield to make those sales.

If we add an extra 5% it adds £37,500.00 sales in just one pub.

Let's extrapolate that up to 2,500 pubs, that is an extra £93,750.000 revenue, yes that's right, 93 million extra cash sales from something that has never even existed, the invented by audit extra 5%.

How can thin air sell for 93 million?

But it does, year after year after year…

The PLC owned pub company branded pub, where you spend all that money on drinks and food, it really is great value every day. Are sure that is a fact?

The pub company spends a fortune in the media convincing the innocent that it's providing exceptionally good value.

THEY are very skilled in deception and twisting truths.

Are you still convinced you are at the heart of the customer service and the most important thing to the bigger bosses?

Yeah right, dream on, that behemoth pub company is holding you upside down by the ankles and will shake your booty harder and faster until every penny falls from your pockets into its coffers...

Trip Advisor and Mystery Guests

Social Media, love it or hate it, it dominates the hospitality business because everyone posts a fucking selfie everywhere they go.

Selfie with my large glass of cola because the crap paper straw has gone limp, selfie with the Yorkshire pudding that looks like 75-year-old twat with chapped lips! Snaps of food, drinks and "filtered" image faces are posted billions of times a day and everywhere is fucking tagged.

Social media can easily cripple a retail business overnight just by going viral with bad reviews, shocking video clips and dodgy product images, so the PLC pub company has to get ahead of the on-line game.

Whopping big PLC Pub Co's employ a certain type of geek to run their on-line world. Any negative posts, public opinions or photos of any big business is always hidden away in a world of gigabytes and silicon chips, big business has to control the content of on-line media, you know, what some people still think is free speech.

The type of people cybering full time for big PLC's only drink green tea, eat vegan cheese (have you ever tried vegan cheese ffs) enjoy Pilates and fully understand what the fuck is going on in the Marvel MCU Multiverse. These keyboard warriors know nothing, zilch, nada, bugger all about pubs or the type of people who use real hostelries. Sitting at a PC posting all day long about upcoming events, publishing imaginary customer reviews, they ensure a company's on-line presence is used exclusively as an influencing tool to increase trade.

PLC pub companies are really heavy with on-line traffic, managing content, blocking unwanted posts, and limiting comments to maintain their positive on-line image!

It's all a frigging con, image manipulation and public perception control is the bread and butter to slick marketing teams.

Pub companies love sending in mystery guests to check the food quality and level of service. Most mystery guests wouldn't normally eat in branded food pubs or pub chains, they spend their own money in high end eateries. Where they eat great food when out socially doesn't matter, apparently it qualifies them to judge the quality of the food you sell and the service you provide in a branded food pub.

The problem with using "foodies" to judge pub is, once you have eaten a slow grown, lean, 35 days matured and perfectly marbled rump steak in The Ivy, when you receive an 8oz cheaply cut fatty rump that costs £5.99 in a branded pub chain, it may disappoint, don't you think?

At the other end of the rainbow, getting some overzealous couple, who only ever eat at Nando's, visiting your pub to judge your food and service will be just as bad. They eat peri peri hot chicken as a regular staple, you have just served the reconstituted breaded scampi and under 15% beef lasagne, this will not end well. Before they even order you are in for a bad score because you don't sell spicy sauce covered chicken or offer bottomless Diet Coke.

On any number of occasions when I was still managing pubs, I would receive a really low mystery guest score detailing bad customer service and poor-quality food.

Award winning pub, fantastic South Yorkshire team and some of the best on duty during the mystery guest visit?

So off I go to watch the CCTV where, once again, I find no trace of these mystery guests anywhere in the building.

Have I got the right time, the right day, am I losing the plot?

The demographic of these mystery guests is described as a 50+ year old couple eating at 7pm according to the mystery guest report. But what I see is an early 20's+ couple eating exactly what is detailed on the receipt. The very same receipt used to prove the mystery guest attended our pub to sample the food and experience the service.

Confused?

What has happened is the well-known and well used con trick to dine "out-for-nowt", some family's do it over and over again to eat out for free.

Still confused? Let me explain…

Someone in the family signs up and joins a mystery guest service, or mystery shopper agency, but it will be their son and his partner who are going out for something to eat at the pub they are asked to visit and assess.

The real mystery guest who signed up to take part is staying at home to watch Eastenders, but he will need the young couple to return with the receipt so the "stay at home dad" can claim he visited the pub and scoffed the food himself.

The receipt is validated by the head office of the company running the mystery guest service, money is refunded by the pub company to the Eastenders watching man for completing all the tasks during the visit, eating the food, making notes while he was in the pub and sending in his report within 48 hours.

In reality what has happened is, the young couple ate out for half price as the TV watching mystery guest refunds his full stomach son half the receipt value in return for taking the receipt back to him quickly.

The lazy TV watching wanker, who has done nothing except fill in a form online, then claims the full amount of the receipt back for completing the mystery visit.

Result?

Eastenders fan farther makes 50% of total receipt value as profit and without moving his arse from his chair he wrote a made-up mystery guest report about somewhere he has never been.

Well-fed son and girlfriend paid just 50% receipt total for the meals and drinks, what a bargain, and the pub company receives NO value at all because the report is just made up lies.

It's a victimless crime, isn't it?

NO IT IS NOT A VICTIMLESS CRIME, AS A MANAGER YOU COULD LOSE YOUR FULL YEARS BONUS, OR EVEN YOUR JOB, THROUGH THIS SIMPLE CON-TRICK, OR PUT MORE SIMPLY, A LIE.

This con has a double whammy:

1: The pub company has been conned out of the cost for food and drinks.

2: The cost of ruining the pubs reputation because the review will end up on-line.

Can you imagine slipping outside the bonus earning criteria because someone lied about a mystery visit, you would be absolutely gutted to say the very least.

Staff Turnover

The actions of the modern prat BDM, or a chief arse Op's manager, will have already killed your chances of hitting this target.

I have never really appreciated why we had to set staff turnover levels as a key performance indicator, surely if you need to remove bad staff you should not be penalised for doing the right thing?

Bosses making you reduce staff at the busiest times hurts team moral, stupidly high yield expectations make for any anxious GM, and making all branded pubs in the same chain use centrally piped in music chosen by a marketing imbecile with an AI profiling App does not deliver great service.

All these backward thinking moves and the fact that your customers don't won't products just because it's cheaper this week than last, honestly, the list of fuckups that are forced upon you as a GM and then present them to guests is fucking limitless.

Circling back to staff turnover, this is one of the daftest loss makers that makes me laugh out loudest now I'm out of pubs.

How does the HR department expect you to lower your staff turnover when it was them who approved this new tosser of a BDM who is forcing you to abuse your pub staff for profit?

Pub companies often operate with a staff turnover rate of 150% or well above. There is a few hard-core long-term staff members who are around forever, most of us know a Jackie or a Karen who have been working at that pub for at least 10 years minimum.

The problem pubs have is generally centred around young staff starting one day with a big smile and leaving very soon after with a long face and the onset of depression.

New pub or the start of a new financial year and you will be set a target of around 120% staff turnover, 30% reduction in current turnover and you think "yeah I can achieve that, I are very friendly manager, a good laugh and very supportive."

In your last pub with your old area manager, it was all good, he knew all my teams names, spent time with them, we all had a great friendly long-term relationship, and really low staff turnover.

Times have changed, now you have this tosser BDM who was obviously bullied at school who wants to get his own back on the cooler type kids who now, unfortunately for them, are reporting to him as the boss of their GM.

You have landed in your new bigger pub, you are now following strict orders to reduce the majority of staffing age to under 21 years old and replace all your old, useless, outdated and ugly full-time staff with part time pretty little things that will make the prat BDM's willy tingle if they smile while looking towards him.

Oh yes, let's not forget, we are reducing NI costs.

After being in your new pub as GM for just a few weeks you are watching the team like a hawk, any infringement, such as a pint head not being big enough to increase the liquor yield by 5% out of thin air, or just pouring Cola without 3/4 of the glass filled with ice first, you will be treating serving infringements like they are a capital crime. The pressure is making you snappy, you are shouting at staff like a ruthless greedy monster the desire to keep your job and earn a bonus has made you.

You no longer recognise yourself...

Most of your staff are being paid under £7.00 per hour for all their smiles, service, and teamwork, you would be paid more than that stacking shelve in Aldi, is that right?

As a team member in your pub, is it worth being treated like a criminal or being shouted at for not pouring a two finger deep head?

Fuck Noooooo. Staff who are being watched intently and barked at for missing one cube of ice from a glass of lemonade don't hang around for long and can blame them!

Badly treated, abused, and undervalued staff move on to businesses who pay adult rate wages, where they become team members and not considered as worthless staff.

Who wants to work where the atmosphere isn't that far from an East European criminal sweatshop?

If treating your team without any humanity is the only way you have any chance to make your bonus, that in itself is a good enough reason why you will NEVER earn a penny more than your basic pay.

Team members are not parts of the machine, they are human beings with emotions and a working brain.

LEARN. Financial Targets

Yet another loaded dice, but you don't know that as you are starting the new financial year.

In your new pub most of your budgets have been changed, adjusted, manipulated since last year's budgets, trimmed for profit creation as I have already described. These changes will make your life, and that of your new team's work-life, much tougher for you, and them, than your predecessor and their team worked last year.

What happens if you hit all these crazy tough targets, you have had forced, unknowingly, on you?

Against all the odds, with the deck well and truly stacked against you, numbers and the results are in showing you have actually on your way to a well-earned stonking big bonus.

If you do deliver the supposedly unreachable targets and land the numbers that were meant to be out of your grasp, based on a true story, this is what happens when the pub company are shitting themselves because bonuses have been triggered for some GM's.

Bigger Bosses have to act really quickly to stop these pay-outs if they can. You see, actually paying out bonuses to anyone below BDM level will reduce the Bigger Bosses bonus total amounts.

PANIC STATIONS...

The final financial weeks of the year are approaching fast and the last, but 1 PandL comes through on email.

There is just two weeks left of the whole financial year so you are just 4 weeks away from knowing how big and juicy your full year bonus will be.

Get in you handsome bastard.

This latest Profit and Loss statement makes great reading, you are 20% up verses sales budget and 25% up verses profit target for the year to date.

Even better, this final financial month is going really well, Easter has just finished, and you smashed it by making Easter Sunday the local Bank Holiday Party of The Year by opening until 4am, so you can expect the profit budget will be smashed in this period by the largest amount of any period throughout the whole year.

But you do deserve a big pay-out, 4am for fuck's sake...

It is looking like you are on for a big, fat, tasty and gorgeous £20,000 plus bonus.

YEAH, YOU ARE THE MAN...

You mind is spinning; the smile is permanently tattooed across your face. That trip to NYC is definitely on, drinking in every hot bar, trendy club, designer shop and fuck it, with this bonus you are flying business class.

Time for a well-deserved 21-Year-Old Malt Whisky, pass the ice.

Next day you are skim reading twitter and you notice one of the financial pages has been posting about a pub company. You click on the link, and it opens.

What you get is a jaw-dropping and stunning shock!

The media site called Propel, it focuses on the leisure trade, has put out in the daily news that one of the largest PLC pub companies has released a statement about a profit warning.

The Headline

(Who you work for) Announces Profit Warning

Hang on a minute, our top bosses have been bragging all year about record breaking sales and dividends, WTF has happened?

Where has this bullshit come from, who the fuck has broken this news, it must be a mistake, surely, they have got it wrong?

You call your BDM to see what he knows, but he hasn't seen the news, so by now you are in a full psychotic head-spin.

Confused, angry, why is the company you work so hard for steeling back the money promised in their bonus scheme before I even get a sniff of it?

What the fuck is going on…?

The anger explodes, into the cellar you go throwing barrels about to let off some steam.

A fierce burning well of frustration stays with you over the next few days, then finally the pub company send out a letter to all its managers explaining what is going on and why a profit warning has been announced.

What trickery is this, dare you read it, yes no yes no yes no YES.

You rip the letter open, and you scan-read it quickly, your beady eyes looking out for key words.

You find a "key statement"

"Bonus will be paid"

The relief washes over you, oh my god, you **ARE** going to get your money, you jump for joy, dance and giggle in a mixture of swearing and laughing.

You had better read it again, but this time slowly and carefully.

"The company has activated the stretch bonus limiter policy because we have not hit our profit targets as a company."

you read on…

"Instead of paying out 30% of any profit above budget as agreed in the bonus terms, we will be paying out a discretionary 3% as a gesture of good-will."

blah blah blah… **WHAT THE FUCK**…

You don't give a flying fuck what everyone else did or didn't do with their bonus scheme, why should someone else's failure mean you don't get your bonus?

Reading on, apparently the brewery lost a shit load of money, why should you care that the brewing arm of the company lost money?

YOU HIT YOUR TARGETS, YOU DID YOUR BIT, SO YOU WANT THE MONEY THAT YOU WERE FUCKING PROMISED!

Still not sure about what has happened.

This is one of the biggest cons the bigger bosses use to save their own bonus payments and deliver dividends to share-holders.

If a PLC pub company boozer smashes it out the park, storm's ahead with bottom line profits even though the odds were stacked hugely against such success, it is then robbed from under the GM's nose by using creative accounting under the instruction of the bigger bosses.

It is publicly announced that because the pub company has not hit its profit target across all divisions, it is a failed year financially speaking.

Even though the branded pub division of the company exceeded its profit budget by 100 million, the accountants can use the "stretch bonus" clause to declare that every part of the company has not met its expectations.

If just one division, such as the brewery, missed its target with just a 5 million loss, the bonus pay-outs at the bottom of the employee pile will be trimmed. Paying out only 3% means the savings made by taking away the other 27% of GM's bonuses allows the city shareholders to receive maximum dividend.

Basically, the PLC pub companies are going to use the bonus money owed to you, and 100's of GM's just like you, as a way to fill the dividend gap.

You, and every other high performing manager is having their bonus stolen to bolster the whole companies bottom line and please the shareholders, and there is nothing you can do about it.

Think back to the numbers?

100 million extra profits over the profit budget in the pubs division.

5 million under profit budget in the brewery division.

That is still an extra 95 million above the total profit budgets for the company, but a simple clause just allows innocent managers to ripped off by bigger bosses once again.

The bigger bosses don't care how the low life pleb pub managers feel, or even suffer, the chef executive and the company board job is to keep the share price high enough, so they all receive their 6 figure salaries and yearly share issue.

Big PLC pub Co's know their priorities, please the city and keep the rich investors investing even more next year.

Do you now understand how important you really are?

The Great VAT Swindle and Carvery Pubs Have you ever bought a cake in a restaurant pub to eat at home?

There is a chain of massive food pubs that actively robs their customers, and the government, at the same time. This is how the great cake con is done.

Let's call this pub chain Barnshed, it is a massive food factory where you will happily queue on a Sunday for 20 or 30 minutes at a hot carvery counter for food. After a long wait in the queue, you then have to spoon the tatty veg and other bits onto your own plates where it immediately begins to cool down at speed.

Next, an ex-Debenhams toilet cleaner dressed in chefs' whites' places wafer thin carved meat to the huge mound of soggy veg and asks, "do you want a Yorkshire pudding?"

Of course, I want a fucking Yorkie Pub ffs, hurry up, my fucking plate is going cold and becoming heavy.

And you are paying for this experience…

Kids running riot, throwing mash and musky peas up the walls, grinding ice cream into the carpet with their feet while spreading chocolate sauce over the tabletop.

Parents don't give as toss because they are both on their 4th pint of 5% strength lager and they know they don't have to clean up after their little bastard feral kids named Chardonnay and Archibald, that's the stupid staffs job lol.

Regular and greedy customers have their carvery plate tactics planned well before they join the snaking hot-plate queue.

Some use roast potatoes laid out like bricks on the outside of the plate, cemented together with mash to create a deep food bowl. Next it is the pile it high within the roast reenforced potato walls, you add so much veg it now takes two hands to just to hold your plate level.

I like to watch the ones who didn't build the circle of Maris Piper strong enough, they pile the plate so deeply, then the mistake that always makes me laugh out loud, they add a least a pint of gravy.

Liquid, as we all know from school, always finds the route with the least resistance. Gravy is no different, it will find the gap it your spud enclosure and run out at speed. What makes it even funnier is that fact that the plate is so heavy it is being held close to the body where the brown warm liquid is seeping out directly onto the space where he has tucked in shirt meets the waist of his jeans.

Enjoy you damp and sticky lunch you greedy bastard…

When carvery users are famished, they pile those piles skilfully high to maximise the value of weight of food vs price, them they scoff every mouthful down leaving the plates completely food morsel free, and that's fine, you paid for it, enjoy yourself.

But when a carvery fan in not particularly dying from starvation and just wants a normal sized meal, they still pile it high, mountains of spuds, carrots, peas, and broccoli swimming in a pool of gravy edged with roasties. They eat half of their carefully balanced food mountain, and just leave the rest as waste. I once asked a friend of mine who did exactly this why he did it, he said "I've paid for it so I'm taking as much as I can, it's my right."

Some of the largest and porkiest people I have ever seen in food pubs were in carvery style branded family pubs. Look around, you never see a person who shops at Marquees R Us with a small plate with a modest amount of food, it's always a solid mass of food tactically placed to maximise yield and quantity.

What drink do you think is waiting for them on the table when they return from the food counter?

it is almost always a supersized diet Cola, it's diet because they are slimming for a beech holiday.

If someone 9 stone heavier now than they were when wearing their wedding dress just 8 years ago, it is not a bad thing to cut something out the weekly food consumption.

I'm sure that drinking diet cola by the pint will help loose the few pounds gained, after all, you did read it would in a magazine.

What did she eat in Barnshed at 1pm on a Tuesday?

While out for a light lunch, she ate 2 kilos of buttered mash, 1/2 a pound of buttered carrots, 4 Yorkshire puddings dripping in cream laced gravy, but she did only have 2 super-sized diet colas while eating her calorie uncontrolled lunch, so that allows her a treat from the fantastic large cake range to eat at home.

After viewing all the colourful iced and creamy baked beauties on display a huge slice of amazing home-made cake is bought for £4.99 to take home and eat later on in the day. It won't be long, just a few hours and she it is starving again due to all the intense regime of sitting on the sofa.

I don't blame anyone for taking cake home in a little box, they look fantastic under the bright lights and are the best thing carvery pubs. And oh, the choice, which one, can you decide?

There is nothing wrong with desiring cake.

Have you ever been to a Starbucks, Greggs, or anywhere that sells take-a-way food or drinks and been asked: "Are you are eating in or taking away?" Why do they ask this?

They ask this question because they are doing things correctly, following HMRC rules and regulations.

If you are taking food or drink away to eat away from the place it was purchased than no VAT is applied to the final cost price.

Not applying VAT because it is take-out saves 20% on the final buying price.

The rule is, if you eat or drink in an area owned, licensed, or controlled by the seller VAT of 20% is applied.

Certain Carvery branded pub chains do ask you if you are eating in or taking away, but it is not asked to drop the price by 20% VAT if you are taking away, they are only asking because they want to know if you need it in a Take-Out box.

The price stays the same, they charge the same eating in price regardless of if you be feasting on the take-out cake at home.

Carvery branded pub chains doing this are selling a piece of cake with 20% VAT to the final price when it doesn't need to.

This means the take-out customer is paying 20%, or 99p more than they need to for every slice of cake purchased.

Do you think the branded Carvery chain owners are giving the government the 99p extra from each sale that includes VAT but doesn't need to?

NO, THEY ARE NOT

Selling cakes to take home is a huge money spinner for the company doing this, if they have 30 sites selling carvery and cakes to take home, each site could sell up to 500 slices of cake that are taken home every week.

That equals 500 slices of cake X 30 carvery pubs X 99p each slice.

This means the carvery PLC owners are ripping off their own customers by around £14,850 every week, or put another way, they are stealing £14,850 per week from the government tax revenues.

Let's take £14,850 x 52 weeks and we get £772,200.00 per year.

Can you imagine someone exposing a Carvery brand owned by a PLC financially controlled pub company aiming at the family market ripping off their regular customers by 3/4 of a million quid every you?

Or highlighting to the tax-man the con trick to with-hold VAT payments to HMRC?

Whoops…

If this carvery business has been open for years, let's add 5 years of missing VAT together and see what we get.

PLC owners of the Carvery brand, you owe the taxpayer approximately £3,861,000.00, nearly 4 million quid.

Pay up, the UK needs it.

And STOP ROBBING innocent people of their hard-earned money.

Friendly, local and wholesome pub company?

You decide now you know…

Chapter 8

Let's talk about the Kingdom of HR and Head Office

There I was, 18 years old and, still very wet behind the ears, troubled by the occasional unwanted boner when sat on the bus or watching a "Block-Buster" rented film, young, loving life and the future was looking great.

How daft was it to place a horny teenager in a position of responsibility for money, H&S and licensing!

Madness…

Joining Whitbread Pub Company as a teenager was a proud moment, this was a big company, a career path working alongside fantastic people, down to earth people who had grown up in the pub trade.

So much to learn, I was like a sponge, tell me everything.

We had a personnel Department at our regional head office in Sheffield who knew everyone name, they took an interest in you as a human being.

All very different to comprehensive school where no one teacher gave a single toss what your name was or if you could actually read or write.

Valley Comprehensive 1976 to 1981, 5 years with bullies and wankers for teachers, and my condition of dyspraxia hadn't even been recognised until the season of Grange Hill featured it as a story line the year after I left full-time education.

I didn't really know what a personnel department did, but they were some of the nicest people I have ever met in any working situation.

Then it clicked, they were the people who looked after me as an employee on a personal level in the big company machine.

David and Jean, they ran the department, and they were so friendly, welcoming, approachable with any concerns you had.

They were there for you, and it felt it like a warm coat, wrapped around you, loose enough to allow the air to flow, you to breath at your own speed, but it kept the wind and storms out.

Training plans were put together for you as an individual, every care was taken to make sure you were taught every skill you needed and made to make sure you continually improved in every area of pub management.

The area managers came across as nice people (they weren't BDM tossers yet) with the odd exception who didn't care about a female manager being punched in her face.

The whole culture was warm, friendly, competitive, and rewarding at the same time.

You didn't fear the BDM, Op's Manager or even the local director popping to say hello, you welcomed it because they we there for you and genuinely supported your pub and the team.

Bigger Bosses were not like the ones we get today, they knew your name, talked to you as an equal, thanked you for your hard work, they were involved with the day-to-day goings on in the pubs in their regions.

The head-office bigger bosses of today are what is known as, "Twice removed up the ivory staircase of power"

sometimes found in CEO suites overlooking the City of London trading floors.

Our Biggest local boss, Ian, was a right character, big smile, powerful voice, commended an audience whenever he spoke and he was not someone who was just a number cruncher, he liked the action, the fun, the creativity of pubs and the people in them.

His most famous quote was: J:F:D:I. This stands for: JUST FUCKING DO IT. He wanted us to try new things, use our imagination and grow our business by being active and fun-loving managers, not sheep.

Any of my old colleagues from Sherwood Inns reading this will be looking back with a board smile.

We also had other senior managers, like Big John, Ian's number two, who came across as business-like, but with a sense of kindness and pragmatism that no longer seems to exist in PLC pub companies.

The whole brewery led pub company culture was all about supporting the front-line manager and their teams. Being so well supported as pub managers we could deliver fantastic service, quality, and fun to the customers.

The area managers, most of them were great people, they were honest and did the right thing, but some of were on the take big time in collusion with some of the manages on their areas.

It was to work out who they were, they always seem to have a villa in Spain or Portugal.

Who else but big-time criminals owned a villa on the Costa Del Sol?

Yep, you guessed it, dodgy pub manages, and area manages.

In the days of J:F:D:I, yes, the bogs in the pubs we're still being ignored and usually in need of some TLC. I know we still served really terrible wine and cheap tonic, but to be honest, we didn't know any better, and what we did with what we had wasn't too bad.

Even the audit team was employed "in-house" by the company, and we knew them all by name.

Malcolm was very strict, Stewart you could have laugh with, but if John turned up, one of the senior auditors, it was stand to attention time and get really for a non-smiling full day of seriousness that only happened when it was John counting everything from the barrels in the cellar to the number of cocktail sticks on the bar.

He was so serious, but he was a fucking good auditor who could pin-point problems, identify weakness with controls and trace every penny.

These day auditors are "outsourced" agencies because GMs are not allowed to get to know them just in case, they collaborate together to steal 2 half pints of lime and soda when the summer heat hits 35°.

Cellar service, you know, that important part of a brewery and pub business that keeps the beer flowing and cold, were also in-house employed technicians. One was always on duty, we had a couple of great guys, Eric, Malc, there supervisor Rod, they all loved their coffee call-ins and our long chats full of giggles and belly laughs.

These fella's had tremendous experience, knowledge and cared about our cellars, the equipment, and the quality of product we served to paying customers. They were assets and brand champions.

Modern cellars a looked after by an ever-changing stream of new contractors who have no loyalty to any products, the cellars, the managers, or the brand they are performing the task issued as a job number.

The point of my ramblings above is this.

We were once just one huge team of people pulling in the same direction, no one got left behind, no one was bigger than the brand, together we were the brand, brand Whitbread, a family working together, every department with the same values, it was all about the people delivering for each other and to a thankful community of drinkers from all works of life.

Now it is time to understand just how far the pub and brewery industry in the UK has changed from the early 90's to where we are now in 2022.

There are no such things as a regional office anymore, all sold off, along with most of the brewery sites to developers who build either warehouse hubs or sprawling Hobbit sized flats that are called apartments just for marketing reasons.

There are no in-house departments anymore, the cellar service team have gone, the audit team have gone, the wagon drivers and dray men have gone, even the canteen ladies have gone and been replaced with "break-out-areas" and vending machines.

And finally, the traditional personnel department has also gone, the people who ran it dumped in the wastepaper basket of computerisation, and with all that loss, the ability to practice face to face management, one to ones with people who cared, the regional family has been dispersed to kitchen tables and motorway phone calls.

Personal Departments are dead and buried leaving a void where the care for the individual once was because that has well and truly fucked right off…

But do not despair, all the above have been replaced by 3 new all-conquering super powerful and perfect in every way department:

9. The Human Resources Department (HR)
10. The Marketing Department (MD)
11. The Compliance Department (CD)

These new centralised departments have taken over all the functions, actions and performance management of each of the pub companies regional departments and amalgamated everything under one roof.

At least the people in this new remote head-office on an industrial estate near Coventry won't have to actually visit the pubs more than 25 miles away.

"I have a job in head office running 1,000's pubs, why would I ever want to actually visit them?"

The pub company now has a "super office" with everyone who is office based all working in trendy "Hot-Desk" rooms, they have a pool table, free muffins and snacks, free hot drinks and a free cold drink vending machine, all because the head office team work so much harder and are valued far higher than a glass collector, line chef, waiter or cleaner.

Personnel Department changed to Human Resources.

Go on tell me, just like so many people try do when I compare these two department names:

"They are the same thing, just a new modern name."

BOLLOCKS TO THAT:

NO, THEY ARE DEFINITELY NOT THE SAME

The difference between the two names comes down to who runs the department and what they are there to do?

I talked about David and Jean earlier and how they ran a fantastic Personnel Department that looked after the people working at every level within the company.

Earlier in this book I also talked about how the Whitbread family still remained part of the company, a family member still sitting as chairman, mainly a figurehead, but those family values had endured and remained at the heart of the values brought forward from the humble beginnings of the Whitbread brewing story.

People meant more to Sam Whitbread than shareholders, than absolute profits, even more than being the biggest brewer.

It was people, pints, and then profits, always in that order, values to be proud of.

So where does the Human Resources department come from?

Over the decades of change, growth, the city getting involved and shareholders demanding bigger and bigger dividends, this is where the HR bastards sneak in.

The new ruthless money grabbing CEO's need HR departments because they who would eat Bambi, if they could be bought for the right price, and then would re-sell the pelt to recover the money spent on Bambi's dead corpse in the first place, needs a department that will always defend the companies' brands and reputation against all those pesky employees and their moaning.

Once the ruthless HR fuckers get inside, a business becomes more of a Fox in the Hen house bloodbath than a family of Elephants caring for their youngsters at any cost, even their owns lives.

The personnel departments only job of looking after the employees is now well and truly over, the main concern will no longer be the people who earn the money to pay the shareholders their dividends, it will be from this point onward simply about one single thing:

PROTECT THE ASSET

This sole role of a HR department is to protect the business from potential risk of litigation.

But what could possibly be risky to our enormously wealthy share-wankers, sorry, I mean shareholders?

People, employees, they are now the RISK.

People can mean anyone from staff members, the public, workmen, official visitors, absolutely anyone.

Each one of the "people" pose a risk to the company so they need to protect the company, or the asset, from people who want to cause it problems, damage it reputation, or cost it any money.

The question now must be asked *"I thought we were in the business of looking after people who use our hospitality business for pleasure?"*

How naive. Once the city gets involved, they will appoint a new BIG BOSS, or CEO who will be focused on the city share-holder's needs.

As soon as you get a greedy, ambitious and monster size cunt CEO in charge of a PLC business, why would they give a fuck about ordinary people anymore?

Unless you are a banker, MP, SPAFFS (MP's advisors), senior civil servant, lobbyist, or they invite the CEO to dine with them on their yacht in Saint-Tropez, fuck-em…

When you get a twat of a CEO in charge of a leisure business the front-line team just become a commodity, a tool to make money and a body to sell brand recognition to future investors.

Let's put it like this, and this game or forever growth is played the same way over and over again.

The CEO wants constant growth, he will challenge his team to find a route to growth.

The team trial a concept pub that turns out to be hugely popular and takes stack of cash in its first month open.

Next, the CEO's minions decide to roll out this new and successful concept pub in 40 more locations across the UK in a desperate hope that joe public will want to visit every single one of them and they will become a successful nationwide brand.

At the same time all the other big PLC pub companies are doing exactly the same, looking for something new to drive footfall and increase revenue.

I have seen soon bat-crack crazy things in pubs!

Ten Pin Bowling, mini golf, over sizer arcade games, football darts, Hot-Tubs (that was mine) oddly shaped pool tables, beds for chairs (yes that did happen in Blackpool, a glass dance floor on the 1st floor so people could stand and stair from below, 54oz steaks, 6-foot-long pizzas, church service, boxing weight-in, foam parties and provocative dance's and even a marriage.

The pub companies will encourage, even push their pub teams hard to extract every penny they can in any way possible to maintain and increase the pubs profit line and eventually the share price.

The CEO with the highest ranking on the footsie must have the biggest bollocks of them all.

Remember, I started this bit telling you how it has all changed, Personnel Departments look after people, Human Resources protect the asset from the people.

How does this protect the PLC's income and reputation?

It is all about mitigating any risks that could affect financial performance and public reputation.

Big PLC pub companies manage their risk by controlling the people to a level of compliance that is beyond lots of tick boxes, it really has become the nanny state in the workplace.

You have all heard about Health and Safety being out of control, stifling, you cannot do fuck all anymore in case someone slips, falls off a chair, bumps their big toe or is trigged by a strobe light.

Years ago, I could stand on a good quality level and solid chair to change a light bulb just above my head night.

Not these days. Of I want to raise myself 45cm off the ground to change a light bulb I need to use a set of step ladders, or steps, with a EN131 European

Union Certification for portable ladders or steps telling me that they are suitable for the task.

I'm not joking, a £70, £100, even £200 set of yellow-coloured steps that EVERY business, school, why not just say every frigging building in the UK, must own to protect the owner from being sued because some twat born to brother and sister parents once tried to change a bulb while balancing on top of an office swivel chair that was set on 5 easy glide wheels.

EVERYTHING, absolutely everything has to be labelled with an instruction, risk, how to use, how not to use, an idiots guide because of something that the Health and Safety madness has created.

Compensation Culture, and it's big business.

Let's go back to changing that light bulb.

Some 24 stone fat prick stands on a flimsy chair that does not sit level because the light bulb is above a wheelchair ramp.

The chair cracks, the human avalanche tips, the chair goes over and oomph, there is a very loud bounce followed by a loud thud and OUCH let out by the bulb changer.

Mr low energy bulb now has a bad back, you know, that condition that cannot be disproved by the medical profession, and he is going to claim for his injuries because it wasn't his fault.

He sends in his claim, he thinks he is in for a big pay-out because his pub doesn't have a set of the EN131 Certificated steps, so he had to use a chair.

He meets with HR partner (I don't know why they are called a "partner"; they work for the PLC same as everyone else) and a Health and Safety auditor from the compliance team.

HR partner leads the investigation meeting into the accident.

They talk through all the decisions made by the injured manager that led him to standing on a chair to change a bulb.

Mr bulb manager explains that the new BDM has told him if he does not get 95% on the next standards audit, he is in for a written warning.

When he is asked why the pubs doesn't have the correct type of steps to do the job Mr Bulb explains that he has tried to order a set of EN131 steps on every single facilities order for the last 6 months, but the BDM keeps trimming the order down to the basics, so the steps have never arrived as requested.

They all watch the CCTV of the accident, they see the chair is placed on the access ramp, they watch intently as Mr Bulb stands on the chair and plummets to the ground with a bang.

The HR business partner and the Health and Safety advisor now ask for a few minutes alone to discuss the claim against the company, Mr Bulb is thinking to himself that HR and H&S people will be taking legal advice.

He is now dreaming of how much they will have to pay him and how soon will he get it?

The HR business partner and H&S advisor call him back and ask him to sit down:

"Ok, Mr Bulb" the HR persons says "We have decided we are going to charge you with gross misconduct for putting the reputation of the business at risk."

"You also risked personal injury by not following the company H&S training that insists you must use EN131 rated portable steps, using a chair is an unacceptable risk."

"We have checked with the induction training team, and it is on record that you have signed and agreed all H&S policies in your induction training stage."

"You are now suspended and will be informed of the investigation date to see if we will be moving to disciplinary action against you."

WHAT THE FUCK JUST HAPPENED?

The Human Resources Department and the Compliance Department have just turned your claim for injuries to yourself into a weapon to kick you in the nuts and remove their problem, *YOU*.

There is now no risk financially to the company as you will be sacked for trying to do the best you could, but because you left yourself open to retaliation by standing on that chair, BASTARDS…

This is what a HR department does, it writes thousands of polices, online training pages that new starters just blindly scroll through without really reading any of it.

Then they suck out any remaining humanity from the cold dead heart that was once a caring, kind, thoughtful, pulsating and vital personnel department turning it into a sinister manipulation machine that works only in the PLC companies' interest, directly in opposition to the hard-working people who run the actual pubs and take the money that pays for the HR department to exist.

Every person working in a pub should be in a union if they have worked for the same employer for over 2 years.

After 2 years employment you have so many more rights to fight back against HR department bullying and harassment.

What the HR department robots know is that the law is in the favour of the employer, not the employee. Big pub companies are PLC's, private limited company, and are owned by shareholders as I have explained before. Shareholders can be individuals, but more often than not they are financial institutions and investment groups who buy and sell huge amounts of shares to make money by receiving dividends.

Who do you think sits on the boards of these "levers of power"? Who controls these hugely influential shareholding capitalist investment machines?

Friends of politicians, lobbyists, political influences, company chairmen, business owners, councillors, and bankers, that who.

It is in the PLC biggest share-holders financial interest that all companies they invest into are protected from litigation.

Being sued by employees who are mistreated, used, abused, and bullied is not a good business model, legal challengers must be quashed asap.

Big PLC pub companies use the massive staff turnover in a way to protect themselves from legal action.

If you have not completed 2 full years you have less than 0.001% of getting you wrongful dismissal into a tribunal and they rely on that fact.

Many young staff complete no more than a couple of seasons, they may even make it to 2 years, but only a very small number stay on beyond 2 years and progress.

A few years ago, the government removed the ability for an employee, or a workers union, to take an employer to a tribunal for unfair dismissal and constructive dismissal.

As most employees don't last a full 2 years as used and abused undervalued and under paid workers in pubs, the companies can do as they wish because there is no way to get them into a tribunal hearing where they can be made to abide by the rules set by ACAS on workers' rights.

PLC pub companies use this weakness in the protection of workers' rights to maintain the low pay and poor conditions staff are forced to work in.

Removing this right to tribunal was a dagger in the heart of pub employees, a real punch to the throat and a kick in the nuts.

No PLC Pub Co's are being sued in tribunals for treating their staff no better than throwaway consumables.

If it is risk free to the company, then replacing any staff before 2 years working is completed with the next unprotected teenager needing money to start a life after school becomes a no brainer.

Win Win

Keeping wages low, keeping staff naive…

Think back to how I explained about pub staff wages being so much lower if the staff are under 21 years old and how part time hours work out much cheaper than full time wages because of NI contributions.

Another chapter ends, Is it all beginning to fit together…?

Chapter 9

Don't Let the Bastards Grind You into Broken Pieces

I've had lots of experience with personality void H.R department empty suits, and to be fair, I can think of a good one, no not even one, that has ever had a team member or managers interest at heart. Yes, they are a walking-talking plug-n-play policy speak and spell robot.

In this chapter I'm going to tell you a story, using props, exerts from actual meetings notes, statements and grievances documents that a H.R department, a BDM so thick if she was a liquid, she couldn't be poured through a playground wire linked fence, and our old friend Op's tosser Mr Knobbush, used to fire an innocent man to save a bit of money.

This manager was once suspended from work on a trumped-up charge because they actually challenged a team member about telling lies and not being able to perform duties they were being paid for.

This is the written record of what happened in the lead up this wrongful suspension, and even though the names and location have been changed, the FACTS have not.

The manager realised all was not right after being suspended and needed to expose the truth. They thought someone may care about an abuse of power by a BDM, so they decided to use the grievance procedure to set the record straight.

This is the actual grievance I sent in with tiny changes to protect the people's identities.

The suspended manager wrote this grievance.

Grievance:

Who is this grievance concerning:
Bruce McSecondplace: BDM
6th November ####
On the 5th of November ####

I was unnecessarily suspended from my duties in what I believe is a way to destabilise my position at The Local Pub and push me towards ending my employment with the pub company for reasons that would only benefit BDM Bruce McSecondplace.

Since around Easter 20## I have been speaking to past BDM's involved with my pub, and my line managers, about the eyesight problem involving employee Meg Beehive.

I have also spoken multiple times about this situation with our HRBP. (Human Resources Business Partner) The BDM before Bruce McSecondplace was appointed fully understood the issues I have faced at my pub; Meg Beehive has always been known as a problem since the financial auditor identified her as a problem to me on an official visit. The previous BDM encouraged me to remove all problem team members as the pub has suffered considerable stock and cash losses for many years and this issue was continuing.

I did not consider Meg Beehive as a priority because I was sure she was not stealing, drinking stock, or using class A drugs while at work, unlike a few other team members who obviously were.

It has taken me far longer to achieve the changes at the pub because a "deputy" was forced into my team, and he came without the skill set to help me manage change in a complex site.

No kitchen ability, almost no experience in dealing with stock problems or HR matters.

I put up with this deputy for almost six months, but when I did finally challenge him about his personal contribution to the pub other than having sex with staff members and customers he decided to move back to his old pub where his life was easy.

It took me so long to deal with this deputy because he was directly appointed to my pub by a senior manager and was also recommended by the previous BDM and Bruce Mc Fucking Secondplace.

I felt under pressure and had to "look after" this deputy as he appeared to have better access to my line managers than I did!

To put this into context, in the seven months my previous BDM had been my line manager I had 2 meetings with him after the site opened. The first was a "catch up" as he put it where we talked about cars and motorbikes, the second was a 15-minute meeting about moving out the dead wood staff and how that process was going.

It was in this very short meeting he told me how the pub was going to get the "rainy day deals" to help sales, but much later I found out he did not actually request these deals for my pub from the marketing team at all?

He lied to me.

The deputy left; I appointed a new assistant who I sauced myself on a probation period of 12 weeks where she would become deputy if she successfully completed her probation period.

At more or less the same time Bruce McSecondplace became my BDM and to start with I was really pleased because I was hoping for a proactive line manager who would help me make this business a great once again using shared ideas.

At our first meeting he asked me to talk through what has been going on, so I did in great detail.

His conclusion was "you really have had your hands full and how many problem staff are left?"

I explained that one of the old team, a waitress, was not really a problem as she was reducing her hours and I could manage her better now I have a new assistant allowing us to manage her consistently when either of us are not at work.

This was the time when Bruce McSecondplace said something along the line of "so Meg Beehive still needs to go, what help do you need?"

I told Bruce McSecondplace that I was hoping to coach her into being better at her job and that I was going to insist she wear her glasses. Bruce Mc was very supportive of this move; she was making mistakes due to eye-sight problems, and it had to be stopped.

A few days later I had a similar conversation with the HR business partner where I asked about changing team members fixed hours and what is the best practice to do this without getting into conflict?

I also asked her opinion about Meg Beehive needing to wear glasses to reduce the number of mistakes that are driving up losses in stock and cash while she is working.

Can I tell her she has to wear them?

I was told I could do that if there was clear proof, she requires glasses to perform her role with continuous mistakes being made.

I had previously sat down with Meg Beehive and our new deputy manager to talk through the eyesight issues informally.

Meg Beehive agreed in that meeting that she needed glasses and would start wearing them when using the tills and reading written word, such as menus, receipts and allergens.

That very same day Meg Beehive put her rather thick lens glasses on when serving, a couple of the regulars, let's call them Mal and Wayne, made fun about the glasses, Meg Beehive laughed along with them, and I thought to myself it was going well.

The next day Meg turned up to work without her glasses, so I sent her home to get them. She went to get them, returned but then decided to refuse to wear them. It was obviously to me, because Mal and Wayne had laughed about her glasses, she now fells self-conscious when wearing glasses.

I did tell Meg that we will get to a point where I will not be able to rota her anymore due to a risk that she is herself creating.

At this point Meg Beehive started to ask for support against me by talking to the regulars she has been serving for many years and lying to them about being bullied.

Over the next few months, I asked Meg daily to wear her glasses and explained is great detail why she needed to.

As soon as I turn my back, she will not wear her glasses.

Just recently she has decided to not wear them at all because of her love life.

I her opinion if someone she fancies sees her wearing glasses, they will not want to take her out on a date.

I have told her I am not interested in her vanity or reasons to not wear the glasses; I have explained why she has to. She insists on NOT wearing glasses and continues to make multiple mistakes on a daily basis due to poor eyesight.

A few weeks ago, Bruce McSecondplace popped in to see me and tell me that the new menus I have written and want to run have been "sort of" approved by Mr Knobbush.

The conversation came around to Meg Beehive once again and her refusal to wear glasses even though she has a prescription to wear glasses when reading.

Bruce McSecondplace said, **"can we not just get rid of her?"**

I just laughed and replied "no, I can manage her, but this will now become a risk assessment required change because she cannot read ingredients, allergens, ABV's etc., etc. and it is all a risk."

Bruce McSecondplace was very supportive again, or so I thought.

The same day the HR business partner was in to meet Bruce Mc, I had the same conversation with her about going down the risk assessment route with Meg, the HR bp also agreed that it was a good course of action.

Bruce has been updated weekly through conversation and multiple emails about Meg, the problems she causes the pub stock and cash levels and her over reactions to wearing glasses.

I have discussed with Bruce Mc how Meg Beehive is trying to use regular customers to support her in a campaign to NOT have to wear glasses, it is Meg Beehive who discusses the glasses problem with the guests and talks about me in the conversations from behind the bar.

I am always trying to stop these conversations by laughing them off when in public view and earshot.

Bruce McSecondplace is totally aware of the problems we are having with Meg Beehive and her glasses situation.

The whole pub leadership team agree that she should not be at work without wearing glasses, she is a risk.

Bruce McSecondplace has also been told about Meg Beehive talking unprofessionally about me while on both sides of the bar in a further attempt to gain support to stop me insisting that she wears glasses, this "slagging me off" is detailed in a statement given by Tracy, a pub team member.

The following week Bruce McSecondplace called me clearly frustrated about a labour cost problem that the pub has.

He laid down the law on wage spending etc, no problem, I except direct instruction from my line manager as part of his, and my job.

Then suddenly, out of the blue and right at the end of the conversation he decided to tell me about a **"possible"** or **"probable"** complaint being submitted against me?

There **is** a complaint coming in, how do you know if it has not yet been entered as a grievance? And if so, far enough, let's sort it out professionally.

But there is no such thing as **"possible complaint"**!

What this tells me is:

Bruce McSecondplace must be giving Meg Beehive advice on how to attack me using the complaints process.

He must have had prior knowledge about this complaint going in and has assisted Meg Beehive with her complaint.

I'm fairly sure he is not supposed to be doing that.

*The reason he said "**possible** or **probable**" will because he could not guarantee when Meg Beehive would finish and submit her homework, issued by himself.*

How else could Bruce McSecondplace have known to hit me with a grievance rumour he could not possibly have known about over 48 hours before he suspended me unless he had planned it?

This was a direct swipe at me over the phone to "put me in my place" and destabilise me into either doing exactly as I am told or hopefully quit.

This is construed as constructive dismissal.

For Bruce McSecondplace to be at my pub on a Monday morning to suspend me was always the plan and Russ Mc is the conspirator.

Through the balance of probability, employment law burden of proof, Bruce McSecondplace is the author of the whole thing.

At no point was there any reason to actually suspend me, he had enough evidence on email and through conversation to know I am not at fault.

Plus, all he had to do was interview the deputy and kitchen manager, who were both on site at the time I was suspended, to prove I have not harassed, bullied, or hounded Meg Beehive in any way. If he had interviewed the deputy and kitchen manager, he could have suspended Meg at 11.30am when she came in for work for lying, it is Meg Beehive that is putting GK at risk, not myself.

But Bruce Mc couldn't suspend a partner in crime could he.

There are a number of reasons why Bruce would be happy to see me gone but using false accusation to remove me for misconduct charges, or forcing me to quit, is not acceptable, unethical, and unfair treatment of myself.

After I had been suspended, I told Bruce McSecondplace in a late-night reply that I did not trust his judgement in this case as I already suspected his motives were hostile towards me. This was evident when he told me about this "possible complaint", it was just enough to hurt me, stop me sleeping and emotionally damage my state of mind over a busy weekend.

He also knew Meg Beehive was off, so he posed no risk to her by teasing me in a harassing way.

Is this protecting your partner in crime I wonder?

There was NO reason for Bruce McSecondplace to tell me about a "possible complaint" unless it was with malicious intent and clearly demonstrates he was involved in the complaint creation.

There was a real "glint in the eye and smirk to the mouth" when Bruce explained how "he had decided" to suspend me, a definite attempt at emasculation and power trip over a subordinate.

The way he delivered the news had no other purpose than to boost the ego of the person delivering this suspension, while at the same time attempting to wound the receiving party to a point of surrender.

The probability that Bruce McSecondplace is involved with this complaint about me is very high, why would he tell me a complaint was on its way, it's either in or it isn't, he is deeply involved, but how far does it go up the management tree?

Why bother telling me about this possible complaint before he could confirm a complaint was made? It could only be that this was his way to entertain himself, he could not contain his excitement as he knew what was going to happen on Monday.

Following my suspension, I have not been given sight of the complaint or been told any detail of it? I can only presume it is about Meg Beehive, but I don't actually know, I don't think I should be suspended without knowing why?

Bruce McSecondplace has acted in a way that can only been derived as misleading, bias, deceitful and with malicious intentions.

I hope that an independent person can be brought in to investigate why I am suspended, after asking ACAS and my union, they also don't understand why I am suspended without any evidence?

They don't understand the timeline between telling me that a complaint "could be" coming in and it actually landing?

If a complaint has not come in, how on earth can I be told about it?
Pub Manager name with-held.

The End

The above was the response to the suspension, a grievance has been entered because they thought they were miss-treated by the manager, and something was not ringing true?

Bruce McSecondplace had always been a dick, a false smiley con-artist and really slimy in the way he operates. He was obviously jealous of always being rated behind this manager in the ranking when he was also a pub manger, it must be tough to always be runner up, but hey, don't fucking blame others, pull your fucking finger out and do better you spiteful twat.

Then it clicked, this was not McSecondplace doing, he has never been smart enough to run this twisted attack on a superior GM, this HAD to be orchestrated by the one and only chief arsehole: Knobbush himself has his oily fingers of hate all over this.

The GM was suspended on 5th November, they waited and waited for an invitation to an investigation meeting where they could clear their name.

Finally, an email comes thought on the 26th of Nov inviting the GM to a hearing on the 27th of Nov!

For Fucks Sake, 21 days to issue an invite and just one day's notice, what the hell has been going on?

In the invitation the GM was FINALLY told what they had supposedly done so awful that the GM had to be suspended?

I refer you back to the grievance the GM has put in against Bruce McSecondplace where they are talking about Meg Beehive and her refusal to wear her glasses.

No, the GM knows the complaint details, only one day to prepare is really unfair and obviously a planned tactic to weaken the defence the GM can put forward due to the lack of time allowed. This HR department clearly like an advantage.

The charge is harassment and bullying a team member by the GM.

These are the defence notes that the GM used in the investigation meeting:

Meg Beehive had contacted Louise earlier in the day and asked her to stay on until 6pm so she could take her son trick or treating.[SEP]*I was unaware of this change as Meg had not asked me if this was ok.*

Meg Beehive arrived at work at 5.50pm on Halloween.

I was working the bar with Meg, and we also had Sue, our waitress, running food.[SEP]*Meg Beehive was her usual self, keeping herself looking busy but avoiding getting involved with taking food out and serving on the bar, as usual.*

I don't like to leave Meg Beehive on the bar on her own as it is easier to correct her till mistakes at the time, she makes them.

We had been very quiet and most of the till sales were being performed by myself while Meg begrudgingly worked the floor, but at least she was offering further drinks at the table and generally giving good customer service.

Then we got a few customers in so Meg started serving on the bar. In one order she made a number of mistakes, including charging for a jug of cocktails for £12.99 that the customer did not want. Meg Beehive asked for payment from the ladies, the ladies did not realise they had been over charged at the time so Meg Beehive took the money and handed the ladies their change and receipt.

The ladies on table 54, called Meg Beehive over and explained to her that they had been over charged by £12.99 for a product they did not ask for or have. Meg Beehive is not authorised to perform refunds, so she had to tell me about this mistake of overcharging.

I was at till 3 serving when Meg started telling me loudly from till 1 about the refund needed. I asked her to lower her voice and tell me in a moment when I had finished serving my current customer. Once I was free, I asked Meg to join me at till 3 while no customers were around to explain the problem.

This is how the conversation went:

me: so what happened?

Meg: I don't know, somehow a jug was rung in, twice, I took one off, but the other was paid for, I'm not sure, someone has moved the button, I wanted a glass, it was there, but someone, or you have moved it, it's not my fault, anyway they need a refund for the mistake the till made.

me: sorry, I'm lost! so you put 2 jugs on when you meant 2 glasses of woo-woo?

Meg: the buttons have been moved, you are always moving buttons, the ladies wanted it, then didn't want it, it was them, they changed their minds, so I voided one but not the other so they need a refund.

me: so they do still want this one but you voided the other one?

Meg: no, they need a refund, then don't want a pitcher.

me: you just said they did want one?

Meg: no I didn't, the button has been moved, if the button had not been moved it would be alright!

me: Meg, do the ladies want, or not want a pitcher?

Meg: no, they want a refund, they want pornstars, not woo-woo.

me: do I need to refund the glasses of woo woo as well.

Meg: no, they have the glasses of woo woo, they want pornstars and I voided the 1st pitcher.

me: the 1st pitcher was voided; do they want the remaining pitcher?

Meg: they have it, it's the buttons, they have been moved arrrgggghhhhhhh.

me: please just answer me one simple question without talking over me please. Has the pitcher of woo woo, that the customer does not want, been paid for?

Meg: no, I voided it, but then I rang it in again and they paid for it so I didn't take the money for that, just the other cocktails.

me: so you looked at the total, took off £12.99 yourself in your head and put that amount of money in the till?

Meg: no, they need a refund, but they still need making.

me: what does?

Meg: the cocktails.

me: you took the money, that wrong money, for drinks you have not poured yet?

Meg: I refunded the pitcher.

me: what.

Meg: voided it and they want a refund.

At this point I sent Meg to make the cocktails I think are still required, I printed off the till receipt while looking over at the table to see what drinks the ladies had on their table. They had no pitcher on their table, a pitcher had been paid for, that told me that at least one pitcher needed refunding.

I went with the refund receipt to Meg to ask her to sign it as required, it was her mistake, you sign for mistakes.

She was making cocktails:

Meg was stood trying to read the poster we use to ensure our cocktails are made correctly with the right measurements etc. Meg was unable to read the size of cranberry to use, after 30 secs or so of standing close and leaning away from the poster she finally discovered that the amount of cranberry required was 100ml.

Please keep in mind the font size on this poster is size 40.

Meg then said, "how do I do that, what size is this?"

She was holding a 125ml wine measure but could not read the size pressed into the side because the letters are too small for her to read without glasses. I said that's a 125ml, so she said "I'll use this and just not fill it to the top"[SEP] I said "no don't do that that, use 2 x 50ml spirit measures please."

I asked Meg to sign the refund slip, she said, "what have you written on it, it's not my fault?" and she started writing her excuse on the slip. I stopped her and said, "that's not true, it was your fault, don't try blaming the customers and the till."

Meg then went on to make terrible glasses of Woo Woo, I was serving so I could not step in quick enough to stop her, and she took them over to the customers.

The Woo Woo's didn't look right to me, and I could not work out what Meg Beehive had used to make them, and Meg would not tell me what she had used when I asked her.

People were waiting so I went back to serving.

About 10 mins later one of the same group of ladies came to the bar and said, "where is our other choc fudge?" I said it will be with you a 1 min, instructed Sue to sort it and get it to the table ASAP, don't even look for a kitchen ticket.

I checked the till, only 1 choc fudge was ordered at the same time as the cocktails. I asked Meg if she had read the order back as required in our customer service policy?

Meg answered "no, I don't when we are taking cocktails" Once the ladies had their missing dessert, I went up to the table and asked if everything is ok? I was told "this has not been good, nothing we ordered seems to be what we got, this is not good at all" At this point I realised that the ladies were genuinely unhappy, so I offered them a £30 gift card, £10 each, as compensation and I explained how a new menu had thrown us off our stride...

They were happy with this and said thank you when leaving.

I went to Meg and asked her: why did you not read the order back as instructed to?

Meg said: "I did, they got it wrong, it was the cocktails and the buttons on the till moving about, it's not fair, arrrgggghhhhhhh" I said to Meg "you are now lying, you told me you didn't read it back, now you say you did, what is going on, is this because you cannot read the till screen and buttons?" Meg walked away and I went to serve waiting customers.

A few minutes later I wondered to where Meg Beehive was as we had a number of customers who needed serving. Next went towards the kitchen and Meg was talking to Felix who lives with our deputy in the pub flat. Meg was in a *great mood, laughing about her Halloween outfit as a ghostbuster. I asked for help on the bar and Meg came out, served one customer, and then vanished again. When I had finished serving, I went to the kitchen to find Meg in the kitchen suddenly telling Sue and Pam (chef) she was feeling sick. I said are you working? Meg said I don't feel well so I said as I walked back to the bar in a very slightly raised voice to be heard above the kitchen extract fans "if you are ill, you need to go home." A minute or so passed, Meg had not reappeared, so I went back to the kitchen. When she saw me, she rushed towards the team toilets. When I pushed the half open toilet door to check on her, I could see Meg Beehive putting her fingers in her mouth in an action that looked like she was trying to make herself vomit. I said, "what are you doing?" Meg: "I'm not well, I'm vomiting" me: I called Pam over as a witness and said to Meg Beehive "as you are ill, I need you to go home because you cannot work, as you know, if you have been vomiting." There was NO vomit in the toilet. I then returned to the bar.*

Meg clocked out shortly after leaving the business short staffed and at risk, but what choice did I have, if she tells me she has vomiting she cannot work.

This question bugged the rest of the night: "what just happened?"

The next day, Thursday 1st November, I was at work at 9am and my deputy was starting at 12pm. I told my deputy what happened the night before with Meg Beehive because my deputy and needs to know.

My deputy then told me that Meg Beehive had requested a holiday that included Wednesday 31st Oct and Thursday 1st November. It just clicked with me what was really going on:

Meg had requested a holiday from our deputy manager on the 20th of November, the 1st day of my weeks holiday, so I wasn't around. Meg Beehive was told no, the rota had been up for 4 weeks, so it was not granted. It is also unacceptable to requested on bits of paper, the team must use the on-line system, but Meg Beehive does not use the online system because she cannot read the screens due to poor eyesight.

So, what happened on Wednesday 31st October was a deliberate con to leave early and also to get the Thursday off: Meg asked Louise to stay on an extra hour so she could take her son somewhere for trick-a-treating. Meg then came to work when it suited her.

Meg Beehive needed to collect her son from the trick-a-treating by 8pm on the 31st, this is why I saw her putting her fingers in her mouth/down her throat to make herself vomit at 7:30pm. She knows I would never allow anyone to work after vomiting so it was the perfect reason to leave at the perfect time to collect her son from his trick-a-treat session.

Meg called the pub at 4.45pm on Thursday 1st November to say she would be back on Friday 2nd. I told Meg Beehive that her return would not be possible as she said she had vomited and needed 48 hours clear from when her symptoms ended.

We had been conned by Meg Beehive so take the time off she had been refused permission to do so.

The Catalogue of problems with Meg Beehive:

Meg Beehive cannot read the allergens folder without her glasses but will not wear her glasses. Meg cannot read labels on products without glasses, but will not wear them. Meg cannot read small print, small print would be anything 24 size or below, I know this because I have a prescription of -1 and -0.5 for my eyes. Without glasses helping my eyes I cannot clearly read the till screens, the kitchen food tickets, the PDQ slips, allergens, how too guides or an H&S instruction for any equipment, such as fire extinguishers, fire blanket, chemicals or COSHH advice.

I have asked Meg to wear her glasses a number of times after witnessing her make hundreds of tills and operational errors due to not being able to see correctly. She refuses saying that she only needs them for reading:

We read as part of the job and need to be able to read the following:

- Till screens: average size 13 font PDQ receipts: average print size 12 font
- Food check: average print size 12 font • Allergens Book: average size 11 font
- Price List: average size 11 font
- Fire Safety: average size 14 font
- COSHH on chemicals etc: font size 10
- ABV on cask ales and other products: average size 10 font.

All Meg Beehive problems stem from her inability to read the things around her because she will not wear glasses, something she openly admits she needs to do, but will not because she believes if make her less attractive.

Evidence Statement End

Off to the investigation meeting the GM goes, talks through the charges made and explains exactly what has happened using the evidence statement.

The presiding officer, who the GM has never met before, is an old school straight talking experienced BDM.

He listens carefully, reads the charges again and dismisses them by declaring NO FURTHER ACTION REQUIRED because the GM have done nothing wrong.

The GM calls his BDM, Mr McSecondplace, and tells him the charges are dismissed and is free to return to work tomorrow with a happy smile.

This fucking prick of a BDM says "oh no you are not returning; we have discovered something else to charge you with, so you are to remain on suspension."

Now what has the GM done? No one is bothering to tell the GM; they will have to wait for another fucking letter to arrive by post.

The GM is incensed, angry, confused, what the hell is going on and you are they keeping the GM out of the pub almost all of November and the build up to Christmas?

Now they are keeping me out again for god knows how long?

There is something very wrong going on, that the GM can be sure of.

The letter comes through confirming the GM's further suspension.

They say the GM has been paying team members cash in hand!

EH? Why the fuck would a GM do that?

No GM is going to hand over their hard-earned wages to pay someone else, who the fuck would do?

The penny drops, this weak and useless twat of a BDM is taking instruction from Mr Knobbush to get the GM out to save on salary costs.

Do you remember how I explained how they remove expensive managers and replace them with cheaper ones to help top up bonuses?

This is just one of the ways it is done, by lying…

Time for an additional grievance by the GM against Bruce McSecondplace.

This is that grievance, as you go through it will become evident to what this utter coward, fucking prick of a BDM is doing…

Read on:

29th November 2018

Grievance concerning Bruce McSecondplace BDM

I was suspended, unnecessarily, on 5th November ####

A grievance has already been submitted following my suspension as it was clearly not required. This suspension was forced by a person because "they could", not because they "had to".

*At the investigation meeting dealing with the charges, I have been suspended over, the investigating BDM actually said to me "**why are you suspended over this?**"*

This is a clear indication that I have been treated unfairly by a bias line-manager with an axe to grind or a hidden agenda.

I attended the investigation hearing on Tuesday 27th November, it was very clear that after 90 mins of investigation, the investigating BDM would have unsuspended me there and then. He could not do that, because revoking the suspension is normally performed by the person that suspended someone in the first place.

Let's examine some of the things I was told, and were said to me, during the investigation meeting on the 27th November:

(IO = Investigating Officer)

IO: "why are you suspended for this?"

IO: "someone has been looking back into watts app messages going back to January 2018, I don't like that."

Even the investigating officer says that trolling back through Watts App is just not on!

When I said to the investigating officer "it feels like a witch hunt" I got no answer of course, but I did get a sympathetic nod. "has Bruce discussed this with you, sat down at all to go through it?"

*I said **no** as he has not.*

I explained how this could have been sorted in 30 mins if Bruce had spoken to my deputy and kitchen manager who was there at work and ready to be spoken to by Bruce. They could have rubbished the allegations against me and disproved everything there and then. The investigating BDM agreed that it should have been done that way.

The investigating BDM said he would speak to HR and Bruce; I got the clear impression that the recommendation was to take no further action.

I went home and waited for a call allowing me to return to work.

What I got was a call from Bruce McSecondplace it was a surprise. He said that I was to remain suspended while he looked into something else.

So, what has happened?

Bruce found out that he has not got the result he wanted, myself dismissed.

Bruce has found out that no further action against me is the result, so he called me to tell me I am to remain on suspension while he investigates alleged cash payments.

I am totally shocked because I have no idea what he is on about.

While on the phone I asked Bruce why the investigation had gone back into watts apps messages from January ####, almost 12 months earlier? He told me does not want to go into that and sounded very flustered when I asked this question. He was very evasive and came across as aggressive.

I thought about what he had said and quickly realised that this new change was in no-way linked to the reason I was suspended, so under ACAS rules why cannot I return to work?

I called Bruce and asked him "if the allegations against me, that I attended the meeting for, are not going forward because I have been cleared, and alleged cash payments is not risk to any team member, why can I return to work?"

Bruce sounded angry with my enquiry, shut me down sharply and said nothing has been "told to him yet".

I said, "but if it has been handed back to you, it is not going to disciplinary?"

He was very sharp and abrupt in his reply about how this new allegation needs to be investigated and nothing is decided yet, he then mentioned a re-investigation.

What the hell if he does not get what he wants he wants it investigating again? A blatant miss use of power and authority.

I just said, "thank you" and got off the line before I angered him anymore.

He is clearly trying to find any way that he can to still use the dismissed allegations when he said something about a "re-investigation"?

Why, when I asked him about this, did he become very defensive and flustered again?

And what did he mean by 'nothing has been told to him yet'?

Does this mean he is waiting for Knobbush to tell him his next move?

I bet that is what it is, it cannot be anything else?

I now feel that Bruce will not accept my innocence and will try to find any reason to make sure I am taken to disciplinary so he can use the escalation process to remove myself and my salary.

Realistically, shouldn't Bruce be allowed to investigate me or any allegation against me, I have lodged grievances against him.

It's like putting a Fox in with the Chickens to protect them.

How I have been treated while suspended?

As someone who has a verified, and recorded on my personal file, anxiety, and clinical depression that I manage with the help of my doctor, I am under clear instructions to see my doctor if any unnecessary stress is placed upon me.

I have also recently been given clear instruction in a meeting with the head of HR that I must always follow medical advice and keep the company informed.

I agreed to do as requested and am happy to do so.

At no point was I told by HR that taking their advice also meant being penalised through loss of pay for taking their advice?

My partner is a heath professional with 30 years of clinical ward, theatre, and intensive care experience, as soon as she realised, I had not slept for 3 nights, due to the way Bruce had "played with my mind" (detailed in the 1st grievance), she insisted I go to the doctors.

I was put on sick leave by my doctor with anxiety and work-related stress. I told to rest.

I followed the advice of my doctor and followed HR instruction to inform my line manager as required.

I did this through the online system.

Bruce McSecondplace then increased the pressure and anxiety on myself by emailing me to tell me I would not be paid my salary; I will only be receiving SSP while I was signed off sick.

This was a cynical attack on me to increase the stress I was under, and a retaliation against me for daring to put in a grievance against Bruce McSecondplace for the unnecessary suspension.

I contacted Bruce, explained that my doctor is overprotective and that I feel perfectly fit to return to work. He told me to stay off, I said no, I'm ok, ready for work, do you want me to work at any other site?

He said no. Why not?

I adjusted my online record to "fit for work" on the Wednesday immediately after telling Bruce McSecondplace I was fit to work, even though a really wasn't.

He had left me no choice after threatening to take away my salary, this is a clear case of bullying and victimisation.

Next, I had to email Bruce McSecondplace and ask him to authorise my online record change very late on Sunday (he had been on email daily so he was aware that the authorisation was required) so that I would receive my salary as I should.

This really is Bruce McSecondplace twisting the knife and doing everything possible to stamp his position as the alfa male, myself just a lowly subordinate.

I am not sure if I will be paid yet?

It would not be surprised if I am not paid.

Bruce McSecondplace decided to punish me for putting in a grievance against him.

He also wanted to remove my costs from the business to show himself in a better light to his bigger bosses, basically fiddling the labour cost down to promote himself.

While suspended I sent my pub 2 emails, both on a Monday just underpinning things that needed doing as the pub is approach Christmas. As I was not supposed to contact anyone in the company, I copied Bruce McSecondplace in so full disclosure was there for all to see, all I was doing was acting in the interest of the team at my pub.

Bruce reprimanded me for this and then added it to the charges against me.

I know this as the investigating BDM brought it up.

The person I contacted at my pub was just the deputy, not the person who has raised this alleged grievance against me that was dismissed anyway, so what harm, I copied him in.

The investigating BDM's response was:

"You were just trying to do your best for the pub, the people and the company."

This is true, why would the cunt Bruce try to use this as another charge against me? It can only be because he will do anything to hurt me, damage my reputation and remove me from the business.

Bruce McSecondplace has an agenda, clearly demonstrated by trolling through watts app team posts back to January, if every BDM did that for every manager, how many GMs and team members would have "miss-spoke" and required further investigation?

Bruce McSecondplace speaks knowingly about policies and following The Winning Ways program, so he is saying openly that he knows right from wrong.

He has willingly chosen wrong.

I know from the investigation meeting that almost every single person who was interviewed about me have said positive things about me, raised no concern over my attitude, behaviour, or respect for others.

All the allegations against me have been dismissed.

Bruce McSecondplace could have moved quickly after the outcome of the investigation meeting and allowed me back to work.

But NO, Bruce kept me on suspension. Why?

Why is Bruce McSecondplace allowed to investigate me after I have put in a grievance against him?

This goes against the ACAS code of conduct and the company are operating against their own policies.

If Bruce McSecondplace is so focused on the company's training system called Winning Ways, why has he decided to hurt me by stopping my wages and intentionally increased my anxiety and work-related stress levels by doing so?

Does Bruce McSecondplace think that driving a person with anxiety and depression towards suicidal thoughts is a reasonable way to manage a fellow human being, or am I just something he can dismiss and wipe off his shoe?

I am astonished that in an enlightened 20## where mental health is such a hot subject in the media, with unions, major employers and throughout Westminster, a company is allowing a BDM to treat someone with a mental illness with such distain and indifference.

It was while working for this company, my partner being "touched up" by my then BDM but being unable to do anything about it as he was my boss, this is when I suffered my first major anxiety attack and I developed clinical depression.

After that BDM had gone from the company, I thought that BDMs of that type who take an unwarranted dislike towards people and use their power to abuse and hurt them and their families just because they can, were long gone in a modern company.

How wrong I was.

It was early in 20## that I had meeting with the head of HR and Bob Angle to discuss how I handled my anxiety issues.

At the end of that meeting everyone was satisfied that I have my issue under full control and needed no further support.

I have strong self-care, friend and family support that keeps me perfectly healthy and completely stable.

No medical professional would be surprised that I had an anxiety peak following Bruce McSecondplace calling me to tease me with his knowledge of a complaint "may be coming in about you" as detailed in the first grievance.

So why is Bruce McSecondplace investigating me now?

He has accused me of making cash payments, so why not simply ask me to explain as to why it is not what he thinks it is, but he didn't, he has left me suspended because he is a spiteful little man or too pathetic to stand up to Mr Knobbush for what is right and the people who are his direct reports.

When I arrived to take over my pub, I faced a unique set of issues:

12. *I had no deputy or assistant because one quit before we opened, she got a job she had applied for at the NHS. The existing deputy allegedly tried to set fire the pub during the refurb, so she moved also.*

13. *We opened with no other pub leadership team on site to help me, we had Jack and Mick who could supervise the bar and cellar but did not have anything other than very basic office knowledge, they didn't even know how to get onto the pub management system in the office.*

14. *I had never seen this computerised management platform either, a much older system was in my last pub.*

15. *We are moving an old and cheap image branded pub into a middle-class brand with a very poor existing team and 6 brand new team members. I was advised by my BDM that we needed to "start again with the whole team."*

16. *The old team, some were passing drinks out free daily, one or two were using class A drugs at work, at least 4 or 5 were drinking while serving on the bar.*

17. *Error corrections were running at 35%*

18. *Wet Stock loses were a £1,000 per week*

19. *Food stock loses were £500 per week*

20. *Cash Loses were £200-£500 per week*

When we opened, it was not easy managing a new development on my own, things were being missed and I was firefighting daily. Things that are important, such as compliance, was getting completed to protect the customers, the team and the company, but other basics were not being focused on. I remember, after about 6 weeks, telling Bob Angle (op's) and Brian (first BDM) that I was struggling to keep up.

I was told I was getting a new deputy just before we opened, but it took 8 weeks.

I was not very experienced with team payment system, I had very limited experience on the system before I got to the pub, but I was doing the best I could.

Things were missed, such as not following up when staff had not clocked in, there was so much missing information that I ended up, after about 12 weeks, owning the team around £700 in wages split across them all, approximately £58.33 per week, or around 5 to 6 staff hours missed per week due to clocking is inconsistency.

Once my deputy had started, I had the time to go through all wage hour reports vs printed rota's and worked out any hours missing. Many team members didn't even know.

We had just completed the latest months payroll input so I could not pay people what we owed them for at least 34 days, or didn't know how to at this point, I was still learning the on-line system.

I knew one of our team needed their money now, so what I did was use my own money to "sub" the team member the missing pay and they would pay me back over the next two pay sessions after I had added their missing hours on onto payroll.

There was also a wage transfer issues with a pub in Bolton, they failed to one of our team members who had help cover illness at their site for 3 weeks, so yet again, I "lent" her the money and she paid me back after I had added her hours to the payroll system the next pay date.

I now know that we can add back pay or missing pay to the online payroll system, so after those isolated incidents any further problems were corrected using the correct process after our new deputy manager showed me how to do it. That system has been used a number of times in the last 3 months to correct all pay.

At no point was there any advantage to myself when I have tried to help my team out. No one lost any NI, holiday pay, tax or pension payments because the hours they had worked, but had been missed, were corrected over the next month's payment cycle.

These errors were the result of being under supported at the time of opening, I'm not trying to blame anyone, a certain set of circumstances led to the failings.

I should have been supplied with experienced pub supervisors to help me, but as I had almost no contact with my new BDM, who I had only met a couple of times, I didn't want to be seen as failing by begging for help.

In hind-site, I should have shouted loudly, then my team would not have been inconvenienced and I would never have been put in a position where I needed to help people with a cash loan to make up for a mistake that was partly their fault for not clocking in and mine for not asking for more support.

Bruce McSecondplace continues to keep me isolated so I cannot not access emails etc.

I didn't expect to be off this long, I thought after a couple of days I would be cleared and back at work.

I realised how calculating Bruce McSecondplace is, and how determined his is to remove me, when he became so adamant about ensuring I have no access to the email system at my pub.

He knows there has been dozens of emails about sales driving ideas and requests for help sent to him and his predecessor from myself, be he wants to hide this fact because it does not fit his narrative.

I expect that these emails are no longer available as they show Bruce McSecondplace has ignored my requests for help with the business performance for months, putting me under further pressure and driving my anxiety and depression deeper.

Luckily for me I have a very disciplined self-care management regime to maintain and support my mental health.

Bruce knows that keeping me away from the business does not allow me to defend myself using the evidence that is electronically stored. I cannot access items that prove my innocence.

With no team are at risk, the evidence Bruce McSecondplace has collected in the form of interviews with my team about me clearly demonstrates that there is no risk, the only reason he does not want me there is to keep me at a distance from any evidence that supports my position.

Keeping me suspended is not about protecting the team anyone, I didn't need to be suspended if he had spent just 30 mins investigating on the 5th of November, it is about increasing my separation anxiety, applying pressure, making me feel worthless and pushing me to quit my job. Constructive Dismissal.

Bruce McSecondplace has demonstrated his tactics to hurt me and damage my mental stability in a number of ways:

- *Teasing me about "a complaint maybe coming in about you."*
- *Suspending me without an explanation of what I was accused of.*
- *Stopping my pay to ramp up my anxiety and push me into a depressive state where a possibility of suicide become a reality.*
- *Isolating me to increase my depression, I offered to work at other sites, but he refused with reason.*
- *Not taking the responsible attitude of talking through any accusations against me.*
- *His intent to "re-investigate" as he did not get what he wanted!*
- *Maintaining my suspension without reason.*

Bruce McSecondplace has also shown total lack of people understanding and business reasoning by putting a pub business at substantial financial risk as it approaches its busiest period:

- *Failing to understand/recognise malicious rummer/allegation even after being informed through conversation/email about the tactics being used to manage a problem employee.*
- *Insisting that an experienced GM remain suspended while a deputy with only 4 months experience and a new kitchen manager are left alone as Christmas approaches fast.*
- *Maintaining my suspension when I could be driving sales into Christmas and beyond.*
- *Risking the business reputation by continuing the uncertainty for the team and customers at my pub without reason.*
- *Using his authority to suspend me instead of using my experience to drive business.*

I submit this grievance
Pub Manager
End Of Grievance

That was the second grievance the pub manager put in against the same person, but strangely, neither of these detailed and accurate grievances were investigated.

What The Fuck? I mean, what type of company allows this type of fuckaboutary to go on in its day-to-day activity?

Here we have a hospitality business, with such wankers at the top, allowing blatant mistreatment, encouraging this level of narcissistic hate for others, and permitting treatment this appalling of its own employees by its preferred employees?

The GM has now been called to a disciplinary hearing on the 20th of December, so another month has passed, what is taking so fucking long?

The GM arrives at the hearing, which is to be chaired by Phoebe Buttress, an ex-manager who has just been promoted to BDM in training by Knobbush himself, and she is accompanied by a HR cuntess Ella Widebottom.

These two idiots are completely out their fucking depth, the following will show just how deeply stupid a female cunt can be.

They go on the attack; they have clearly had a plan to crack the GM into submission.

Yeah, right lol. By the end of the hearing, they are so confused, outsmarted, outwitted and shellshocked they have to make contact with the mothership for advice.

They had obviously been told that this was an open and shut case and that the GM was to be dismissed today.

The GM and union rep were called back in after a short break only to be told they were adjourning the hearing until January.

Everyone knew this was far from over, Bruce McSecondplace and Mr Knobbush still wanted their pound of flesh, bring it on.

The GM went away and decided to write up how they had been mistreated, lied to, berated, and dehumanised by Buttress and Widebottom.

This is what the GM wrote about the now adjourned hearing and after receiving the hearing notes.

Response to Hearing Notes and The Hearing Itself 27th December 20##

Dear Phoebe Buttress

Re:

1. Meeting note corrections
2. Concerns about the hearing held on 20th December
3. Response to actions taken by you following the hearing adjournment

Point 1: Meeting note corrections

After reading the notes, sent by email at 3.30pm on Christmas Eve, there are a number of corrections that need to make, and inclusions added to ensure the notes are accurate and not biased against me.

I was asked if I was covertly recording the hearing, I confirmed I was not, but now I wish I had been so the meeting could have been transcribed accurately.

It is now fully apparent that only small parts of my reply's to your leading questions have been recorded and do not include most of my explanations, corrections and comments that clearly demonstrate my innocence to accusations had they been included.

As part of myself answering questions I also presented evidence that proves the allegations against me are false using prints from the company's own payroll and email system. This evidence, that includes statements from witnesses, clearly demonstrate that all hours have been paid to all team members through the payroll system. As a matter of substance and accuracy I hope these pieces of evidence are being taken into consideration. I am very concerned that I have, or the evidence is, either being ignored or not listened to because it does not fit a set narrative.

No one cannot reasonably expect a perfect word for word record of a hearing, but as these false allegations require a detailed defence and my ability to disavow any "cash for hours worked" payments have been made, surely, I can expect my defence to be included and not "short-handed" into a limited defence and explanation.

Being falsely accused of any charge is upsetting, but this is also of life changing importance to me, this is my job and would a huge impact on myself and my family if I was to be judged unfairly.

I am not receiving a fair hearing and so will not receive the adjudication that my answers and defence evidence demand.

In the notes I have identified six areas where I delivered a very detailed explanation and defence to the allegations.

These statements have been omitted from these notes. SEP These omitted statements, made by myself, are a reaction to comments made by the chair and HR representative that were an attempt to push me into an admission to something I have not done by "re-wording" what I said. These must be included in the statement because they balance the hearing towards an innocent verdict.

Or is this why they have not been included?

For example, going through 24 weeks of team timesheet prints clearly shows no hours have been un-paid to any team member, so no cash for hours was necessary.

I offered a full explanation as to why hours had not gone through the payroll in the week they should have, lack of support, lack of knowledge, other pubs not adding shared hours and team members not using hours recording system correctly.

As the evidence says, no hours are owed: that is because I corrected all hours through payroll as required where taxation and contributions are calculated as required to meet the company HMRC obligations.

Point 2: Hearing Concerns

No notes were taken when Ella Widebottom spoke to me in a way to belittle me and insist, I was in the wrong. My union rep stepped in and talked about how I was being treated was unacceptable and making the defendant and union rep herself very uncomfortable.

This was not a hearing; it was an interrogation!

A question was asked, answered by myself, then it was asked again and again and again over two hours. I answered the question within the first two minutes of the hearing, but the same question came back almost every 10 minutes for the whole hearing.

It is a tactic that criminal interrogators use to break down suspects and get them to admit to something. Asking the same question twenty different ways, trying to catch me out, trick me into admitting something I have not done is not a hearing, it is the pursuit of an agenda. But I am not a criminal, this is not a police state and persons chairing any hearing should not be playing "tag-team" with the note taker in a focused attempt to twist my words to fit a required result.

My union rep stepped in a number of times to request for me to treated fairly and the HR person tried to shut my union rep down. This was supposed to be hearing, a fair hearing, not a forceful and oppressive interrogation.

Point 3: The Chair / HRBP actions following the hearing

I was asked if it was ok for the chair to have copies of all my evidence. No problem, I said I have access to my evidence from my laptop by going into the company system. So, I handed the evidence over including the printed files from team time worked recording system.

On Saturday 22nd December 20## I went to reprint this evidence only to find I no longer have any access to the prints or the company system itself.

In fact, my username has been deleted from within the company systems, as the printout I got from trying to access the system told me. This action of cutting my access has now put me in a very unfair position where I can no longer access much of the evidence that I have used to prove my innocence.

If I have no username on the wage system, I am no longer employed at my pub, or indeed, with the company?

I have complied with every rule, request and restriction that has been placed on me. I haven't even sent Christmas cards to lifelong friends who work for the company to protect myself from further chargers.

Can I refer you to the letter emailed to me on 24th December 20## where my suspension in continued? That letter does not restrict me any access to company systems so removing me from payroll system is just wilful harassment intended to cause hurt to feelings and damage my defence.

Why else do it?

No doubt you will now re-issue the letter to restrict my access to systems, but as I don't have any access, the point is mute.

As the DPS and GM of My Pub (or so I thought) I have a valid interest in the performance of the business. I have not interfered in any way, so cutting me off from the computer system is a hostile act that demonstrates persons within the company are on a mission to weaken my defence and so reach the predetermined result of dismissal.

May I thank you for taking the time to read my notes, all points can be discussed when we reconvene on the 4th of January 20##.
Kind regards
Pub Manager

End Reply

They reconvene the hearing on the 4th of January as requested.
Phoebe Buttress and Ella Widebottom are in no mood for chat.

The union rep wanted to talk about the mistakes made in the meeting notes that have been identified to Phoebe and Ella and had sent them over email.

Phoebe Buttress looked very angry and dismissed the corrections that were required to correct the meeting notes as:

"Not admissible and we will not be discussing it any further."

WHAT THE FUCK? Mistakes have been clearly identified, errors and missing items in the meeting notes. The GM was not allowed to read these notes when the first hearing was adjourned, they were told the notes would be emailed and the GM could ask for changes at a later date.

The GM is now being DENIED their basic workers' rights!

Phoebe then went into a well-rehearsed speech saying that on review she has decided the GM was not guilty of gross misconduct, but was going to dismiss the GM anyway using the escalation process.

To say the GM was shocked is a ball busting understatement, the union rep and GM just stared at each other in bewilderment.

The GM said "*I don't understand, I have been found not guilty of the gross misconduct offence, paying staff cash for hours, and rightly so, but you are now claiming that this is connected to a previous offence I committed on social media?*"

In employment law is not possible in any way to link these two disciplinary offences together, this is sheer madness.

Phoebe Buttress and Ella Widebottom just clammed up, shuffled papers while staring down at the tabletop, they no longer wanted to converse with us.

The GM told them they would lodge an appeal and they left.

The union man said he had never seen anything like it and urged the GM to appeal because what had just happened was a clusterfuck by the company and the union will happily take the case all the way, as far as it needs to go to put this miscarriage of justice right.

The GM drove home in a trance, stunned at how badly they were treated by a company they have delivered millions in profit for, given much of their adult life to and spent many years putting the company ahead of their own family needs.

But the GM knows they can win the appeal, all the evidence was there, they have now withheld if, but the union man witnessed the evidence, it is undeniable.

Then, yet again, the penny dropped…

This had all the hallmarks of the slimy evil fingers protruding from the cloven hoofs of Knobbush all over it.

This is why Phoebe Buttress looked like a scared cat in the headlights of a speeding car, she had disappointed her puppet-master by not sacking me before Christmas.

The reconvened hearing was basically a staged act written and directed by the twat that is Knobbush. Phoebe was now under his total control and has been instructed exactly what to do if she wants to confirm her full-time appointment as a BDM.

And that is exactly what she did, ignoring the truth, acting in her own job interest against the innocent employee, ending someone's career for brownie points from her hero, Mr Knobbush who is probably slipping her a finger knuckle deep under the table at meetings as well.

Off the GM goes the write the appeal, which went something like this:

*8th January 20## **Appeal: Disciplinary decision on 4th January 20##.***

Dear HR

I want to appeal against the decision to dismiss me from the company.
The reasons for this appeal are:

- *1: The hearing was not a fair hearing; it was an interrogation that was intended to break me down and admit I had done something I had not done.*
- *2: The evidence presented by the chair contained statements that exonerate me from the charges against me. This evidence seems to have been ignored.*
- *3: The charges against are not relevant: The charges are about paying team members cash for hours worked, that would mean failing in compliance to payroll/payee/tax! No team members are claiming that any hours have been paid cash instead of through payroll systems. All team confirm that all their hours have been put through payroll and processed correctly.*
- *4: I was found innocent of the Gross Misconduct charge; this means that I had proved I had not paid anyone cash. I had only ever given people, who were desperate for money, a "bridging loan" from my own pocket. These amounts of money were not calculated to "hours missed", the*

amount was a lump sum of £60.00 and then another £60.00. The team member was paid minimum wage, not £10.00 per hour! The chair says in the decision that I "paid an amount of cash". This was proved to NOT be the case and the words "paid or paying cash" have been used against me even though I proved that I had NEVER paid anyone cash for hours, I simply lent some cash to people, who were desperate, from my own pocket.

- *5: The decision says I did NOT take the appropriate action to correcting mistakes made in the payroll process. I produced evidence that clearly proved I did take actions to correct any mistakes using the payroll system and had contacted my BDM about the issues we had with pay not being processed. I did not receive any response from my BDM, in fact I only had two very short meetings with the BDM at in the 7 months he was my line manager.*
- *6: The words "compensated them by paying an amount of money" are use in the decision. This never took place, I proved that no money was "paid", I just offered a small personal loan to help people in distress!*
- *7: The decision says "failed to ensure certain employees were clocking in and out" correctly. The decision maker has ignored the facts that I was not fully trained in the wages system, was left completely unsupported and on my own managing a new business without any trained supervisors. I was stretched to a point of exhaustion; the evidence is available in old emails where I am begging for help. It took nearly 3 months to get me an assistant manager. As soon as he started, he taught me what I did not know about missing payments and how to process them. That process was followed from that day onwards. The evidence I supplied supports that fact.*

The decision maker refers to my disciplinary record. I need to clear up some issues with what she is referring to.

I was given a final written warning for a rather silly thing that was blown out of proportion by an overzealous HR rep who was new to the company and had to "show what she was about" to her new employer. Eight months later she is no longer with the company. The hearing was meant to be conducted by my BDM with the HR rep taking notes and assisting. What actually happened was the HR rep took over completely, my BDM hardly spoke.

The hearing was adjourned, and I was told I would be contacted.

I waited 15 days for a decision that came by letter only, so when I got the letter informing me of a final written warning, I was very shocked. I was going to appeal, but I had waited so long to receive the decision we were now into the World Cup build up in May, time slipped by, and I realised I had allowed the 7-day limit to pass by.

What is important about this is, this inappropriate level of action against me has now been used to dismiss me through the escalation process. During the investigation into the recent charges, the investigation chair said very clearly that I should not have been given a final written warning for contacting a complaining customer on-line in a private message.

The escalation process should be used when the allegation is connected to any previous warnings. The final written warning I received back in April 20## is not even similar to the allegations I have recently proved false.

Allegations made against me in April 20##:

serious misuse of social media reasonably bringing our name into disrepute serious breach of the duty of trust and confidence owed by an employee to his or her employer.

Allegations used to escalate and dismiss me on 4th January 2018.

breach of trust and confidence: namely relating to cash in hand payments being made. There are two problems with how this has been used.

1: Comparing the allegations I do not think it is fair to use the words "trust and confidence" as an escalation when they are just an introduction the actual allegation Social Media and Cash in Hand Payments are NOT the same thing so the second allegation cannot be used to escalate the previous warning up to dismissal.

2: Cash Payments Is Gross Misconduct When reading her decision at the reconvened hearing, the decision maker clearly stated that NO Gross Misconduct action had to be answered for. I had proved my innocence and that the allegations are false. But in the escalation to dismiss me, the decision maker used the "proved false" allegation as the reason for the escalation? Paying cash is a gross misconduct offence, if I had done that, the decision would have been summary dismissal for gross misconduct. How can something be used as an escalation if it has not happened?

A number of ACAS codes of practice have not been followed in procedure and conduct by the company

- *When suspended I was not told why, no explanation was given and I did not know anything for 48 hours when I received an email confirming the false allegations, two charges that even the investigation chair told me he did not understand!*
- *In the disciplinary I was told that I could not ask questions by the chair and HR representative. This is wrong, ACAS say I can ask questions and when I did the chair refused to respond, unless it was in an attempt to shut me down.*
- *The HR rep told me early in the two-hour hearing I was guilty in a statement telling me how I should conduct myself in a hearing. This is when she was telling me I could not ask questions!*
- *I have put in two grievances against the person who has suspended me. Both grievances clearly indicate that he is bias against me. Why was he allowed to continue to investigate the allegations he had made against me?*
- *Code of practice clearly states that suspension should be reviewed, and the status changed if applicable. I offered to work at different sites, anywhere, but this request was refused.*
- *Any employee is entitled to a speedy investigation, and hearing if required. It took nearly 30 days (6 days at the start I was signed off ill) but it still took over 20 days to hold an investigation meeting! This was just adding stress to me as an employee and creating a separation between myself and my pub team.*
- *My line managers know I have a depression history and have tried to use this long-term suspension, threats of "none-payment of salary" to push me into handing in my notice due to the increasing stress placed upon myself.*
- *I have had no communication about the two grievances I have entered from the company, not a single up-date. The company thought I would either walk away or be dismissed at the hearing on 20th December so the grievances could then be dropped without investigating.*
- *At the point of dismissal, I have been suspended for 9 weeks. This is not an effective process that is fair to the employee.*

I believe there are serious concerns to be addressed with the decision to dismiss me. The evidence presented against me contained evidence that actually proved my innocents. The investigation meeting notes are being taken out of context by the decision maker. A hearing is supposed to be an opportunity for the defendant to explain any misunderstandings etc. I explained everything I was asked, but the chair was intent on reaching a final decision of dismissal in any way she could.

Because Gross Misconduct was proved false, the decision maker used the only way left to impose dismissal. But let's think it through, add some common sense and look at what has happened. My innocents to charges left the chair with a gamble to take, try to use the escalation process in a very loose and ambiguous way. But the escalation is not appropriate in this case as the allegations are governed by different polices.

It would be appropriate for this appeal to be chaired by someone not connected to the North team. My case has clearly been discussed amongst Mr Knobbush's BDM team over the last 10 weeks since I was first suspended.

Appeal End

After reading my appeal you can see the GM had strong grounds of appeal, far too many holes, mistakes, and misrepresentation of the evidence.

So now the GM back in the waiting game, relying on the company to do the right thing and reinstate them as a manager.

The only explanation for what has happened can only be the hatred the GM faces for my Op's manager Mr Knobbush, he must be the one pulling the strings. Just think back to the money saving tricks used but nasty wankers like Knobbush, the GM had refused to treat their team that way, it is not moral or right and should be exposed for what it is, abuse of employees. That is why he needs the GM gone, what if the GM was followed by other managers and they also refused to work their staff to death to line Knobbush's pocket and ego, it would be chaos, the GM had to go…

The appeal finally comes around, and the union rep and the GM attend the planned hearing with a certain amount of confidence.

The meeting goes very well, the challengers are listened to, talked through for a couple of hours, then they need to adjourn to investigate the information they have been given.

The GM leaves the meeting fairly confident, this James fella chairing the meeting didn't seem like a wanker, what a relief and a huge change from recent meetings.

They reconvened the meeting again and talked through even more detail, another couple of hours go by with the GM's case getting stronger and stronger, they were feeling good, this chair was doing his job properly.

They had to adjourn yet again as the GM had brought up even more items that proved his innocents and the miss-treatment showed further enquiries were needed.

Then a letter arrived through the GM's door.

The decision to dismiss the GM has been upheld.

WHAT THE ACTUAL FUCK

This cannot be right, the GM has proved without a doubt that the ass-licking silly bitch who sacked the GM was wrong, the GM had not committed gross misconduct and the escalator warning system could not possibly be applied under ACAS rules.

Throughout the appeal the GM has clearly demonstrated a plot to remove him and why the original decision was un-sound?

Then they had their final "The Penny Drops" moment…

A couple of years ago the GM left this pub company after being tempted away by big promises. They stayed with the other company for 10 months only because they turned out to be the type of company, I have described earlier on in the money saving tricks chapter.

The Op's manager in this new company, let's call him the fat controller, was also a real cunt. Bonus obsessed and greedy, the worst the Op's had ever come across, well until they met Knobbush who soon nicked that crown for himself.

Leaving this "other company" the old pub company immediately gave the GM a manager's job in a big pub on a good salary, it was nice to be back at home and happy.

Because the GM had left the employer for under a year the personnel department man who was over seeing their return said he only needed a very brief induction covering basic legal stuff like not drinking bleach not sticking your dick in the meat slicer, you know the type of stuff.

The HR man said to the GM "we will call this a continuation of your employment from before and they were even issued their old original employee number."

It was like they had never been away.

The only problem for the GM, they were living 250 miles from home most of the time and never seeing their family.

The GM's family were also looking at moving to New Zealand in around a year's time, so the GM dropped the hint to some senior people about missing their family and possibly moving to NZ.

A few days later the GM was offered a new pub that was being refurbed and rebranded near to their family home.

The GM jumped at the chance and said yes yes yes.

But there did turn out to be a problem, the GM's salary.

Just like in earlier chapters, certain types of idiot BDM's and tosser Op's managers don't like paying high salaries to pub managers.

This is one of the two reasons the GM was sanctioned to be booted, dumped, removed painfully from the company by Mr Knobbush, who if you remember came across to our company after he personally helped ruin the one that was bought for pennies because he helped make it fucking worthless.

The second reason is, the GM will not follow "the slash the staff hours rules" enforced by bonus greedy middle management to cut wage cost and stop NI payments because it is just not right to do this to fellow human beings.

Where are the morals? The union rep is now chomping at the bit, "I cannot wait to take these fuckers to tribunal, we will screw them to the fucking wall."

Off he goes to start the proceedings to take my case to the courts because he knows that the GM has been fired unfairly, without warrant, and by the legal term "unfair dismissal".

After the GM received the outcome of the appeal, they felt they had one last response to make to the people at the company who had done this to them.

Here was the GM's final response:

Final Statement Regardless of Outcome

I was very surprised how the appeal went! As the decision had already been made that I was not guilty of "paying cash wages", and so not guilty of "gross misconduct", I thought the appeal would be focused on the reason for my dismissal and the way the escalation process was used incorrectly?

I was asked, in the appeal, questions that I had already answered in the disciplinary hearing. I proved myself to be innocent of all charges using the detailed, neatly tagged and ordered, structured defence evidence. It was with this evidence that I presented at the disciplinary hearing I explained every question asked, disproved every allegation.

I was promised verbally by the chair that my evidence would be returned to me for the appeal. This evidence has been withheld from me, not made available for my appeal, so without my evidence that proves my innocence, a different outcome could result because "who would believe someone without evidence?"

My access to re-print the evidence was removed from the company system the day after the hearing held on 20th December 20##. We were due to reconvene on January 4th 20## where a decision would be made.

Why was my access removed, I had not been dismissed? Why had the chairperson asked to hold onto my evidence? I only agreed because I said to the chair, it's no problem, I will reprint everything. It would appear very suspicious that my access was removed the next day.

I was asked questions about an email "I had sent" about wages owed? It was not me who sent that email! What this tells me is that the evidence you were handed to review the decision to dismiss me was filed poorly and in no coherent order. This is a lack of care by the chair that can only lead to evidence / notes going missing and so hurting my appeal.

If you were given the evidence against me, why were you not given the evidence proving my innocence?

The way I had "allowed" the handing of the hearing notes was questioned and said to be "disappointing". I accept that the note signing process was an issue and I could have done more, but: I did question the notes, ask for changes, and was denied any alteration flatly by the chair at the reconvened hearing on 4th January. This has made a mockery of the note taking process. As chair of the appeal, you have executed notes correctly, as I also do it when I acted as chair in many meetings and dictated how the notes process was to be completed.

This is exactly what the chair of the hearing did, dictated the process to us and gave us reassurances that any amendments would be agreed when we reconvened. Yes, I could have done more, but as the chair is my superior at the hearing, I have a duty to trust her and the process, including those involved.

I had no reason to suspect what was to follow, a complete disregard for the process I myself had been instructed to follow and dismissal of any changes I asked to make to the notes after being assured this would be the case.

The reconvened hearing was rushed, we sat down, I was told my requests for changes and my complaints about the first hearing were not accepted and the chair went on to read the decision from a prepared statement. I was found not guilty of gross misconduct (paying cash wages) but was told I was being dismissed because I have a final written warning for the same reason when I didn't?

The reason for my dismissal was not told or explained to me at the hearing. I was told verbally that the gross misconduct charge had been dropped and not proven. This was the cash for wages charge. So why in the dismissal letter was the "paying cash for wages" used as a dismissal lever in the escalation process? It had been proven not the case so how could an unproven and dismissed charge be used if not shown as an offence? I was proven innocent so how can a dismissed charge be used to escalate if it no longer exists?

After the decision to dismiss was given at the disciplinary hearing the chair quickly explained the notes would be sent by email and we were dismissed from the room. We were asked if we wanted to check the notes, we said no because there was no point as no notes were required for a pre-written statement that we were not given the opportunity to respond to. We will check on email but, as the amendments had been refused for the earlier hearing notes, we were not hopeful.

A full break down in trust of the chair and HR rep had taken place.

The final decision notes have never been sent to me.

I have an expectation that any person conducting a hearing follows ACAS code of conduct and best practice, as advocated by the company HR policy. This has not been followed. The company has to ensure that anyone conducting a hearing has the ability and integrity to follow a fair process.

A HR rep who represents the company in a hearing should be able to follow ACAS code of conduct and understand what is, and what is not allowed. A HR rep who shouts me down with anger by telling me "I am not allowed to ask questions" and helped conduct a hearing that was in fact an interrogation, is incompetent.

The chair, with poorly filed notes, hiding of my defence evidence, dismissing my amendments, interrogation tactics, failing to understand the escalation process or explaining my dismissal reasons, plus a HR rep who should be advising the chair on correct procedure, but instead does not know the ACAS code of conduct herself, the hearing should have ended with my acquittal, but instead it was adjourned to "find a reason to dismiss me" or to take instructions from above.

As I was found not guilty of gross misconduct, I have to question the level of punishment proscribed to me?

As we all know, a person can have multiple warnings running alongside each other, it is only escalation when the charges are a repeat of a similar type of offence.

A number of options were available to the chair but given any warning I would have appealed because a person cannot be issued with a warning after being found innocent. Dismissal is drastic overkill when I have been found innocent of gross misconduct.

The options are:

No further action. Why was I not given a written warning? Why was my current warning not extended?

Other Questions: If Dismissal upheld, After I was dismissed, I received a letter telling me I was dismissed on the 4th of January.

But I was not summary dismissed, I was paid 4 weeks' notice, so I was given notice of my dismissal on the 4th of January.

According to AXA PPP my employment ended on 4th March?

All these mistakes show that the Chair, Phoebe Buttress, was totally out of her depth, completely unfit and far too thick to be allowed to make decisions on someone career and livelihood.

The appeal was going my way, James adjourned twice to reinvestigate information that was pointed in my favour, and the whole thing was being drawn out proclaiming my innocents.

The company continued to pay me my salary in February and March because they had lost and knew that they would have to pay me any salary I had lost after the dismissal date and up to winning the appeal win.

We were winning and putting a wrong right…

But then, someone in the HR department turned very nasty indeed.

Remember when I explained how the HR department mitigates risk to the company and will act against all employees every-time to protect the company finances, well this is what they did to me.

I had been re-employed as a continuation of my previous employment with the company because I had been away for under a full year. I had even been given my old employment number back on my return.

But some bright cunt in the HR department realised they could make it all go away by repealing the decision of "continuation" part of my employment.

This made me a recent new starter with under two years employment with the company.

This meant I was no longer entitled to take this case to a tribunal.

So, in the end they WON, they chucked me on the scrap heap of life like a dead rat would be discarded, without care or thought of what they were doing to a loyal and dependable employee who had earned them millions over the years.

What was done to me was a disgusting abuse of the rules.

I was lied about, trolled on Watts App, bullied, framed, deceived, and even had defence evidence stollen from me, but I still won because I had NOT done what they said I had done, but in the end a technicality killed me off.

My union were gutted, but they cannot take a company to the cleaners when the law prevents them from doing so.

Fucking Tory changes to employment law…

I have talked a lot about how companies can hurt, wound, and crush employees in so many ways.

I have given details on how they save money by deceit, trickery and legal theft using their employees to drive up profits at the cost of the people on the front line.

Most of the PLC pub companies, not all, but the majority will crush a person, swat them like fly's if they can save a few quid or drive up the share price.

Now ask yourself, did this really happen to the author writing these pages?

Would a PLC company actually sink so low as to steel evidence, lie, ignore facts and decide an outcome before the invitation letter to a disciplinary hearing has been out?

Can the people involved in this sort of injustice and act in such a malicious way sleep at night, are they not kept up by guilt and remorse for what they have done to an innocent people?

If you have worked for some of the companies running UK branded pubs owned by PLC financial institutions, you will know already if this story is just fiction, or if fact, the truth.

Anyone wants to take on a huge legal claim for hundreds, or thousands, of ex-pub staff and managers who have experienced similar to the GM above…

Contact the author…

Chapter 10

The Good, The Bad and The Worse Than Ugly...

In this chapter I'm going to talk about a few people I have met, hated, respected, admired, loathed, and loved to spend time with.

Derby

In my 35+ years of managing pubs I have met some strange, very weird, and some amazing people.

I want to share some of these people with you.

The first one I want to share with you, I have no idea about his name, his history, nothing.

What I do know is, in Derby in the early 90's financial cuts to public care facilities were the same as everywhere else in the UK, facilities were being closed down with what seemed little or no interest in what happened to the people these closures directly affected, the residents, patients and anyone in need of the care community.

I was managing a unique below ground cask ale pub that I had opened for Whitbread. Luckily, I was working with some amazing people such as Beccy, rock chick and lifelong friend, Debbie, fit, sexy dancing lady, Matt, my assistant, top lad, one in a million, Emma our super supervisor and Paul, our doorman, top bloke and good friend.

All I can say is we were fantastic small team who delivered amazing service to our regulars, people like Tara, fruit wine loving piss head but such a laugh, below the street level of Irongate in Derby.

One day, mid-week, a fella wanders in, we were underground, so he had walked down the 18 steps where he entered the bar area.

This young man coming in to have a drink was not a concern, why would it be, we welcomed people every day for this very same reason.

It was what he was carrying that raised concern.

As he entered the bar a guitar came through the door first followed by a mid-20's man neatly dressed and smiling broadly.

As I glanced towards him, I could see he was not alone, but something was off, why did he appear to have a friend hanging onto him so tightly?

As he came further into our little underground pub, I suddenly realised who was with the man.

It wasn't a person after all, it was a headless female manikin wearing a stripy dress, socks and no shoes.

Hmmmmmmm, One other odd thing I noticed; the guitar had no strings?

Most of the pub's seating consisted of old church pews facing each other, the type that just about held two reasonably sized arses on a flat wooden seat with a table in-between.

The man seated the headless female manikin on one of the pews, carefully adjusting the legs and arms into an upright seated position with the hands face down on to the tabletop.

He sat across from his plastic, non-talkative friend, and started playing his guitar enthusiastically even though there was no string too pluck.

I was witnessing full on air-guitar competition action but without the usual judgers and screaming fans looking on. His hands, the fingers, all going through the motions to a sound that only he, and his faceless friend I presume, could hear.

What The Fuck is going on? He "played" for about 10 minutes, stopped and came to the bar.

He polity asked for a coke, so that's what I served him, without ice or fruit as requested.

He returned to his seat and while he sipped the cold black fizzy soda he chatted to his female friend and laughed at her responses as if they were on a date.

I could not take my eyes off what I was watching!

A few customers walked in and as they passed our new friend with his headless date they double-checked a look, smiled and even giggled a little bit.

"What's going on with him?" one customer asked me.

I just smiled and shrugged my shoulders as I didn't know what to say and certainly could not explain what we were witnessing.

After around 30 minutes of being the pubs free entertainment, the man stood up, collected his silent guitar and incomplete lady-friend and left without saying another word.

I didn't expect to see this man and his friend again, I presumed he was on day release or something from some type of home, but we did see him again a few weeks later, and he was a very different person this time.

My shift was over, and I had handed over to Emma to manage the pub for the evening and until close at 11pm. I was having a pint and playing pool with my friend Paul when I noticed the silent Romeo man was back and standing at the bar talking to Becci.

She had a look on her face that was not quite right, the way she was slightly leaning back and looking away from the man made me think she was feeling uncomfortable, and after around 30 seconds the man who had been so calm while quietly serenading his lifeless lady friend was becoming more and more agitated, so I put down my pool cue and made my way over to where he was still speaking "at" Becci with a force I did not like.

As I got near, I could see it was definitely the man with a headless friend, but this time he didn't have a fake friend with him, he had a dagger and now he was pulling it out of his jacket...

So, I punched him square in the face...

Just once, but luckily that was all it took.

On occasion, as humans, we can freakily do something that you are not normally very good at, but that one time you absolutely nail it and that is what had happened.

The punch I hit him with was an accidental perfect hammer blow and he was out cold.

I disarmed him and the Fuzz was called to collect him.

He did wake up, put I kept him pinned to the floor with my foot pushing heavily on his chest.

We never saw or heard from him again, I don't even know what happened to him once he was taken away in police bracelets, but that was a valuable lesson in my early years as a full-time licensee.

A switch is flicked in the mind for a reason we may never know and what seems to be a mild-mannered harmless person can change into anything, even a potential killer.

York

What a fantastic place to work, the culture, the history, tourists, friendly Yorkshire people:

but not everyone is nice even though they are living idealistic surroundings.

It's January 1995 and I have been asked to go and manage a pub in York City centre out of the blue.

Another underground pub, I've just spent 18 months in the frigging dark, now I'm starting a new chapter of my life selling beer from a hole in the ground again, but at least it's a new city.

But first things first, I need to granted permission to hold the liquor license for the pub, so first port of call, the local courts building.

Before February 2005 no one held a personal liquor license that allows the holder to manage any pub in England or Wales.

The way you were granted your license was by going to court in a suit, tie, polished shoes and just standing still. Occasionally a solicitor requested a judge to grant you a license.

In most towns and cities, the licensee could go to court on their own because it was little more than a formality to be granted a license. The local police had been given prior notice of your name, they checked out your history, no red flags, no risk to people and if no criminal record you were granted permission after answering a couple of simple questions.

The judge, and any witnesses, just want to know one thing and it fits into one simple, but formal question:

Are you a-
Fit And Proper Person to Hold the Position of Licensee

If you have previously been a licensee, it's all pretty straight forward and over in minutes. Not in 1995 York it wasn't.

The historic ways of how things are done had been clung onto like nowhere else in the UK, no not the history of the city, buildings and city walls, I'm talking about legal administration.

Modernisation was not a done thing in York's court systems.

I was informed that I would be represented in court by a senior partner from the breweries retained legal company.

Into court I go, suit and booted, ready for my five-minute hearing and then off to the pub to start my new position as a GM in York.

My appearance in court did not go as smoothly as I had expected.

The judge, oh my god, looked like one of the walking dead, I still remember his name nearly 30 years later, but I won't use it as it's not a nice thing to do, I will just call him judge; he must have been 85 years old if a day!

Don't misunderstand me, there is possibly a million 85-year old's out there in the UK who are vital, on the ball, current, progressive and modernised with every legal up-date ever. But NOT this judge.

I was being asked questions about my history, my experience, and if I'm really up to the job as I am still in my 20's?

To say I was a little surprised with this judge's tone is an understatement, he was being a condescending ageist twat.

I answered all his questions, and our solicitor was trying to bring the judge back into expected parameters, but this judge wasn't having any of that.

Next, he asked me about my brother?

My older brother was no angle, no boy scout, but I'm not responsible for him and I hadn't seen him for years.

He asked me about being single and who was going to help me run the pub?

Just a few years earlier it had been frowned upon to employee single managers in big pub companies. When I moved to York, I was working for a big brewery that owned 100's of pubs and when I was appointed as a single manager a fair few years earlier many of the old-fashioned older area managers thought this was the beginning of the end, single people could not be trusted to run pubs apparently.

When the judge asked me these outdated, out-of-touch and slightly offensive questions our solicitor remarked that this line of questions was not acceptable.

But the judge just continued to look at me and was waiting for my answers.

When I was working in Derby in our basement home from home beer cellar, a young lady with big blond hair came to work for me called Becci. I had known Becci for a few years because she had been a very young and talented waitress in my friend's pub near Chesterfield.

Becci had come to Derby for Uni a few years before I landed there, but when we met again, she become part of my team in the pub while finishing her Derby Uni years.

When I was asked to move to York early in 1995, I asked Becci to move also and be my new deputy manager in York. I knew I would need someone I could trust in a strange city, a new pub and an old team in a poorly performing pub.

Back to answering the question posed by man in a black robe whose understanding of the world was still somewhere in the 1920's...

So, to my reply on who would be helping me manage the pub?

"I have a young lady joining me at the pub and she will be my assistant manager."

This was the genuine judgers response:

"do you think it is wise having a young lady in a position of management in a pub?"

WHAT THE FUCK DID HE JUST SAY!

Our solicitor jumped all over this, then the man who I think was the court clerk quickly had a quiet word in the ear of this misogynist judge and my application for a license suddenly was granted.

Following this remarkable comment about females holding positions in management I took a close look at the night-time economy that existed in York.

There was so little, just a couple of small clubs and no more than a couple of pubs held licenses that let them open past 11pm.

No wonder the University was classed as really good, no students were drinking or eating curry while shit-faced late into the night.

I can remember after I had been in York a couple of months, a few of us wanted a late-night drink after working till 11:30pm on a mid-weekday. We had to go to a Chinese restaurant because it was the only place in York open after 11pm. Even the clubs were closed as it was mid-week, fuck me, we are in a time-warp.

I had moved to York from Derby, as city where I could leave work at 11:30pm, get a drink in loads of late bars and the Rock House, and after that, go to the Eastern Curry house at 2am for even more booze. The number of times I went straight to work for a 7am beer delivery after crawling out the Eastern curry house at 6am lol.

Now I was in York, I had stepped back in time to the 1950's, let's hope a city this beautiful will make spending time here enjoying the history worth it?

Not everyone in York was a nice person.

The pub I took over had been a disappointment to brewery owner for decades. We had a new Op's manager, smart man called Martin and he wanted change. Martin had appointed a new area manager to the pub, and he wanted me in York to work with the new area manager.

For the last few years, I had been on an area of pubs managed by an area manager who was a little bit on the naughty side of honesty.

He had his fingers in lots of pies, the **P** key till con, buying beer in, using tills that didn't belonging to the company, you name it, he was part of it.

But I was never involved in the dodgy dealings, I was the young kid manager on an area of old-time licensees who had all worked together on this area for many years.

When the opportunity came up in York Martin wanted me moved off the area managers team so I couldn't be tainted with any future investigation. I had spent 18 months working with this team of managers and too be honest I really liked them, except one, he was fucking scary, I had learned so much from so many of them, but I used the knowledge for good, not lining my pockets.

For me it was pastures new with fresh, squeaky-clean people.

The pub in York had a big problem, a group of men, 50 years old +, used the pub as their regular daily boozer. They all sat just inside the main doors sipping beer all day and basically growling at any person, especially tourists, who dared to open the door looking for a refreshing drink or bite to eat.

They had to go, but how do I get rid of these entrenched men?

This group of men had a leader, Roy, a hard man with a big reputation and an even harder stare. He disliked everyone, didn't work, he just sat in my pub every day scaring people away if they risked opening the door to this underground unknown mystery vaulted space. It was a magnet to tourists, until they faced Roy and his minions' glaring stares by cracking open the stained-glass window centred in the antique wooded main entrance door.

I had heard of this pub chain called Wetherspoons, but they hadn't reached York yet, so what do I do with Roy and his crew until Wetherspoons lands nearby and welcomes him with open arms?

I had to find a way of getting this man and his mates to voluntarily leave the pub FOREVER.

My BDM, Glenn, had confirmed to me that the company wanted to spend money on the pub turning it into a quality cask ale pub in May, so I only have 5 months left to "make Roy and his band of merry men" wander off into the Yorkshire sunset.

Hmmmmmmm, I needed a plan.

This is how I did it…

From this point on I tried to always be the person who served Roy when he needed a refill of his half of Boddingtons.

I was working 7 days a week anyway trying to sort out the huge staffing problems I had inherited.

There was just one existing team member I wanted to keep from old current team, and she was a young lady called Kerry, a nice young lady with great customer service, a far cry from the other team members.

I started to chat to Roy every day at the bar, just stuff like "hi, how are you today" or "did you see the England game"? simple stuff to get us acquainted and break to ice and get my plan started.

After a couple of weeks, the hard stare faded and Roy began to talk back to me, just one-word answers to start with, but this was significant progress.

May was now just 4 months away, the timing was tight, but I really could make this happen.

The weeks were flying by, and I needed to change tactics a little.

I stated walking around the pub with a tape measure, clip board and old plans for a refurb from the last time the pub had been fettled around 8 years earlier. I had found the plans in the back of the office filing cabinet.

This peaked Roy's interest, so after a few days of me writing notes about total bullshit on page after page, Roy eventually asked me while trying to suppress his interest "what going on"?

This was it; this was the opportunity I had been waiting for, an opening to spin my web of lies…

It was finally time to use my elaborate and many times rehearsed spiel to get the result I needed, to provide the company with a Roy-less pub or the investment into my new pub may not go ahead.

"You're not going to believe this Roy, the company have decided to turn this place into a family pub, it will be all about food, families, they are even going to put a creche in."

Roy's reaction was priceless, he looked shocked and asked me what I thought about it?

"Well, I don't really get a say in it, it's a stupid idea in my opinion, families in pubs, where are people like us meant to go for a pint?"

That was it, without a doubt, one of the best white-lie I have ever spun, and I even managed to keep a straight face, brilliant.

We didn't have the internet, mobile phones, nothing, we had no choice but to ask other people what the hell is going on. It was not possible for Roy to know I was spinning him a yarn.

Over the next few weeks Roy and I chatted about "the companies stupid plans" and how daft they were, how much money the pub would lose without the locals and how kids running about and screaming will empty any pub.

No man wants to sup in a place with screaming kids ffs.

This was perfect, Roy's was now driving the conversation, asking me about details, plans and dates.

I needed to sow the seeds for the end game that was saying goodbye to Roy and his band on not-so-merry men.

We were down to just 4 weeks until the builders were due on site, and I had guaranteed my BDM that Roy will be gone.

It was time to load the final bullet in the chamber of deceit.

Roy was approaching the bar, so I put on a really angry face and acted very pissed off.

Roy asked what was up?

"I've had instructions from up-high that we will not be allowed single men in here when we reopen, apparently it will not fit our new family image, I cannot fucking believe it Roy."

Roy didn't say a word.

I then explained to Roy that the builders were starting work late in May so I explained I would do a countdown to the day when the old single men regulars were being barred by the company.

"The faceless company Roy, those twats at head office don't care about people like me and you, I'm embarrassed to work for them."

This was my best acting ever, I deserved a BAFTA…

It was at this point I told my BDM, Glenn, how I was getting rid of Roy, I hadn't known him long enough to trust him with the truth yet.

He was a little flabbergasted with my plan, but I assured him it would work.

Time was passing fast and soon the builders will be in to change it from an old man's pub to a student orientated cask ale emporium.

Time rolled on, every other day Roy and I would remind each other of how many days were left until it was finally the moving on day.

Final week made me nervous, 7, 6, 5, 4, then Roy didn't come in with just 3 days to go. 2 days left and still no Roy, was that it, the final day was tomorrow, Roy barred by 3pm without saying goodbye?

The final day began at opening time, 11am and no Roy.

Then out of the blue at 2:30pm Roy came to the bar with just 30 minutes left before the deadline.

He ordered a 1/2 pint of Boddies, and I pulled it for him.

"This one is on the house" I said, Roy smiled at me, held out his hand and we shuck hands warmly. Roy took his drink over to the table near the door and took a sip of his beer.

At 3:10pm I took a walk towards the front door; Roy was gone, and I never saw him or any of his cronies ever again.

I don't even know where they moved on to, all I knew was that they were gone with just a single weekend left before the builders turned up to do their stuff. When I arrived in York almost 5 months earlier, I was told by the old pub staff that I would never see the back of Roy and his mates, he was a violent man who takes no crap, he rules the pub, and no one has ever been able to change this Status Quo!

I had done it, and I was thanked with a handshake for barring the person offering their hand.

I did what I had to do, but I still felt dirty…

The pub re-opened under a new brand aimed at a much younger clientele based around York's large university population.

The pub went from strength to strength, we had amazing sales growth, income climbing like Whitbread had never seen before from a pub that had failed for the last 6 years.

But it wasn't the cheap refurb that made the difference, it was down to the fantastic team we had put together in just 6 months.

Becci joined me in February, and yes, I really needed an ally, thank god Becci came along just a few weeks after I started because apart from Kerry, it was a tough place and people to manage.

Next came Alison, our new chef.

She was quite simply a tour de-force of nature, big blond hair, thick well applied make-up and a very loud sweary voice.

For a non-trained chef, I have never come across a person so organised at getting food out of a kitchen so fast.

We also recruited Karen for the kitchen, and when Alison was not there, we needed Karen, and she had the best collection of kitchen hats ever, inspired I think by Jamiroquai's JK.

Heather, very cool team member, but she went weak at the knees every-time our BDM, Glenn, visited us. Possibly the biggest swoon I have ever seen come over a young lady.

Chris, a hardworking and reliable young man, always wanted to do his best, but never really understood being cool. The business needed him.

Lisa, tiny pocket rocket with tight curly hair, she was always so fast, disciplined and so committed, a single mum if I remember and a super star worker.

Rob and his sister Sarah, a bit posh compared to the rest of us, but they pulled their weight even in the busiest sessions.

Helen, 18, full of life, bracers on her teeth and looked like she would snap if bumped into behind the bar, but a total firebrand and what a force of nature.

Steve, ex-military and not tall, he was also very ginger, but great lad, good friend, and a great bloke to work, and drink with. Top fella.

Joanne, who became my assistant after Becci went off to manage her own pub, famous because she once told us she slipped a finger up her boyfriend's arse at the moment of truth.

Just think, no one had heard of porn-hub at this time, what an imagination.

Liz, a real star who always set herself apart the rest of us, real talent, very smart, but had this huge defensive wall in place at all times. Extremely bright and diligent young lady who is probably a millionaire by now.

Anna is the last one I will mention, a student, quiet and genuine.

I had so much time for Anna, and she did end up working for me in Nottingham and eventually because a paramedic, public hero Anna, I wish we had kept in touch.

The York team were a remarkable group of people, they really gelled as one unit, we had real teamwork, we sweated together, choked on cigarette smoke together, laughed, and celebrated success together.

There are lots of other team members I could mention, Garvey, Kerry, John the KP, and a young lady who was amazing at Fast-Show impressions.

I spent 2 and a half years in York, loved it, great team, great area manager, bought my 1st mobile phone in 1996, a Nokia 232, and a fantastic city to live in and enjoy.

Except for the fucking traffic…

Oh yeah, and by the time I left Yorkshire the old Judge from the courts was gone and licensing changes were transforming the city, it had become vibrant, exciting and a huge late-night economy for everyone in North Yorkshire and the millions of worldwide visitors.

Nottingham 1

In 1997 I arrived in Nottingham to open a new concept cafe bar themed on Spanish sunshine. Nicky (BDM) and Malcolm (designer) had this crazy idea about opening a new style of cafe bar, this was 1997, there was only a few cafe bars in the UK and the market was open and ready for a revolution.

This is where I fit in, they needed someone who thought outside the box and was always looking far ahead.

But I was never going to be good enough on my own, just like in York a GM needs a wingman, or woman, to help bring it all together.

I had the crazy ideas, the new ways of working, the invention, the BIG stuff, but I would never be able to make it work like clockwork day to day, I needed someone with really disciplined customer service values, a true understanding of what a cafe bar could be, we couldn't just rely on just my crazy ambitions, I needed Clare.

Back in the day when I worked in Derby, Clare was the assistant manager for the very cool bar at street level directly above our subterranean cask ale pub.

She absolutely hated me, I don't know why, she didn't really know me, but the dislike was almost visible whenever she was near me, total indifference.

But I didn't care about that, like me or not, we needed Clare on board to create the new cafe bar brand we were building.

Nicky, BDM, was charged with tempting Clare to come on board, God knows how she did it, but Claire joined as part of the opening team, we just needed to recruit a full team from out of thin air now.

So, I'm now in Nottingham preparing the brand-new concept cafe bar to open and interviewing for was not fun. You sit in a hotel room with someone coming through the door every 15 mins trying to impress us just enough to offer them a job in our new super cool cafe bar.

To be honest, I only remember 2 people who stood out on that day, many more became our fantastic CASA team, but Adam and Lynn stood out.

Lynn arrived at the interview, huge blonde hair, around 30 years old and a giggle that never stopped. She also had bar experience; she was signed up straight away.

Adam, down beaten, looked broken as a young, no spark, I asked him why he was unemployed? He told me he got caught with his hand in the till.

Without going into detail, Adam explained what had happened.

I gave hive a job, he didn't let me down and became successful a few years later as a pub manager in his own right.

I also met Yasa, a DJ who I thought was pretty special.

What we were doing was something new, we wanted live DJ music without anyone asking the DJ to play Dancing Queen.

So, the DJ booth was fitted near the back of the bar, to the far left and facing the wall. If Yasa wanted to check out the crowd, he would be looking over his left shoulder, no, he did NOT have a microphone where he could shout SHABBA or wish Karen a happy birthday.

We wanted Balearic House tunes smoothly played to a more sophisticated crowd.

Our new cafe bar concept was a huge success and they started opening all over England from Newcastle to Epson.

Opening a new cafe bar was not the only thing the brewery wanted me doing, I was also given another pub to manage just 300 meters away, one of the oldest pubs in the UK and overrun with hells angel types who were weighing out drugs on the 1st floor tables.

For Fuck Sake, how did it get like this?

How do you take back control of a pub being used as a drug dealing base?

Without going into detail, the process is called fussing tables.

I will save all the details of dealing with drug dealers for the follow up book, lots of juicy stories in that one.

Nottingham 2

I moved from the new cafe bar and the really old, but no longer a dealer's pub, to open a brand-new cask ale bar to be built in a modernised version of what we had created in York.

I stayed in Nottingham which felt like home as it always had to me, or as much as a wandering nomad can claim a home city.

I was working with Glenn again, so things were looking good.

Recruiting for the new cask ale emporium seemed so easy, I was attracting people who had worked with me in Nottingham and York in the recent years, my old troopers, and friends returning to work as a family once again, nothing better.

Chris, Anna from York, and Lynn from the Cafe Bar joined the team to help get it started.

Next, I found new superstars to join our amazing team, Tracy, Minda, Karen, Lesley, Ralph, Little Lisa, Wendy, Sarah, Vivian, and many more would join our team ready for the big opening.

Sorry if I missed anyone, not intended, old age and all that.

We opened with a modernised the style of food delivery, I took what I learned from Clare while at The Cafe Bar and improved customer service in the new site with real WOW factors that are not normally used in that type of environment. We were using trays and legs to take food to tables, our new team were outstanding, we suddenly become the highest taking food site in the brand, we were unstoppable, and we had a massive success story on our hands in little old Nottingham.

But not all was well with the national brand managers, they are not happy that we were trading so well, a pub in the East Midlands could not be allowed to be the star site of the brand, that position had to be a site under the brand located in London.

When I left York there was no national brand manager, it was area manager and pub manager sticking to a loose brief, so all the sites were very similar, but not exactly the same. This was still the 1990's and the city was only just getting involved with breweries and pub companies, refer to earlier chapters.

I was summoned to a meeting.

In recent weeks a new cask ale emporium super site had opened in the City of London, and this was to be the flagship of the brand.

The opening was at a similar time to the opening of my new site in humble East of England Nottingham.

The new super-site opened in the wealthy financial district, and it was meant to be the biggest food sales site of the whole brand meaning everyone involved could claim success in The City, the home of shareholders, the ones the company and breweries want to attract.

(Have you just fitted another key piece of the jigsaw?) Things didn't go in London as they expected!

My new Nottingham site was the number the 1 food sales site, and it was bursting with the volume of sales, 7 days a week.

Admittedly The City site only opened Monday to Friday because that part of London was a ghost town at weekends, but it was still a huge shock to the system that this maverick manager with a fantastic team and brilliantly supportive area manager were showing every other pub in the brand the way to do it big style.

In the meeting I was asked by Bigger Bosses about our pub and what was so good about it, why was it performing so well?

I explained about the service style, the atmosphere we had created as a team, the fun we were having and the specials boards we were using to drive our food sales.

I expected a big old pat-on-the-back and a hearty thank you.

What I received was not a pat-anywhere, I got kicked in the fucking nuts by a prick in a suit telling me I had to cut sales by removing every none-brand finesse, every up-skill, all our improvements, no more trays and legs and scale back the atmosphere, I was told that sales MUST GO DOWN!

My area manager and I were stunned, gobsmacked, was this a fucked up "Watch Out Beadles About" ITV show joke?

No, this was the instruction, stop being so successful so that our planned super site can become the super site we need it to be when we brag to our potential shareholders.

What had happened to the freedoms we had when we were in York?

While I was opening the Cafe Bar a new national company had been formed within the parent company. All the newly branded sites were taken out of regional head office control and centralised into a national head office. We no longer had regional bosses that new who us as people and supported our work, we now had the beginnings of the future remote faceless bosses that I have described in earlier chapters.

My area manager left not long after we had been told to slow our sales, he returned to work for the regional head office team in Sheffield and a few months on, so did I, following the hope of a more friendly and local work life.

Off to Sheffield I went to team up with the same area manager once again and create even bigger success stories.

Sheffield

I was given the opportunity to return an American themed bar and restaurant back to its glory days. I do like a challenge.

I only really have one main story that comes to mind from Sheffield.

It is about the day I met a self-important wanker who left feeling utterly embarrassed.

The year is 2000, we have just managed to evade the millennium bug, nuclear power stations had NOT blown and sunk the UK below the surface of the North Atlantic, all was good as the clock struck midnight to bring in a new millennium.

Spring was starting to show in the sky, lighter and longer days were just around the corner and the business was doing really well after last year's refurbishment.

I was still controlling the music to suit our site and customer base, at the time I would have slipped a Cafe-Del-Mar CD into our 5-disc player, pressed play and parked my arse in the bar area with a coffee and today paper.

I had done something that I found fun approximately 15 minutes earlier that needed me to sit where I was and wait, just wait.

Around another 30 minutes passed, I am now drinking a second cup of coffee and a man rushed past me to the bar where I heard him ask loudly:

"Who put a clamp on my car?"

The bar staff just pointed at me, but my face was hidden behind the newspaper pagers, and I was listening with a naught smirk across my face.

This bar and restaurant just outside the centre of Sheffield had very limited car parking spaces but we were across from a large hospital multi-story car park with a pay for parking system.

Our small car park had very large, very clear signage to read before entering our car park, and when any driver did park, the signage was clear and unmissable.

"PARKING FOR CUSTOMERS / CLAMPING IN OPERATION."

I was clamping 3 or 4 cars per weeks, I didn't charge anyone to have the clamp removed, I just let them go with a gentile warning and hoped they had learned a lesson, leave our car park for our customers please.

The man who had spoken loudly at the bar was now standing over me, he was not a happy bunny.

I asked him "how I could help?"

"Have you clamped my car?" he asked.

"Yes," I replied.

I was now looking at him with my best customer service face mode engaged.

"WHY" he asked aggressively?

So, I politely explained our car parking rules to him in detail and told him he could park in the hospital car park next time.

He was still not a happy man.

I recognised this man from somewhere, then I realised he had been a footballer, played for England I think, I now had two or three names rattling around my head, but which one is he?

At this point in my life, I had never watched a game of football at a game or on TV, in fact I had never seen any more than a few minutes of Match Of The Day while channel surfing.

It was time to tell him that I will remove the clamp in a few minutes and would he mind waiting by his car.

Off he went, I finished my coffee and set off down the steps to the car park with the clamp release keys but on my way to the car park one of our cocktail experts waved me over, spoke quietly into my ear, and that would be very important in just a few minutes time.

This footballer was stood by the car, driver's door open, one foot on the sill staring at me over the car roof.

I started to take the clamp off, he was looking at his watch that seemed to push him into saying something to get a reaction out of me:

"Come on come on, I haven't got all day, I've got training to get to, don't you know who I am?"

I stopped dead, slowly looked up at this man who until a few moments ago I could not name and replied:

"Yes, yes I do, you are that cunt who missed the England penalty so shut the fuck up"

His eyes widened, he looked physically shocked, and he slowly sat in the driver's seat of his car, closed the door, and didn't speak again while I finished taking off the clamp.

He drove away without waving goodbye, how rude… tosser. I never saw him again, well not in real life, just on the box working as a football pundit.

Nottingham 3

The bar restaurant in Sheffield performed so well and received such a public reaction that our regional part of our company decided to open another one, based on the same principles, in Nottingham on the banks of the river Trent.

I wasn't there long, but I did open it, but not as what we had planned it was going to be, let me explain.

Do you remember the man in the suit who told me to cut sales in Nottingham because we were doing far too well in the north of England and making some of the Bigger Bosses look stupid?

The very ungrateful suit wearing plonker that preferred fake London success over East Midlands brilliance had become the head of the recently created national branded pub group within our now ex-brewery company.

It called itself something like the High-Street group and was based just north of the M25 near the M1.

By now the brewery arm of the business had been sold off, so as worker bee's we all knew something was going but we hoped the changes would stop with no longer brewing our own beer.

What our ex-brewery owners, now just a retail pub company, was actually up to was a much bigger project indeed.

Within the next 2 years they would be selling off most of company's pubs turning it into a coffee and room business.

This explained, in hindsight, why the centralisation of the pub company and the closure of regional head-offices now made sense, it much easier to break up a company from a central office.

Back to Nottingham 3, we started the project overlooking to Trent River as a regional pub company, but within a few weeks the new national branded and centralised arm of the pub company took over lock-stock-and-barrel. My area manager was gone, the whole project was changed to the cafe bar brand I had opening in Nottingham a few years ago, but that cool brand as I had left it was now watered down, cheapened, branded and managed by people who just didn't get it.

This was a big snatch of pubs and cafe bars by the new High Street group. It meant that my old super successful site in Sheffield, my new site in Nottingham under development, all the Cafe Bars from Nottingham to Epson were all lumped together under the Cafe Bar brand. Next, the trendy high street sites were also added, and we now had a large High Street division headed up by this pillock in a suit who told me to cut sales for fuck sake.

We were now no longer recreating my hard work from Sheffield; we were told that the designers are coming back, and this new site will now be a Cafe Bar just like the others.

I had committed to opening this site, so I stayed to do that, but I knew soon after I would be gone, this was my first taste of the modern managers who were beginning to appear in the industry, yep, just like the ones I have extensively bitched about in earlier chapters.

The good area manager, Glenn, he had, like me, left the infant High Street group to return to working for the regional head office, so he was out, yet again he returned to the local head office just before it closed for good with the grand pub sale coming soon.

Time to explain what happened to the Our Pub Company.

What the humble pub mangers didn't know was what the company had visions, a much bigger picture and they was why they had restructured from a multiple regional operation into national centralised business.

The was the prelude to Our Pub Company selling off all its high street and local pubs, so by putting certain styles of pubs into groups it made it easier to sell for a bigger price.

I told you before, branding adds city value…

Any type of company could buy a load of pubs, we didn't know our future and most of the GM's hoped it was going to be another pub company wanting a bigger estate where we could stay in our pubs. What we did NOT want was a financial institution looking to make fast profits.

Turns out it was both, an investment group bought the high street pubs, a local, but newly ambitious local brewery, one with a financial backer appointed greedy new CEO, bought the local pubs. Does this ring any alarm bells from previous chapters?

And we, as employees at all levels, were sold down the river.

Leeds

Nottingham 3 was open, trading not too bad, so I was off to go and work with Glenn again.

I arrived in Leeds and took over a student focused pub/club with a 2am license. Nearby was 10,000 people studying and working in the Uni's and hospitals, but strangely they were unable to eat in the pub I had just taken over.

Soon sorted that out when Mark joined us as our chef, food turned out to be a really big winner, sales boomed within weeks, we were onto another success story.

Next, I got hold of a huge barista coffee machine and grinder from another of our companies' pubs, they were a beast of a site in Headingly but had hidden the machine behind a liquor display.

I installed this large two group 3 phase coffee machine in the conservatory area of my pub, sorting all the plumbing and wiring out myself, and bingo, we have an overnight coffee business that did rather well.

We went from being a night-time only venue surrounded by huge numbers of people between 10am and 6pm going about their business and university life and became a great day time food and coffee hot spot with a new menu written by myself, simple, fresh food, and quality coffee all day every day.

Our Pub Company was by now was in complete chaos, or so it seemed to the pub managers working for it.

The big sell off was underway, the rumour mill was rotating at maximum speed, we had entered the transition phase.

Bosses, many we had never heard of before, were coming and going, pubs were swapping in and out of divisions as the company traded which pubs packaged together would drive the highest selling price. What the GM's saw as light relief and amusement was all these new bosses fighting to keep their jobs with whoever or whatever bought the pubs.

We were removed off Glenn's patch and placed onto Pete's.

Pete and myself didn't get on at the time, but years later we make a great team when I moved to Derby the work once again.

Pete reported to an Op's manager from the Northwest, let's call him Mr Pillarky shall we.

What a cunt. I had been lucky enough to be a bit of a shining star in the old regional division of our old company, so my name was fairly well known. Pillarky was from a rival regional head office based in the Northwest called managing everything west of the Pennines.

I met him, he saw that I had taken this failing site "out of brand" and sales were growing through using our team's skill and ideas that had built a very different offer to what had gone before.

The tacky nightclub days were long gone, we were now a well-rounded pub and venue for everyone.

Once again, I am doomed because I was just doing my job, creating a better environment, better service and driving sales.

Many years earlier a dickhead BDM tried telling me something about the shape or the PandL.

Eh? PandL is the document that details every financial fact of a business. Normally a PandL tells the story of the most recent financial month and the year to date in numbers.

It contains everything, sales (the top line), margins, machine income, repair costs, utilities, wages cost, the very finest details, and then finally the bottom-line profit, the bit that is the actual monetary value created by the business after every possible cost is calculated and taken away.

What matters on a PandL?

If we simplify it, all that matters is that the sales are matching the set budget on the top line and profit is exceeding budget on the bottom line.

Who gives a flying fuck how it is done, the numbers that matter have been delivered, another successful sales period and financial year making money is behind us.

It was one of those times when a new BDM turned up at my door with a filofax, lap-top and clipboard in his rucksack.

Out comes the PandL and HE is going to talk me through the PandL I contributed to using his gender studies 2.1 business skills. kill me, kill me now.

I happily explained how we had smashed the bottom-line profit budget, exceeded conversion rate, so I'm happy boy.

The BDM goes into a speech about "The Shape Or The PandL" and how we could perform better while gesturing long waves with his hands up, down, and round and round.

He was going on about making a small saving on this line and a 0.1% increase on this other one will help "shape" the PandL.

I would like to explain what he was talking about, but to be honest, my mind slipped into "self-protect from wankers" mode and tuned out his voice.

I didn't hear a fucking word he said from that point. So, Mr Pillarky doesn't really like me, Our Pub Co are selling us to anyone with the cash to splash, it was time to abandon ship.

Sheffield 2

I was recommended by someone high up in property to a nightclub owner in Sheffield. This club owner had a failing club and wanted it performing better. Who wouldn't?

It was becoming very much the normal that those asking me to do a job for them was telling me a pack of lies.

After being sold the spiel, read a fairy story dressed up by big numbers and false promises, it always seen to come down to the same thing, all they want you to do is save them.

What I was not being told during the talks I had with the owner was that the club needed to produce a better set of accounts enabling him to lease it out to a Lap Dancing Club chain for a big profit.

The owner needed someone to grow the business and drive-up footfall. If this growth could be achieved, then the ass twerking brand would see a viable building in that part of a major UK city.

I had no idea what we were getting ourselves into, the owner, let's call him Mr Skint, was propping up the business with pennies, it was barely surviving.

I asked Tracy, Jonny and Mark to join me in this new adventure, as usual I needed allies and they had the quality we needed.

We committed to a mini refurb, I asked designers and project managers I knew to help out and we re-opened with a new look and with a very different focus from its recent hard-core dance and RnB.

Success meant mainstream music as a base, daytime opening of the lower bar, and big nights promoted by experts.

This club had a fairly bad reputation with the public and police, so I brought in a new head doorman, very experienced, to manage door team and prevent any trouble.

If you ever watched a series on late night Channel 4 (I think) called "Bounces" where old school doormen talked about their times and experiences working the doors in major cities and huge venues, our new head doorman had featured on that program.

244

It was all looking good, we were about to open our re-imagined venue, the right look, the right people, a fresh vibe to attract new footfall.

Then I tried to put in a beer and drinks order from the owners contracted supplier…

Flatly refused unless paid up-front.

I tried to call the owner, no answer, we were opening in 2 days with DJ's booked, a promotor had invested in the marketing, and we were a dry bar for fucks sake!

Bollocks, now what do I do, everything is in place except the booze, so I reached for my own credit card and placed an order worth over £3,000.00 on a new account in my own name.

We traded well over the weekend, ran out of a few drink lines and by now I realised that the booze sales were not the main draw to this venue, it was the hard-core dancing and tiny plastic bags.

I took my money out of the weekends takings and banked the rest into the owner accounts as I was supposed to do.

But by now I had doubts creeping in and started to think wider about what could be going on?

Over the next weekend I noticed a lot of bad behaviour, pills, powder, skunk and at times even weapons, what the fuck have I got myself into?

I started to talk to the music promoter and their teams about my concerns, they just laughed it off as no problem, it's all under control, nothing for me to be concerned about.

But this was now VERY concerning!

I asked for a meeting with the music promoter before the next weekend came around in the daytime so we could talk.

He turned up with others, it was like a scene from the film 8 Mile.

It was in this meeting I realised that the real promoter was not the man sat in front of me, it was an unnamed gangster type drug dealer with a large mob of foot soldiers doing his dirty work.

I was managing what I could only describe as a one stop shop of highs and lows in the 4th largest city in the UK: *FUCK*. I found out his name, I had never heard of him myself, but plenty of people I know had, their faces displayed a very deep concern whenever his name was mentioned.

As a manager I have been around a long time, I was 36 years old, finally stopped smoking after 24 years, and I am very strong willed. I wasn't going to be pushed around by a dealer and his troops, if anyone was the right person to stop the dealing in this club it was me.

Or so I thought…

I started pushing back against the drug use and encouraged the door team to adopt a zero tolerance, and I was getting results, the drug using, and dealing was beginning to drop off as we barred anyone, we caught dabbling.

Then I was told that the main man, who had been in Europe for a few months, was due back and coming to see what was going on.

This was great news, I needed to speak to him directly and let him know my thoughts on what had been going on, and the way the future was going to be for this venue, clean, anti-drug, a safe space for everyone.

I was told he was on his way one evening so I went to stand outside the main doors. We met just outside the doors, and he was completely dismissive of me with a level of arrogance I had never experienced or seem before.

This man was cold…

His attitude throws me off my metal balance, now what?

I still hadn't heard from Mr Skint, in fact I hadn't heard from him for a few months. I was still buying the bar stock with my own money and claiming it back from the cash takings every week, so I stuck in a loop, buying a beer delivery on a Wednesday, and taking my money back on a Monday and depositing what was left in Mr Skint's bank account.

By now we had been open about 3 months and I had tried to ensure all payroll owed to staff was paid every week.

I was submitting all the staff wages, but more often than not, the staff, and including myself, were not paid through the bacs system set up for payroll, so I was also taking the missing staff wage payments out of the cash takings after every weekend.

It was a fucking nightmare, but people were relying on me to keep the place going because they had bills to pay in their private lives.

The door team were trying their best to minimise drugs and keep everyone safe, but now the main man was back from abroad to check on his non HMRC declared income, how would he respond to minimising his income?

A couple more months rolled by.

No one told me if he had gone away again or was in hiding or whatever, but I hadn't seen or heard of him for a while, had he given up and we were winning the battle against drugs?

Then the big announcement, the club would be hosting the launch event for Radio 1X, a new RnB / Rap radio channel on the BBC's new digital service in just 3 months' time.

This would be a huge event.

Weeks rolled by, same old stuff, I would buy liquor stock, opening up 7b days per week, solid night-time trading, footfall was going up and up and I was depositing more and more cash into My Skint's bank account.

Against the odds we had turned it around.

Then came Radio1X launch night.

The police roadblocks were set up, metal detectors like those in a courthouse set up, and a far few of the dozens of the police were armed.

What The Hell Is Going On?

I had never managed a venue for an event like this before. Launch nights and opening venues is bread and butter to me, but this was something far beyond what I expected, imagined, and was prepared for.

I can honestly tell you it looked like a 50cent music video, people in loud clothes, bandanas, snakeskin boots, cowboy hats and pinned up cars, were we in South Yorkshire or Hollywood?

Our very own missing gangster friend turned up on this night, it would appear he was the star attraction from Sheffield, and he was the one hosting this huge launch party for other similar gangsters from Leeds, Birmingham, Newcastle and London, they came from everywhere.

I saw people wearing mad brightly coloured leather jackets, huge amounts of gold hung around necks and wrists, it was like a film set, I have never seen this type of dress or bling in the UK before, these people surely cannot be for real?

Guns were found, not 1, not 2, dozens of guns were found on some of these out of towner's, the police defiantly had better intelligence than I did about the people coming that night.

Thank God the police were there.

I didn't see one person arrested for gun possession, I'm not saying no one was, but I certainly didn't see it happen.

I was stood their gob smacked at the crowds and type of people coming through the doors, I had never seen anything like it, some very scary people, very big personalities, attitudes so huge they had their own gravity, Snoop Dog, Tupac and Dr Dra "in da club", well not really, but these were certainly the UK's versions.

I asked the police if they would be patrolling inside the club as well, but no, they were only going to be policing the outside.

This night was something beyond my night-time economy experience, totally alien to me, a different world, but there was still more to come that I wasn't expecting.

Drugs, the place was awash with drugs, more than I had ever seen before in a single place, the smell of weed was thick in air, chocking any non-smoker with its sweet heavy stench, and powder was ringed around almost every nostril in the building.

If I had turned the fans on high it would have looked like it was snowing, inside a building, in July!

I have always had a hatred for drugs, I haven't even tried cannabis, not even once, and I find myself acting against drug use whenever and however I can. I went to see our head doorman and asked him if we could do anything to stop or reduce the drugs?

He said, "I'll have a word."

He went off looking for our local big-time gangster.

My head doorman came back about 15 minutes later, his head down, almost shuffling around with drooped shoulders.

He was slightly shaking, his voice soft and pathetic.

"Neil, can I have a word"

We walked outside to a quiet spot.

"I quit with immediate effect" he said *"What The Fuck, you cannot do that and leave me tonight of all nights"* I relied sternly.

His reply makes me feel sick, scared, for me, and sorry for him...

"If I didn't go now, I will die within the next few days"

He believed it, whatever someone had said to him made him utterly convinced that he will be killed if he does not leave right now.

WOW, JUST WOW

The ultimatum was really simple, something like:

"Try to stop my mates selling or taking drugs and enjoying themselves, you will be a sliced-up body found dead and need to identify by your family."

248

The job was not worth a life, his mine, things had taken a sudden and acute upturn and I had to take notice.

I shook this honourable, experienced, but now broken man's hand and he walked away into the night.

I never saw him again.

A couple of hours later and the big radio launch was now in full swing, live on the radio to the whole country after the huge marketing campaign to launch Radio1X.

BANG!

What the fuck was that?

Had a gun really just been fired LIVE on radio?

A dozen or so people ran out the doors shouting and screaming, the music dropped, and everything fell silent, except for the voices of people panicking, scared and shocked on the dance floor.

"Can someone tell what has just happened" I shouted to my team, I wanted to know if a gun had been fired in the club, was anyone hurt, this was madness, I had lost control of what was going on, for the first time in my hospitality life I was out of my depth... and very scared...

It was at that exact moment I decided that this was my last night at this club, when I lock up tonight I would never, ever, return.

The night finally ended, we watched the last of the bling covered 2PAC wannabes drive off in their pimped-up cars housing at least 20 speakers and 2000 watts of rap battle power ended, we closed the doors, locked them tight, and sighed a huge relief that it was finally over.

I had never been so thankful for a night to end; the relief was so strong I was on the verge of weeping.

I took the money for the liquor that the club owed to me, paid any money owed to the team, thanked them all, and then I drove away. I didn't return to the building ever again.

To this day, I still have NO clue if it was a real gun shot that rang around the acoustic amplifying club dance floor, every rumour I heard said it was genuine, but in reality, I just don't know?

The local supposably "gangster" who instilled such fear into so many, approximately 6 months later he was killed by a gunshot to the head as he was driving away from his house around New Year.

I wasn't very keen on him, but no one deserves that...

I, always on the move.

The big pub company I had left were still not finished selling off their pub estate, I guess it takes more than a few months to sell off 2000+ pubs, so I rejoiced the big company once again cos I needed a job, it was that simple.

I took over a pub in Sheffield that had been bullied and manipulated by a local football mob who called themselves the BBC, basically a gang of thugs who thought they were important for fuck's sake.

In reality they BBC were a bunch of losers who had watched far too many films, such as Green Street and anything starting cockney legend Danny Dyer.

My old BDM gave me the GM position to help wrestle the reputation of the pub back from a period of dark times driving the pubs sales and status down and down.

The football World Cup was hitting TV everywhere in a few months' time, so the job was urgent to say the least.

Dee (fantastic assistant) and I got stuck in transformed the fortunes of that little pub, by the time the World Cup started we were managing a safe environment for families, females and couples.

More importantly football supporters with any colours draped around their shoulders were welcome, so had a very successful World Cup season with a small, but top-quality team.

A compulsory purchase order was slapped on the pub to make way for a new city centre, so it was time to move on.

I stayed with the same company and moved onto Lincoln to mend a pub that had lost its mojo!

I had a plan, but I needed help to sort this one out, the customer service was non-existent, and I wasn't going to live-in the pub, I need eyes, ears and quality on the ground. I asked Tracy and Jonny to join me in Lincoln, and I developed yet another plan.

Tracy, assisted by Jonny, was already a good enough manager to be a GM in her own right, so right from the start I didn't intend staying in Lincoln to long, I prefer bigger cities, but I knew I wanted Tracy to be the GM of her first pub within a year.

Working with such quality as Tracy and Jonny we had that pub ticking like a Swiss Watch within 6 months.

Something else had changed also, the sale of the pubs had finally gone through, and we were sold with our pubs. This meant the high street; city types of pubs went to one company and all the local boozers and food brands went to another company. I have lost my normal BDM, he has been transferred with the local food branded pubs, I have been moved into the high street gang.

Not long after being transferred into the new company a position came up is Derby, it was for a Cafe Bar, one of those opened after the success of Cafe Bar in Nottingham, plus it was the bar directly above my old underground pub below the paving-stones of Irongate, you remember, the place the man took his mannequin date out to serenade with any strings.

It's a very small world and we meet the same people many times.

I left Tracy in Lincoln to manage the pub with the assistance of Jonny. I was so proud that my friends had finally got their own pub and that Tracy had become what I had always seen in her, a fantastic general manager in her own right and I knew huge success was just around the corner for her.

I stayed in Derby for nearly 2 years and came across a few memorable people. To start with I inherited an assistant manager who was really keen but came across as ready to give up.

I know that makes no sense, but I cannot think of any other way I can describe the situation. After talking to the assistant, her name is Kelly, I understood the problem, she had been overlooked and underdeveloped. Over the next few months Kelly began to redevelop her natural spark and we spend two amazing years working together, I enjoyed helping her start to path to become the hugely admired GM she is today.

Over 20 years later and Kelly is still a top performing manager based in a jewel of a pub in Nottingham city centre.

I also met a young man called Adin, a very tall, very slim, awkward but a very stylish fella who had something really special about him. He joined our team and came on the incredible journey of sales and profit growth at 20% in the 1st year and 22% in the 2nd without any investment.

Adin worked so hard, he was like a sponge, soaking every bit of knowledge and information up about pubs, bars, food and total hospitality business.

He was going to be a big player on day, and he was so funny as well. Adin would do an impression of a man who came across to us for a happy hour pint every day. This man, I have forgotten his name, would walk in at exactly the same time every day and just say:

"WWooonneeee" … while poking one finger in the air.

Adin nailed the tone, the pitch, get it down exactly and I still smile now when I think about it.

This one pint regular eventually told us how he could afford to drink all day every day?

In his own word he told us how he goes to "the social" and picks up his daily beer allowance! I have no idea if that was actually true in 2005 but we were gobsmacked to say the least.

Adin is now, and has been for many years, one of the top venue managers and a star of the night-time economy of Birmingham and long may his success continue.

The other person who stands out is Claire, a tiny little blonde haired young thing that was fairly new to customer service, she was behind the coffee counter and greeted our guests with the widest smile you have ever seen. I know she has a spray tan business and a family these days, Claire you were a pleasure to work with.

I cannot forget Karl, a tall and quiet young bar man. I didn't work that long with Karl before I was moving again, but he did stay working in the Cafe Bar long after I had moved on and has also become a very successful GM in Nottingham city centre where he managers a treasure of a pub cut into the stone foundations of the castle.

While managing the Cafe Bar and the subterranean pub in Derby I was also asked to manage another glass curved bar 200 meters up the road, and also an experimental bar in Nottingham.

I was a very busy boy, but I was also very lucky, I had great people working with me and together we worked our magic in all four bars across two cities and did our best as a team for our customers and our new shareholders.

Times were changing, fast.

Manchester came next, I was persuaded that Manchester was my future by the high street company, they wanted me there to introduce the same high service standards and levels of control that had made the Derby bars work so well.

It was already a busy bar in central Manchester, so yeah, I can do that.

Manchester
I have 3 short stories about Manchester city centre:

Story 1

One summer Saturday it was late afternoon, and I was on the floor overseeing service because we were fairly busy and there was a massive gig at the arena in a couple of hours.

The layout of the bar was split level to one side, the main dining area was raised and overlooking a large vertical drinking and dance floor zone in front of the very long curved bar. An informal lounging type of area was towards the front that consisted of sofas, low lounge tables and leather bucket chairs, and finally we had high stools along the front window bench.

I was looking around for glasses, empty plates, and dirty ask-trays when I noticed a man stood on top one of the coffee tables and he was sort of dad dancing without moving his feet.

This was not on, what does this knob think he is doing, he must be 50 years old, its fucking teatime, is he pissed or fucking what?

He has a couple of much younger ladies swooning over him, laughing at everything he said, their eyes were fixed on him, and every crutch trust he made.

Right, he we go, time for me to get him down.

I walk over to where he was slowly, stopped about a meter from the table, I calmly waited for the man to acknowledge me before I spoke "excuse me sir but could you come down please?"

He didn't reply, he stared at me for a few second and then stopped swinging his pants so much.

As his swaying hips came to a complete stop, he turned towards me and with his left hand he pulled the left side of his suit jacket open to reveal what looked like a guitar strap looping over his shoulder.

Clipped to the bottom of the stripped 2-inch-wide material strap was:

A MACHINE GUN, SMALL, BLACK, AND FUCKING SCARY
OH MY GOD, I ALMOST SHIT MYSELF

This man has now introduced himself not only by trusting his pelvis towards my face I am now looking at an automatic firearm.

I've seen mini-machine guns in lots of films, but never in real life, was it real, was it fake, how the fuck should I know.

What I did know from the films I have seen is that these pistol sized automatics can pump 100's of small, glowing red and pointed metal objects into my body in a matter of seconds.

I took a deep breath, I had to reach deep inside my fear and steady myself, I'm at that critical point of flight or fight, who am I trying to kid, the only thing I'm fighting is my impulse to RUN VERY FAST!

But I stand there, calmly, and say "*I'll give you 10 minutes before I call the police*" I turned a full 180 and started walking towards the glass-wash area behind the bar. I had to force myself to NOT increase my pace, breathing in through the mouth and out the nose slowly, there was no fucking chance I was looking back over my shoulder!

As I stepped into the glass-wash I was using my hands held firmly down by my sides to urge my bar team to follow me into the glass-wash out of potential bullet trajectory.

I felt like a coward, I was hiding from a man with a gun and not protecting my team, our customers, but what could I do?

I had stood my ground and remained calm when facing this man, all the time concentrating on keeping my arse cheeks firmly clenched and given him the opportunity to walk away and not escalate the situation.

Surely that was the only play, to reduce the risk anyone being hurt.

So why do I feel like a snivelling tosser for hiding in the back?

What I had done was the right thing, or so I was fucking praying it was the best thing I could do for everyone in the building.

I leaned to my left and peered through the open door into the bar where the gun carrying twat had been standing on the low table, he was gone, the girls he was with were no-where to be seen, oh my god, the relief, I was shaking, sweating, and needed to sit down.

A few minutes later I called the police.

Story 2

In the Manchester site we had just won our companies national award of customer service pub/bar of the year.

Because we were doing so well the bigger bosses decided they needed to protect the asset. We were having a little refresh, the painters were in, new lamp shades, just a little tarting up and modernisation to keep up with the competition.

Part of the work being done was a bit of joinery, repairs and replacement to furniture and replacement of technology.

One thing that was being upgraded was the alarm system, new sensors, rewiring, thinks like that, no big deal, it was all done over one week, and we reopened.

With the site open and trading it was time for me to have a week off and do some decorating at home.

I had been off for a couple of days, and I was fast asleep, tucked up and enjoying the fact that didn't need to get up in the morning, then my phone rang at just after 2am.

"Are you the key holder to this bar?"

"Yes."

"We are the police, and we need you to come down immediately."

When I got there, FUCK ME, it was like a bomb site as people often say when they face devastation.

Turns out, it WAS an actual fucking bomb site.

The bar I was managing in Manchester city centre was built in an old banking type secure unit, so the basement had lots of rooms with walls ranging between 30cm's to over a meter thick.

The bars kitchen, loo's, offices, staff areas and safe room were all in the basement protected by these intimidating heavy duty vaulted walls.

The original walk-in lockable vault was long gone from its subterranean home, but we did have the biggest and tallest safe I had ever worked with where we kept the money, till draws and anything else of value.

The safe sat against the wall that separated its home in the safe room from the coriander that ran the length of the basement.

It was put there for a good reason, when the door to the safe room is opened the safe itself remains hidden behind the heavy metal door.

The safe was also being watched by the hard drive CCTV system, but yes, you guessed it, the CCTV recorder was located in the safe room in clear view.

Fucking Idiots, will they ever learn.

On arrival at my bar at around 2:40am I introduced myself to the police and they confirmed it was safe to go in, but I must not touch anything.

Every surface was covered in thick dust, there was broken glass on the floor, glass shelves on the back bar had tipped, emptying yet more glass and debris onto dust covered piles of shards.

I noticed the fire door on the right hand outside wall was hanging off it hingers, had someone have battered their way in?

Off I go downstairs to the basement, dust was still floating in the air, it was just hanging there like white mist.

I was following the footprints of the police already investigating the crime, what would I find?

What had actually happened to make such a mess?

The stone floor beneath my feet was becoming crunchy the further I went into the basement, a few more yards in and I was stepping over bricks and rubble.

Then I saw it, a massive fucking hole in the safe room wall, and you can be sure it was no coincidence the safe sat on the other side of the wall.

This was professional precision and in-house knowledge.

I wasn't allowed near the room or the hole in the wall, but I could see black soot marks around the hole and what looked like burn marks on the ceiling.

Looking around and as my brain was started to churn everything, I was taking in it felt like I was in a TV crime show.

Had a thief actually blown through the wall to reach the back of the safe?

This was crazy, fucking madness, Hollywood script writer type of things going on in my bar located Northwest England, I was stunned as the magnitude of what has happened started to sink in.

Hang on, why didn't the alarm go off, I would have been alerted if it had?

The police came to the site because of a report of noise and a fire door being open, not because the alarm alerted them, how the fuck did the newly up-dated alarm not go off?

As I was just a lowly pub manger, I wasn't involved in the investigations being made by the company and police, except to confirm where I had been earlier that night.

I was never told if it was an explosive, pickaxes, or firebomb that destroyed the wall, I was not privy to any subsequent report.

I wasn't told about the amount of money that has been nicked, if any at all?

I was still on holiday for the week and by the time I was back we were reopened; the basement was still a mess and I had to move into a new room as the office was also wreaked by what had gone on.

The one thing I did find out, the alarm.

The fire door alarm sensor had been looped out so it would not detect a break-in. The motion sensors had been set in a way so they will not pick up any movement between the fire door and the basement entrance.

Basically, setting the alarm was a waste of time, it wouldn't have picked up an Elephant charging through locked front doors.

This was an inside job and had started with the mini-refurb and ended with a serious robbery and major rebuild.

Story 3

My last thing to say about Manchester is how I ended up leaving that pub company and moving to another where I was working with colleagues from the old Sheffield regional head office once again.

We were trading really well, our customer service scores were fantastic, our reputation as a daytime cafe bar and night-time venue was going from strength to strength. I was happy, my team were happy, things were going great.

The newly created Pub Company from the sale of the high street sites was doing well, all indicators showed the future looked really promising.

I have tried to use as few pubs brand names, pub company names and brewery names as possible in my writing, but there comes a time when only the name of a bar will do it justice…

when you know you know?

Have you ever heard of a branded bar called Yates?

Have you ever been in a Yates?

Would you go on a 1st date, a romantic meal, a family lunch, a wake or hold a business meeting in your local Yates?

The Pub Company I was working for in Manchester bought the Yates group for practically pennies because as a company it was on its arse, almost finished with nothing in the bank.

Pubs and bars were changing fast, culture was evolving faster than ever before and places to socialise were becoming sophisticated, stylish, even designer uber chic to match the Italian made handbags carried by the customers.

Yates attracted, and still does, lads on stag-nights or looking for someone to finger while sat in a booth after she has downed two premade and poured from a bottle Porn Star Martini's, tree shots of tequila and a large Zinfandel.

The lads often shopped in Burtons and BHS while the girls who wanted to meet these future chav boyfriends bought their own glad rags from CandA and Dorothy Perkins.

Yates has never really changed, it was still aiming at the same customers base mid-2000 and using the same tactics, that just may be a small clue to why it was failing.

Those of you old enough may remember when Yates was known as The Blob Shop due to the particular drink it reinvested in 1984.

I enjoyed Yates as 19 years old in 1984, not really my type of place in 2005.

Late in the 90's a new type of drinking had emerged, pre-loading.

It has always happened small scale, a small glass of wine before you go out at 7pm, a cheeky WKD Blue before the taxi into town at 7:30pm, that was the done thing.

What is the harm with a small glass of wine before you go out?

It becomes a bottle of wine before you hit the town at 10:30pm, that's what is wrong, no sales for the pub but bigger profits for supermarkets.

Eventually you miss out the pub altogether and have 10 shots of vodka in the kitchen at home before the taxi comes to take you direct to the club at midnight.

Pre-Loading become a phenomenon, no one was power drinking in the pubs early-doors anymore, a huge part of the drinking session died an early death on the high streets of towns and cities in every corner of the UK.

The Go-Large mirror ball and flashing disco light type of pubs that sell booze by the bucket load were now fucked, their standard customer demographic were all at home getting tanked up for a couple of quid, and if you had grown up and had money to spend, you went to a nice, cool, stylish place, somewhere to be seen wearing your Louboutin red souled shoes that cost £1,500.00.

You no longer mixed with people wearing a Sports Direct hoodie and George by Asda trainers, not a fucking chance, now pass me the Grey Goose Vodka and a plate of olives.

Now the pub company I worked for suddenly owned the Yates group, I was in an award-winning stylish bar delivering high end cocktails, great food and Balearic sun-down music sets to cool people who oozed style and class, and now we owned Yates.

It was decided within the company's bigger bosses to mix up the area managers, or BDM's as they are called by now.

The "blue sky thinking" came up with the idea of an area of pubs and bars within a geographical area to minimise travel, travel cost, and increase visits by the BDM to each site.

Sounds like a cracking idea doesn't it.

It was total bollocks, utter clusterfuck and that's putting it mildly!

A few weeks happened and the reorganisation happened, I was informed I had a new BDM and he had come across from the Yates group.

So our area now consisted of classy city centre bars, uber cool music bars, and now pubs along the sea front in Blackpool and a number of run-down ramshackle Yates.

Yeah, Whoopee, feel my joy…*NOT.*

Let's call my new BDM Mr Ballsack.

I was given a date and time for my first meeting with this new BDM, someone I had not met before, and it went a bit like this:

"Hello Neil, nice to meet you. So, tell me about this place?"

So, I go about explaining our philosophy around combining assisted service with style, cool Balearic music, cutting edge cocktails, freshly food made to order and a top-rated coffee on offer.

In the mid 2000's all these qualities were rarely found together under one roof, we had become one of the choice sites to be seen in by the people who knew the Manchester scene.

It had taken 18 months to get where we were, with the robbery, the bad reputation for food and service when I took over, we had a lot to be shouting about in a cut-throat marketplace.

I talked about our awards, and sales growth, our night-time focus on culture cool swoon, not dance music policy, if I was to describe my mood as I was regaling Mr Ballsack, I would say I was very proud of what we had done and how the business was growing, we were smashing it and the future was looking good.

Mr Ballsack gave his reply: **"what we need in here is Tit's n Teeth, Tit's n Teeth, no-one wants all this posh shite, lemon grass, star fruit, coffee, naaaawwhhhh, we don't need any of that shit, I'll get you one of my DJ's down to play next weekend."**

Oh, sweet Jesus, what the fuck just happened, are we were going to be pushed down the Yates route?

Next week some wanker DJ will be playing I*ts Raining Men* and *Come On Eileen* for fuck-tards in my bar for fucks sake.

This is a nightmare

Ballsack left, his mission to destroy everything we had built was being put in place just because he could not understand the reason our bar worked so well.

Fucking imbecile.

I decided there and then I was off, no fucking way was I hanging around to serve tossers wearing hoodies and sweet pants.

Not in a million years am I pouring lager for white picks who try to talk like a Jamaican because it makes him sound "Gangster".

Hen Parties pilling in and requesting the latest boy band crap spewed out by Cowell and his cronies, bollocks to that, every type of Karen in the world pissed out of their head projecting vomit down the back of a radiator where it can never be cleaned deeply enough to rid the area of the foul aroma.

Arguing with slappers, the type who watch Jeremy Kyle, because her kid, little Chardonnay, is throwing food about hitting other tables, but she doesn't give a fuck, she paid for it and these posh cunts can do one.

"Nope, I'm worth more than that, I need a new job ASAP."

It takes time to find a new job, and in the time it took This Pub Company went mad, barking mad, crazy offers started coming through with stupidity like 2 for 2 deals, half price food deals that we did not need, for the last 12 months we have had customers queuing for tables, which brainless knob-head wants to give it away for half price when it is selling for full price and growing?

The ex-Yates marketing team, who had ruined that company by applying far too many discounts and driving down the reputation of a once very busy brand, were now intent on bombing another set of bars and making them just as worthless.

Companies have business shuffles, area changes, initiatives, cross-pollinate thinking type crap that no customer understands, and no staff members want to be involved in.

The new big idea was: *"let's increase the price of all products on weekend nights, no one will care or notice."*

You might be right about that in London you tosser, but up North in Manchester, as sure as your ass crack has a hole in the middle, they will, and did notice.

And your bar is next to one of the biggest Wetherspoons in the country, it cost 1,000 of people in foot fall every weekend.

Seriously, the bollocks we were having to put up with as managers, stupid sales strategies that were losing us more trade than it could ever gain, what a fucking joke.

I Interviewed for a major pub company, I know a lot of my old friends and colleagues are now with this brewery led pub company because it bought the locals pub estate during the big pub sell off.

I didn't let anyone I was friends within that company know I was going for an assessment day, and I wasn't interviewed by anyone I knew, I attended the assessment day just as anyone else and passed the tests on the day.

I was offered a job with this major brewing pub company; the job was to be a GM of a pub on the waterfront in Liverpool.

It came with a decent salary, better than I had been on with the company I was leaving, so it was time to hand in my resignation to Mr Ballsack.

Hmmmmmmm what should I write, how should a word such an important resignation letter to a man I had little too no respect for? He needed to feel the impact of my words in a way that he could not mistake what I was saying loud and clear:

This is the actual resignation letter I sent in, I did copy a couple of lines from a funny one I had seen many years before, but the majority of it is all mine, all mine…

Dear Pub Company

RE: Neil J Moore-Resignation and Unconditional Surrender

I am very happy to announce that as of this moment, I resign.

As you have no doubt noticed, many of your managers and team members have decided not to accompany you on your journey of snatching failure from the jaws of success.

I have decided to join them.

The 2nd half of last year and before the last reorganisation my bar was booming with double digit growth and the highest food growth year on year throughout the company! Our new senior managers have now led us into decline through ineffective management of process, systems and people.

I cannot take being strategized, reorganised and redirected anymore and I find myself unable to take this company seriously any longer.

I understand that this Yates led "new pub company" look upon me as a relic of a by gone age, a time when the customer was king, service was priority, support was there and managers managed the business to meet their customer needs, so after 23 years in the business I feel qualified to pass on a few pearls of wisdom.

The fact that we are now giving away more wine and spirits then we are selling may be seen by some as a bad sign, but not our clueless marketing department whose insane directives compounded by the middle managements seemingly limitless ability to de-motivate and pass the buck have turned a once profitable managed estate into the disaster it is today.

Each day I dread another e-mail containing yet another, "Fad/Directive/Strategy/Initiative" from up high in the never-ending list of bosses, and if I am told about COMPLIANCE one more time, I think I will shoot myself!

Please accept this letter as my official notification of resignation.

This letter serves you with 4 weeks' notice. As you have sucked the life out of me for the last 4 months, I shall continue to suck a pay check out of you for the next 4 weeks.

£1,000,000 and free sex with the model of my choice could not convince me to continue to work for this company!

A position as a junior goat herder in Outer Mongolia would be a more positive career step and lead to better prospects than working in the companies Circuit/Yates division.

I have enjoyed my time at my bar (but the fact that I am leaving may be an indication that I no longer do so) and I wish you continued success with the current Circuit BDM's goal of turning skilled, dedicated team members and managers into aimless, shambling, tick box focused groups of dry, lifeless husks, a far cry from pre-Yates' leadership.

Like many others I look back at the days of the company before the introduction of a nasty cheap high street brand, for some reason some people still think they work for that company, the one that was bought for peanuts due to its poor leadership, skill base and bullying tactics that had served them so well in the past!

Finally, maybe I'm just not a "team player", but I feel it's high time I "self out-sourced" to a better run organisation, one where a simple act like "putting sales into a till as the product it should be and for a price everyone knows will still be the same price tomorrow" actually works. One where the area manager, operation manager, systems manager, audit manager, purchasing manager and marketing manager are at least sane!

I look forward to seeing the company losing the poor people soon and returning to being a great company, then you never know, managers like me who can think for themselves could once again find good jobs and careers...

Yours with respect for the bullied masses and 1 finger in the air to the bullies...

Neil J Moore

It was goodbye to the old company and onto the new one with my pub based in Liverpool.

Liverpool

I had one job to do in my new water side pub, make it a pub for everyone and sort the food out because the offer was just terrible and not fit for purpose.

The previous manager was a mad Liverpool FC fan, the whole fucking pub was decked out with Liverpool paraphernalia, it was everywhere, hanging off lights, covering mirrors, red and white bunting along the back bar, I know people love their football clubs but come on, it just looked so tacky and it also stuck two fingers up at the blue half of Liverpool, no blue money was being spent in this pub and that had to change.

I ripped it all down, we became neutral in colour, everyone from Merseyside and beyond, even the Wirral, are now welcome was the message we were sending out.

Next it was onto the food.

The only food offer we had to sell was a glass fronted unit where pre-prepared food could be pointed at and served from.

The kitchen team would bake a quiche, fill a few French sticks with salad and cheese, easy to make food that could be prepared, placed in the cold counter, and handed to a customer. It was like working in a Greggs, but at the same time, nothing like Greggs at all because our range was rubbish.

This was a truly awful food offering in the heart of one of the busiest visitor attractions in the UK, Liverpool waterfront.

The area was packed out with tourists, wall to wall Americans, Asians, every day we would serve someone from Oz, Japan, and South America, and what were we offering as food?

A jacket potato with tuna mayo, cheese, or beans to the 1st 25 people that came through the door looking for hot food.

We only had room to cook off 25 jacket spuds at a time, so once they were gone, we had no more hot food to sell that day.

The kitchen was fairly large, but it had no extraction system meaning we could not cook over a naked flame, no grilling and no shallow or deep fat frying could take place in the kitchen.

I found out that when the building was first converted into a pub it was expected to be a success as just a cheese and wine bar.

What dumb fuck thought that in 1984 it was a good idea to open a cheese and wine bar in the city that was at war with Thatcher's government? After all, this is the city where Boys From The Black Stuff and GBH was based, what a prized prick bad idea, cheese, and wine in the city full of hardened socialists.

When the pub opened in 1984 there was almost no tourists milling around Liverpool's waterfront, but over the next 20 years this had changed beyond recognition, the waterfront was mobbed with the people of the world every day, but my new pub had continued to trade in almost exactly the same way since 1984 up to 2006 when I arrived.

Things had to change, and I was the right person to deliver...

Coincidentally, it was not long before I started with my new employer that it revealed to the city its strategy to become the UK's biggest pub company.

This policy, strategy, mission, whatever you want to call it, had been kicked into life by the ego maniac new Chief Executive.

Earlier in this book I talked about the changes to how a pub business operates in modern times compared to 2 decades earlier, especially with a financially owned CEO appointment.

Due to the installation of this CEO the process of becoming a money-making machine has hit full speed ahead and is charging full-on towards customer service sacrifice for bigger profits.

I had jumped right into the middle of this crazy spin cycle...

It was not a time for politics that was not affecting me, yet, the day job still had to be completed to the best of my ability.

How did I make this poorly facilitated pub serve food all day every day?

The answer was the miracle known as Merry-Chef.

No that isn't a chef with a fat wide smile singing cheerfully as he peels onions, it's a clever type of microwave / grill / oven / roaster that can cook almost anything, as long as it does not need to be deep fried.

I wrote a menu that consisted of items that could be reheated in microwaves, cooked fresh in the Merry-Chef, or heated by placing pots into a bath of boiling water called a bain-marie.

We served rice, jackets, curries, stews, wedges, lots of veg, pies, Yorkshire Wraps and it was all cooked to order.

We won Green King food pub of the year and the sales had shown that this Liverpool pub was worthy of a 1-million-pound investment where the company would finally put in a fully equipped kitchen completed with extraction.

My work here was done…

Where to next?

South Yorkshire Village

In my late teenage years and early 20's I had spent many-a-night in South Yorkshires Greatest Pub (SYGP) in the village near Rotherham.

What a pub it was back in the day, rammed with skirt every disco night, all the top totty was in this one pub.

For everyone who calls it "The Masons Arms", just fuck right off, you drive me mad-bastard angry, it's not called "The", there is NO "The" in its fucking name, so stop it once and for all, please.

It was one of those places people from miles around flocked to, a real magnet for fun lovers and seeking out the opposite sex.

In my much younger days I was barred twice by Richard and Janet, they were landlord and landlady for 19 years, what a stint. First time was scooping a ladies boob out of her top, it was an accident, and it was hanging out anyway, honest, the second time was for being far to wankered to walk through to door and calling Richard a cunt, I think that's what I called him?

When I was originally working for Whitbread, Masons Arms was also a Whitbread pub before being bought by the company I was now working for as part of the big sell off.

But all those years before, long before the sell off, I was a fellow Whitbread pub manager and a colleague on the same area as Richard, calling him a cunt was probably not that wise.

Anyway.

Richard and Janet decide to retire after 19 years at the pub, they had been fantastic managers in what I earlier described, in the genuine landlord and landlady style. The pub had performed so well every year they had been in charge, but they were winding down now so things had started to slip just a little.

My old BDM, Glenn, and I ended up chatting on the phone. Glenn was the BDM of Masons Arms, and he needed a new manager.

It had been at least 10 years since I had been in Masons, so I said I go and have a look, then I'll call him on Monday.

It was early in 2007 and the Liverpool City of Culture build was blocking most of the city centre access to the water front, it was freezing cold, no one was out and about on the water front, not because they didn't want to be, they couldn't get to it because of an enormous building site that was to eventually become the superb new Liverpool city centre.

Sod it, I jumped in my car and headed towards South Yorkshire to take a look at my potential new pub.

I got to Masons Arms about 7pm and parked up in the car park.

It was busy, lots of people in and out the rears doors, but something was wrong, what was it, the feeling was not the same as it had been all those years ago when I once, accidentally, had a large left boob cupped in my right hand?

Then it hit me like a slap across the face, everyone was wearing tracksuits, hoodies, base-ball caps and nylon.

What The Fuck Has Happened to my old tash hunting ground?

I drop the driver's window to hear what was going on and 2 things slapped me even harder.

I could hear a Spice Girls track being played far too loudly and the stink of weed was so strong I was genuinely shocked.

Did I take a wrong turn, how the fuck did I end up in somewhere I could compare to 1985 Asda car park in Moss Side Manchester?

I had an ex-girlfriend from many years ago with me, she said *"come on, let's go, you don't want anything to do with this dump do you?"*

"OH YES I DO" I SAID, "YES I DO"

Masons Arms needed me, my experience, Glenn's support, I was the right person at the right time to take on Masons Arms and return it to its glory days.

So I walked away from the 1million refurb on Liverpool's amazing water front to take on a job near Rotherham.

This would take all my strength and determination channelled as drive, commitment, and personal discipline, but I was up for the challenge.

I moved in, at the start of May, it was an unusually warm week and I stayed largely in the background observing, learning, working out who the key players were.

It was my first Sunday evening and I was taking my dogs for a walk. On my return I was walking through Masons car park past the rear doors I had watched a few months earlier from my car.

The door man was stood there, no shirt on, smoking a joint!

I could not believe what I was seeing.

After walking over to the door, I said *"what do you think you are doing?"*

He asked *"who the fuck are you?"*

He never worked at Masons Arms again, wanker.

This was the beginning of a two-year journey that led to a huge refurb that changed the pub for ever, or at least until I moved on after 8 glorious years of being a very proud GM at my favourite pub of all time.

Let's pick out a few special mentions to the biggest cunts who were kicked the fuck out, Masons was better without them!

My first one could easily be top of my all time, self-appointed, and thoroughly deserved "Fucking Wanker and Chief Cunt" list.

This award is given to an Asian taxi driver who thought he was some kind of super model.

I sussed him within minutes of watching him perform his "charming act" to all the fawning impressionable silly girls, and that is exactly what he was, nothing more than a wind-up toy banding two symbols together to attract attention. I found him a bit pathetic to be honest, his only purpose in life was to be the court jester trying so hard to entertain an even more pathetic audience.

When you have been around this business a long time you spot these false and shallow knobs from miles away, but they think they are untouchable because their attitude and arrogance creates an imaginary world where they are untouchable because everybody is fooled.

Actually, it is those two flamboyant flaws that combine to pin a fucking great big target on their backs.

All I had to do was watch him for a while, he will fuck up…

A couple of weeks in and I had already worked out his preferred drug selling method. The car park had two entrances and the rear pub doors were at that time almost central to the car park.

He would climb into his taxi, drive to the pubs rear doors and his passenger would slip aboard. He would then drive out the car park with his fake fare and drive around the round-a-bout and straight back into the car park using the other entrance.

In the time he had driven off and returned his passenger, to exactly where he had picked them up, he had sold the passenger drugs in his taxi.

I wanted to catch him at it, but better was still to come.

One Sunday afternoon he was sat with a group of silly girls who worshipped him for some reason. I remember he was wearing a cowboy hat and looking like a complete dick.

His attention seeking was off the scale, laughing far too loud, talking at an annoying volume, and acting in a very animated fashion, he was at the very centre of his universe.

I don't know why he did this, but he took his cock out under the table and pissed onto the floor.

Disgusting drug-dealing wanker.

But I still wanted the drugs offence, that was my main goal.

Later on, in the same weekend my targeted cunt and his mates, steroid pumping tossers with way too much product in their hair and perm-a-tans, were stood at one end of the building in the car park. It was a flat roofed area, so I crept across the roof and sat above them listening while they were talking.

The conversation featured drugs very heavily, mainly cocaine, so I rushed down to the car park and screamed in his face to. FUCK OFF FOR GOOD.

He argued, they all did, I didn't give a toss, he was out, the carpet pissing wanker was done, never to darken the doors of Masons again.

I had done this in full view of all his muscle-bound boy band wanker mates as a clear warning, I don't stand for shit…

One final twist to the barring of a drug dealing taxi driving prick, one of the girls from his fan club, apparently an intelligent lady and the daughter of a wealthy local plumber, wrote to my employers calling me a racist for barring an Asian man.

My BDM, Glenn, has known me a long time, he knows that was not true, so that attack on me failed.

What happened to his friends, you know the type, FHM boys, the pretty pricks in designer clothes worn in that weird cat-walk type of way, dressed up to a point of looking like a bit of a dick. I always thought some of them were showing off as a man's man a little too much, you know, to hide their urges to suck cock for themselves.

The barred taxi drivers' dealers' mates continued to use Masons on a weekly basis, were they really all such good friends, or did they just get a new dealer?

Who knows…?

Full Circle

Getting too Masons Arms has brought me full circle towards me leaving there and moving on to the Food Factory Carvery family pub, and eventually leaving the company through manipulation of evidence and blatant lies.

I could talk about characters I have worked with, fought with, rowed with, drank with, and snogged with, so much to say it could go on for days and days, and maybe I will in a follow up book where I name the names lol.

But for now, let's put the people to bed…

Chapter 11

It's Not Just the Idiots Paying the Price

Stupid Things Customers Say

Facts don't lie, pub would be nothing without people, customers, punters or whatever you call them, hospitality doesn't survive without two legs walking through the door.

No, I am not being disabled-phobic, it's just a figure of speech.

I also know, for a fact, every single person working in a pub has at some point called a customer a fucking dickhead, twat, prick, arsehole, bellend, plonker, massive cunt or just a fucking idiot.

The thing is, more often than not customers deserve being called a stupid twat, after all, acting like one deserves the verbal medal awarded to them for being such a total and absolute cunt.

People say really stupid things to professional hospitality people, but what they don't always realise is that very often the staff working behind that bar or delivering the plate of gammon and eggs to your table is far better educated, verbally skilled and quick witted than the person they are serving.

It amazes me that many of the general public view bar staff and waiters though a moral superiority set of googles.

Some of these idiots think wiping someone's arse in a car-home because you only managed 3 E's in your GCSE's means you must be more qualified than bar staff.

No, I am not belittling care-home workers, they are far nicer people than I could ever be, what they do is awesome and as a society they should be held up as heroes, but I'm sure you get my point.

Being kind is one thing, being smart witted leads to something else completely, sarcasm that can punch holes in anyone's ego.

Most new pub managers have been to university, hold a degree, often a pointless one in something like crochet or football culture, but at least they do have a proven ability to learn.

This doesn't make them great people leaders.

Bar staff and floor teams, these people are very different and will make far better managers if given the chance.

They are often highly in-trade educated by the companies they work for.

Never underestimate bar staff, many are at Uni themselves, and those who are not at Uni are put through extensive, detailed learning and development by the pub companies because a PLC knows that better educated teams will generate more income.

The average Joe will treat almost all pub staff and managers with at least some respect, but there is a lot of scum out there that talk down to anyone serving them as they think being served by another human automatically make them superior to those serving.

WRONG

Not only is this wrong every time, but these thick cunts abusing pub staff are so fucking stupid that they don't realise the, possibly fatal, risk they are taking.

Pub, restaurant, and kitchen teams are some of the most dangerous people you will ever meet, they hold your health, your guts and your ring piece in the cross hairs of a food poisoning bug every time you converse with them.

I'll give you an example:

A man shouts at a waitress, needlessly embarrassing her and he is totally inappropriate and unnecessary aggressive towards the innocent young lady just to feed his own ego.

He ordered his meal 22 minutes ago on his lunch break and yes, he needs to get back to the office. But this wanker has ordered a well-done steak with gluten free bread as a side order.

The steak takes 20 minutes to cook on the low heat section of the grill, so it doesn't burn, and the gluten free bread is kept in the freezer because so little of it is sold daily. It needs defrosting before sending out by laying it under the gantry heat lamps.

Defrosting the bread takes around 15 minutes before its ready to eat.

The worst thing about ordering gluten free bread, this man is not a celiac, he can eat bread with gluten without harming himself in any way what-so-ever, but his wife read him a clip in a magazine that said eating bread free of gluten reduces retaining water.

Absolute Bollocks of cause. Yet another totally unproven myth written to make women think they are doing trendy things that helps them self-medicate and improve body image, for themselves…

If this arrogant customer had ordered a medium cooked steak and normal bread, he would have received his lunch within 15 minutes.

The steak is cooked perfectly to the customers requested standard, well done, but not charred, rested for two minutes before being plated, it is now on the heated gantry about to be delivered to the rude prick, but not just yet.

The waitress who was unfairly scolded by this awful man picks up a fork, sticks it into the perfectly, carefully and thoughtfully prepared 8oz sirloin and walks across the kitchen with the steak dangling in the air and enters the bin yard where she wipes both sides of the steak against the insides of the 1100 litre waste food bin that is empty, but has not been washed out for 6 months.

The abused waitress returns to the gantry and carefully places the steak back onto the plate, wipes any bits of food waste that shouldn't be stuck to the juice meat surface and delivers the food to the arrogant customer.

"enjoy your food sir, sorry for the delay, can I get you anything else?"

The man ignorantly waves the waitress away with obvious attitude and she walks away with dignity and unruffled grace, but she does have a very wide smile beaming across her pretty face.

Who do you think is the winner, the wanker or the waitress?

Being rude to hospitality staff is exposing yourself to a viciousness that cannot be warned about enough, the retribution will be calm, quick, and extreme if you deserve to pay the price for being an asshole.

Is risking to your guts twisting so tightly you involuntary doubled over in public, and that poor sphincter muscle that you wipe so gently with aloe-vera bog roll, it will become a real sting-ring fire spitting black hole releasing gallons of foul, shit nearing the temperature of magma for 6 to 10 hours.

Is being a prick to a waitress worth it?

Before being a cunt to hospitality staff, think first, bite your lip and if there is an issue, not a problem, just be respectful.

Experienced pub staff genuinely know exactly how to ensure your ring-piece explodes like the surface of the sun sometime later in your, about to be very ruined, day.

This knowledge is handed down by the experienced to their own replacements willingly because it's not the young staff at fault or pushing to reduce labour costs, and one day they will suffer the same fate.

The pub staff who listened carefully during their detailed and extensive training sessions know that the scummy thick and creamy build up around the seals in the glass washer is listeria, and that will have you crippled in pain and spraying anything within 2 meters of your but-hole with liquid dark brown shit with the texture of badly stirred powdered gravy.

Thin but with lumps…

The people that you treat like a piece of crap you wipe off your shoe know exactly how to make you shit yourself so fast with pressurised liquid diarrhoea.

I would advise any dickhead stupid enough to verbally attack pub staff to hold your fucking tongue, you may think you won the battle, but your lower half and but-crack will definitely burn as you lose the war later that day.

Imagine, while your bum is still being cradled softly in your Calvin's, you could be on the bus, the tube, driving your car, in a coffee shop with only one, but occupied toilet, shitting yourself so hard that it runs down your legs onto your shoes, and don't forget the projectile vomiting onto strangers sat across from you, nice.

This could be the price you will pay for being an absolute prised prick for no reason to hospitality staff.

Imagine it happening while you are driving, try explaining that to the car valeting team, a shit-stained seat and vomit splattered dashboard and windscreen!

It has never ceased to amaze me the things that stupid customer say form up on their oh so high horse.

One of my absolute favourites is always thrown in the conversation when someone is complaining about the food they have been served. They actually think this loudly spoken statement will put you, highly experienced in professional, on your back foot.

Tell me if you have ever heard this line from a moaning customer?

"I was a chef." So fucking what?

I have a standard response to that statement, but only if I'm dealing with a knob-head who has no idea what they are talking:

"So, you weren't a very good chef because you're not doing it now?"

I don't use it often, but it generally slips out my mouth when an idiot complains about how a steak has been cooked wrong.

Let leave stupid things said for a while talk about chefs.

Many people know what a good steak is, they know when it's been cooked exactly to their liking, chefs understand how to cook that piece of meat to maximise its taste, they have been trained, practiced, and perfected their skills through hours of dedicated hours working in hot, airless, almost inhuman conditions to be able to grill the perfect piece of beef as requested, rare, I hope?

Grilled, pan fried, sprinkled with Oxo, sautéed in butter just before resting, I can guarantee college trained chefs know more about cooking steaks than any smart-arse who only eats rump steak once a year on their birthday in a Wetherspoons.

Man comes to the pub with his newish girlfriend, this is the first time they have eaten together, it's a very big deal.

He orders a well-done steak.

A well-trained server will ask "are you sure you want it well-done?"

The man, dripping with testosterone, speaks with confidence, showing off to the women he is hoping to be poking later on top of his Star Wars duvet before midnight, he knows his food, he makes out he eats steak on a regular basis. "yes I'm sure I want it well done"

Just over 20 minutes later the steak arrives, and he cuts into it with the super sharp wooden handled steak knife.

It is bone dry inside, dark coloured all the way through, not a single spec of moisture in any part of the dried-out meat, it has the texture of Gandhi's flip-flop and could be used if crunched up as an odd shaped squash ball, this dried lump of cows ass is fucked beyond human consumption, but it was done AT HIS REQUEST.

He calls the waitress over. "this steak is over cooked" he says with attitude, he needs to keep up the act to help loosen his dates clothes, he is "all man".

There will now be lots of running about by the waitress, the supervisor, and the chef are asked to look at the offending shrunken piece of beef imitating a used paratroopers insole.

The supervisor now checks that the order was entered correctly, did we ask him if he really wanted it well-done?

Yes, we did.

Eventually, as GM, I am called in to talk to the tracksuit wearing, LOVE HATE tattooed on his knuckles, prat of a customer about the problem with his steak and he says:

"I used to be a chef"

You can guess my response?

Not this time, I follow the company guidelines.

He leaves with a full refund, a bad attitude, and a belief he won because we refunded him the money he paid for the food.

Of course we refunded him, it's not fair to take money from those afflicted with such stupidity.

He shouts as he leaves that he will tell everyone we cannot cook, who fucking cares what he says, he doesn't understand how to use Trip-Advisor anyway.

He will know take his date to MacDonalds for a burger, and if I was his date no way would a fast-food burger loosen my knicker elastic, he is now in self-service mode for being a cheap bastard, and if he is really lucky, she will pass him a tissue.

Why do people who think saying that they are, or was once, a chef, is going to force a total capitulation and make highly trained staff beg to be bathed in all their culinary past glory?

Spending 6 months frying chips in burger joint does not make you a twating chef.

Yes, you passed some sort of on-line questionnaire that apparently "qualifies" you to fry chips, but this is it, its fuck all really.

Most real chef's feel pretty insulted when non-qualified people claim to be a chef, and I don't blame them one bit.

Being a chef is a highly skilled job, it takes between 2- and 4-years basic training, not just working in a kitchen, actually training under supervised conditions, being assessed, meeting qualification standards, and producing the finished goods to be a real chef.

Chefs have to know detailed knowledge about nutrition, heath, very strict hygiene rules, there is just as much time spent on paperwork as there is actual cooking when you are a real, fully qualified chef.

Trained chefs are currently a very rare find, you will find more rocking horse shit than qualified chefs who are struggling to find work. Every large food company, fast food outlet, most restaurants, hotels, just about everywhere is short of chefs who can actually cook, at speed and with the quality required to meet the needs of the ever-increasing expectations of the public driven by TV chefs who have the option to say "stop, let's shoot that scene again."

The chef in your local branded pub does not have that luxury.

Recruiting chefs is a huge, big problem for pubs in 2022, and that won't be changing soon. Almost all pubs sell food in this modern age, chefs do need to be paid a reasonable hourly wage or salary for their skills that have taken years to develop, but as I have explained much earlier within these pages, pub companies do not pay well, in fact, they pay very poorly.

If you are a chef who is skilled, produces top-notch food, and hold great qualifications, it is very doubtful you are working in a pub on a poverty-line wage rate, you will be somewhere that pays well because you have been poached with better money and conditions.

So, who the hell is cooking is cooking pub food?

Most pub menus are basically the same, they offer a microwaveable lasagne, combi-oven cooked half roast chicken, easy cook burgers, pre-coated deep-fried fish and chips that are seasoned before the leave the factory.

The only thing the cooks in a pub kitchen create with their hands is the Marie-Rose sauce by mixing pre-made mayonnaise with pre-made ketchup!

Such skill…

To help you understand how far some plc backed pub companies will go to control what their cooks produce, and control costs, I will give you a real example of total control.

Let's take a great British fried breakfast in a certain big pub co.

Take 2 rashers of bacon, 1 sausage, 4 mushrooms, half a tomato, 2 hash browns, baked beans, a slice of black pudding and eggs that have been taken out of their shells and put into a small plastic pouch.

All these ingredients are not delivered by the poorly rewarded trade food supplier as individual items, oh no, the pub company would never trust a kitchen worker on minimum wage to make any food related decisions that could affect profitability.

This is how all preparation options are removed allowing only the pre-specked meal to be cooked while maintaining perfect margin control.

Each breakfast item is delivered between two flexible sheets of plastic. All items are squeezed into place by sucking the air out of a plastic surrounding the measured portion of tomato, bacon, black pudding etc and then the sheets are heat sealed together.

You get the picture.

One vacuumed pack roll contains the exact amount of each ingredient the company wants included as a cooked breakfast for a particular controlled price point displayed on the menu.

Pub chefs, or cooks as most of them should be called, vary in skills from utterly useless, but they can work a microwave, but only just, through to highly effective self-taught cooks who really are chefs because they have earned that right for doing such a fantastic job of delivering quality food in a pub without ever attending chef training college.

Now let's talk big plc pub companies and their underpaid kitchen teams shall we.

Hopefully you really want to know the truths about kitchens in cheap branded pubs, and you also may not want to or care, but here it comes anyway.

I have described in detail how the pubs of old have been turned into Pasta Grill type branded food pubs, and in doing so they have put themselves in direct competition with well-resourced and successful restaurants, not only when it comes to attracting quality employees, but also in dish selection and menu direction.

How does a fancy looking branded food pub owned by a financial institution managed pub company tempt people into their pubs and away from fresh cook genuine restaurants?

Menu, price, and atmosphere.

I have already written about pricing and atmosphere, so let's delve into producing menu items at a competitive price for hungry customers.

The menus in the pubs of the 80's started out as very simple, ping ding microwave food with a pile deep fried chips, easy, almost anyone with two brain cells could whip up do a few plates per hour in a slow kitchen.

But pub company bigger bosses, pushed on by the new CEO, want a much larger slice of the eat-out market, so in comes a whole new range of dishes that can rival restaurant quality and choice.

Well, the wording could if not the end product…

Probably the biggest con of all is the public's perception of pub chefs, industrious highly trained food experts in gleaming white chef togs and 12-inch-high bright white hats.

This is intentional of course, no pub company wants you to think there is 20-year-old man wearing a T shirt, old chinos, lace less and tatty trainers and a grubby sports cap, the customer must think that their food is being cooked by a chef, after all, it takes a chef to create the following dishes:

Schezuan Pork.

Boil-in-a-bag meal added to microwave rice and steam in bag veggies.

Chicken Milanese.

Microwave chicken with pasta meal with a pre-sized side salad.

Miso-Glazed Haddock Ramin.

Microwave in a bag, sprinkle the finely chopped spring onions on top that come in a separate bag.

Lamb Shank with mash, veggies, and gravy.

Vacuum packed lamb is taken out the packet, placed in the combi-oven for a pre-set time. Mash in microwave, veggies in microwave, gravy pack in boil-in-a-bag.

And so, the menu goes on and on, each carefully named dish is added to the basic lasagne and scampi-based pub menu to create the image it can rival a real restaurant for quality and taste.

Can you identify one single trained chef required input needed in getting these dishes from the fridge to the table?

No, you can't because there isn't any. But this pubs menu is selling food dishes that makes it sound like a gastro pub with freshly prepared meals by a skilled team of chefs and kitchen operatives.

In reality, Tom is 20 years old, paid just £6.83 per hour and he is managing the kitchen tonight.

Tom is assisted tonight by Connor, a 17-year-old student paid just £4.81 per hour. Connor is good a fetching stuff from the fridge and pressing microwave buttons.

Any good gastro pub must sell a couple of expensive steaks on the menu, it's some of the dishes that cannot be left off any good menu because there is always a high demand.

Since the first-time food was cooked and sold to someone paying to have a meal served to them by someone being paid to ready their meal, the steak has always been a way to celebrate, indulge, show off or display social position. Men eat steak in an attempt to impress the woman or man they are hoping to shag later tonight.

The branded pub company will present a pub as a foodie heaven, all the right dishes, the quality is not exactly The Ivy or Piccolino levels of culinary skill, but it's not too bad for what is mainly ping-ding ready meals.

The biggest win with an upgraded image is what it has allowed the pub company to do, increase prices.

Unfortunately pushing up the pricing is to increase profits and not because of improved staff pay rates or ingredient quality, no such moral compass exists, it is done just to drive the bottom-line profit.

And we all remember what profit increases don't we, BONUS…

The menu contains a 10oz Ribeye, a flavoursome and tender cut with gentile marbling of fat making it perfect for fast searing style cooking.

On a £14.99

Now comes the 10oz Filet Mignon, one of the finest cuts of beef that is best grilled with care over a scorching charcoal flame to seal in it juicy body and melt in your mouth texture.

On at £19.99

And finally, it's the 14% Aberdeen Angus Sirloin, certified Scottish, grass fed with a slim strip of fat left on to prevent drying out while increasing flavour.

On at £24.99

The family sit around their branded food pub booked table on dad's birthday, mum and the kids insist dad tuck into a well-earned Aberdeen Angus Steak on his special day, and why not, he works hard, pays his taxes, his bills, is a good dad and a great husband, he should get his reward for just £24.99.

Would the family be thinking the same if they knew that this £25 slab of meat, the most expensive item on the menu, the price of 3 meals in the local Italian, was being cooked by two un-trained, inexperienced, underpaid kids, one of which hasn't washed his hands since completing his mid-morning wank!

You are reading this thinking that this cannot be true, just a load of bollocks for effect, but I am telling you the truth, I promise you.

This poor practice is not the normal in all pubs, when I was back in South Yorkshire I had 3 chefs, long in the tooth quality foodies who genuinely cared. Karen, Greg and Nick where great guys, they stayed with me through the years because we understood how to treat each other, respected each other and I protected them.

These 3 were assisted by Nat's, Lisa, Nicky, and many other team members, we grafted together making it work.

I was always relegated to pot washer, but it's teamwork, we all pulled as one team, and I fought for them from the occasional harshness of the company because they were worth far more than the new BDM's or people like Knobbush will ever understand.

Sadly, my old kitchen team left after I moved on, wages cuts, hours cut, all those things I talk about earlier in the book happened to three great team players, so the country lost a further 3 talented Chef's because of one company's relentless drive to continually reduce wage costs.

Anyway, back to the stupid thing some people say.

Gluten has become some kind of mythical secret murderer, if manufactures can remove it from products, doesn't matter if no one is actually affected by it, society health will spontaneously improve.

Bollocks you gullible turd.

I am really pleased that allergens are taken so seriously these days, it's the right thing to do, I have worked tirelessly to improve any food I have ever offered with the best allergens information I can provide, and the vast majority of food businesses do the same.

But, when people come to the bar and say the following, I do sometimes think we should remove the warning labels off everything and allow natural selection to do its thing.

"Hello, what can I get you?"

"I'll have the hand battered cod and chips please."

"Great, would you like any sides, such as bread to go with that?"

"Yes, I'll have bread, but it must be gluten free."

"Are you sure you want a battered fish as the fish batter contains gluten?"

"Yeah, it's ok, once it's been deep fried it's ok to eat."

This dumbass lady seems to think that deep frying batter changes the chemical composition of gluten, it doesn't.

I warned her, if she is now fucked up and doubled over in pain for the next two days, I tried my best.

"Don't put more than one ice cube in my drink because it will water it down."

Oh, my fucking god, IQs have shrunk to an all-time low with today's millennials, it's basic physics you stupid twats.

Putting one ice cube into a body of liquid that is far larger than the volume of the ice cube causes the ice to melt so fast it will be gone in minutes watering down the drink.

Increasing the amount of ice changes, the volume ratio, so lots of ice in an a much more equal volume of liquid will reduce melting speed because the ice brings the liquid temperature down instead of the liquid melting the ice.

Do you now get-it Thick-O's…?

"Have you watered down the orange cordial?"

Fuck You! I have not watered it down, keep up with the times you twat, all the nasty e-numbers were taken out so the artificial colour making it deep orange in colour have been fucked off by the EU.

It tastes exactly the same, but I'll tell you what, why not add another 25p shot to your glass to satisfy your stupidity.

"How many can I have and still drive home under the limit?"

I have been asked this so many times, often by academically intelligent people.

I don't know, everybody is different, take some responsibility and have a soft drink!

"I worked on a bar, and I know how it is done" Just fuck off. you did a few shifts on a bar while at Uni, a student bar managed by ex-students who have no fucking idea what they are doing.

If you had any knowledge of bar work in the real world you would know that you cannot replace Worcestershire sauce with watered down HP brown sauce in a Bloody Mary for fucks sake.

"My Mum and Dad were licensees" So fucking what, they were probably crap at it and why does their experience qualify you to tell me how to do things are done properly?

Just do one you stupid wanker and don't try telling a professional how to do their job ever again. I was managing a pub in York; an underground pub and we were in the middle of a major refurbishment.

The bar had been ripped out completely, the whole thing was gone, all that was left was a few pipes, wires, and a few 50-year-old beer stains.

I'm stood exactly where "behind the bar" had been, before the bar counter had been demolished, talking to one of the workmen when I notice two men walking in through the front doors.

They had squeezed past the metal fence keeping the public safe from our building site, they must be really thirsty.

They walked up to where the bar once was and one man said without any sense of irony or sense of humour, with a completely straight face: *"are you open?"*

I cannot remember my reply, but it was not my finest customer service delivery day.

"Can I have a neat scotch, on the rocks, make it a Hennessy" I don't even know where to start with this one, but I can tell you, I just stood there for about 10 seconds trying to fathom what this fucking prick actually wanted. *"do your peanuts have allergies?"*

Have you ever tried reading a book?

Start with reading the back of this nut packet, here, have this packet on me…

"You know your lasagne; can you take the meat out?"

Errrrrr not really. *"Is there any sinks in the toilets?"*

No, they are built into a unit that is fixed to the wall, there is just water and blue cleaning cubes in the toilets.

"That fruit machine isn't working?"

Ok I'll have a look, everything seems ok, I'll put a £1 in myself, yep, it's working fine, what was the problem you had with it? *"it's says Free Spin there in the front but it didn't"*

Have you put any money in it? *"No, I just wanted my free spin"*

Go away, just leave now… *"is there anywhere in that smoking area outside where people cannot smoke cos, I want to eat out there?"*

Errrrrr no, sorry. *"Do you have a separate chef in a meat free kitchen to make vegan meals?"*

Yes of course we do, all pubs have two kitchens these days.

"Why is that door marked Private?"

I cannot tell you, it's private.

"Will you be closing in the daytime and only opening up overnight for the Rugby World Cup?"

We will consider it, where is your nurse?

"I can get a bottle of that wine for £4.99 in the CO-OP"

Good for you, sit on their ice cream freezer, wave you £5 in the air and ask them to serve it to you in a clean glass.

"Can I get a flat coke please?"

Yes, I'll pure it now, leave it on the bar for about an hour, then come back for it.

"Does scampi grow in its shell; it looks just like breadcrumbs?"

That was new kitchen team member, first kitchen he had worked in if you had not guessed.

"I was in the bar across the road and a lady had a pinky-coloured cocktail with fruit and a sparkler in it, can I get one of those please?"

Yes, you can, in the bar you saw the lady drinking it.

"You know TGI's, they do a jug with loads of fruit and ice, what's in it?"

Next time I go to TGI's I'll ask for you, ok.

"Is sherry the same as port?"

No. *"is Malibu a strong spirit?"*

it's not a spirit, it was a spirit called rum, but it was diluted to make it Malibu.

"Is the dish marked VE really vegan?"

Me: The regulations allow for an 'average of around 75 insect fragments per 25 grams of paprika, as well as an average of more than 11 rodent hairs.

Chocolate is even worse because 100 grams of chocolate is allowed to contain 60 insect fragments, as well as one rodent hair. Wheat flour is legally allowed 75 insect fragments per 50 grams, plus one rodent hair per 50 grams.

The vegan dish contains paprika and wheat flour.

This so I'll leave you to make up your own mind, ok.

"Today I drove past Ranby prison near Retford earlier today. All the cars parked outside, are they the prisoner cars?"

Yeah, of course they are, they get reserved spaces for up to 15 years. *"Is venison meat?"*

No, it's a special veggies type of meat that vegans can eat. *"Oh right, good to know."*

For Fucks Sake, look it up on Google. *"You know in America you can't drink until you are 21. Do American kids grow up slower the us in England?"*

Yeah, that right, they don't get pubes until they are 18 years old.

"I don't want the 1st pint from a new barrel, you never get a full pint if it's the first one." You do realise that the glass IS a pint, don't you? *"Really, I thought the pump measured a pint."*

"Are those bottles in that bottle fridge to keep them cold?"

No, we use the fridge just to light them up so people can see what's in the bottle fridge.

"What does lime cordial taste like?"

Here, try a bit.

"It's a bit like lemon." shoot me, shoot me now.

"Do the chips come in already fried so you just need to microwave them?"

No.

"To make rosé wine do they just mix red and white together?"

Yeah, I do it myself in the cellar.

"How many gallons do you get in a 22-gallon barrel?"

About18

"What you need in here is drum and base nights, can I DJ it"

NO and fuck off now you skanky weed stinking, Argos gold wearing track suited chav. *"It is illegal to put a shot of every spirit into one glass and sell it"*

No, it is not, it's irresponsible, but not illegal.

Ok that's enough of stupid things said in pubs.

Now we move on to pay the price…

Wagon Wheels Are Becoming Smaller?

The magical Wagon Wheel Fish is a phenomenon that I realised was happening over and over again and again many years ago.

Anyone reading this old enough to remember when we thought Wagon Wheels were as big as your head?

The vast majority of us genuinely remember them as a massive chocolate and marshmallow disc that no one could possibly fit into their gaping hole of a mouth.

I now, when young, I tried, I failed.

We have become convinced that Wagon Wheels have shrunk every year since we were very young and now Wagon Wheels seems to be tiny verses the good old days.

It is true, Wagon Wheels have actually become smaller, in the 80's they went from 79mm down to 74mm, a 12% reduction, but in our heads, they are at least 50% smaller, and that's the minimum.

Where the fuck does fish fit into this so-called Wagon Wheel phenomenon you are asking?

Fish is cut as a fillet, the larger the size, the more it costs.

You would expect that, but that is only half the story.

Larger fish with the larger fillets are not in the same abundance as the smaller fish, so the larger fish not only cost more because of the size of the fillets are much bigger, but also because the demand for a product that is not so readily available also drives up the price.

The Wagon Wheel phenomenon occurs at menu change.

Thinking far back into this tail of pubs over past decades do you remember the local pub being turned into a Paster Grill food pub?

This was the first time the pub has had a full menu and the 1st time the food offer includes fish and chips because they now have deep fat frier and extraction.

The brand-new shiny menu says "large" fish and chips, the battered fish fillet being served up to customers starts out as 285 grams, or 10oz, it's a whale on the plate and everybody loves it.

After 6 months everyone is used to the large fish, it has become the normal fish in the regular's psyche, so no one is wowed anymore when it arrived at the table, it is just a battered and fried fish.

Then the time comes to refresh the menu, the food team at head office have to justify their jobs and salaries, so they need to deliver the same, or more sales, but at a much lower purchasing cost.

It may seem odd, but each department within a plc pub company has to deliver its own profit, not just the pubs.

I'll come back to this!

Some bright spark in marketing decides to reduce the fish fillet from 10oz, down to 8oz, or as described on most menus, 285 grams cut to just 225 grams.

That is a weight reduction of 60 grams per fish fillet, or a shrinkage of fish to be eaten by a whopping 21%!

So, the cost of each fish fillet supplied to the pub company is greatly reduced because it is now over 20% smaller, and then reduced even further because the smaller fish fillets are much cheaper to buy because they are more readily available.

The food development team and marketing mob have them BIG WINNER, more profit for less.

The new menu is reprinted, refreshed, new colours, new fonts, pub companies normally change around 30% of a menu content at each menu change, but certain core items stay remain forever due to customer demand of certain big sellers like lasagne and scampi.

Companies will also leave high margin dishes on a menu forever if they are still selling well and earning a healthy profit...

One of these "stay on the menu forever" items is good old British classic fish and chips.

Two things will eventually change about the fish and chips on the menu, and one thing definitely won't.

The word "large" will be removed from the description on the reprinted menu and the way the fish is presented on the plate will be completely different to the old menu plate layout specification.

This is crucial because it is part of hiding the fish size reduction.

There are two simple marketing tricks used to fool the public into believing the dish is better than before and the same size.

The first trick requires the new fish and chips to be presented in a whole new style. The old fish and chips was a whale covering half an oval plate, the new version is much more artisan style with the fish balanced on top of the of the chips.

The second part of the trickery is plating the new menu fish and chips on a 1inch smaller plate.

It really is that simple, and if you are old enough you will now be able to think back to the old days of eating fish and chip in the early pub restaurant.

Every fish and chips came out on an oval plate, and there was no way of balancing that huge slab of battered cod on top of the chips, it was far too heavy.

The new "balanced on top" presentation looks amazing, especially on the smaller plate, there is even a photo of this "new improved" fish and chips on the menu cover, very soon no one will remember the old whale on a plate from the last menu.

We now understand the two things that will change on the menu, the change in wording and presentation.

But what about the one thing that won't change?

The price. Yep, that's right, the one thing that has not changed is the price, or if it has it will go cup.

Kerching, the marketing team have robbed you yet again, you are probably paying more for cheaper, smaller fish.

I talked about changing recipes, sizes, ingredients, all in the interest of driving up margins early in this book, all the trickery that takes place to increase profits.

The Wagon Wheel Fish Phenomenon is my explanation of how menu changing is a tactic being used in the real world to fool the customers into receiving less on their plate, paying just as much, if not more, and then thanking the pub company for ripping them off.

It's a PR stroke of genius, a switcheroo that even Dynamo would be proud of.

Pies become smaller, contain less meat, steaks are cut from 8oz to 7oz, burgers drop from 8oz to 6oz, the cuts are always hidden behind a menu change, but you, the customer, will always pay the maximum price while believing you are enjoying a genuine bargain.

Paying the price is more than branded pub chains fiddling about with menu's and reducing the size of your Cumberland sausage.

The government takes the biggest piss to be honest, rips drinkers off at every opportunity and are forcing the pub companies to delve even deeper into our cash-strapped pockets.

The Great British Tax-Rip-Off

We all know we have to pay VAT at 20% on drinks and food we buy in pubs. We know that the 20% VAT goes to the government to pay for pensions, the NHS, social care, it helps keep people alive in a harsh modern world and rightly so.

But what else does the government take from every drink we buy through taxing alcohol with something called "Duty"?

Breweries make alcoholic drinks for us to enjoy, but the government do something that I think is absolutely despicable!

HMRC charges our enjoyment of drinking alcohol, either alone, with family, with friends, weddings, wakes, you name it, the government are taxing every one of your good, or sad times.

Fucking ridiculous.

When breweries make alcoholic drinks in the UK, they have to pay HMRC a taxable Duty on the volume of alcohol made.

Most of you have heard the term alcohol duty, but how much does it increase the price of your alcoholic drinks?

Breweries don't absorb the duty levy they pay to the taxman; they pass the duty tax cost on to YOU through purchase price.

Here are a few examples of how much alcohol duty effects the cost of your favourite tipple.

I'll give you the product, alcohol by volume level, the amount of duty the brewer or distillery has paid from creating the alcohol and the VAT paid on the duty, yes that right, the tax is taxed.

1 X Pint of Lager or Beer at 5% strength = 52p duty + 10p VAT. so your pint is 62p more expensive than it should be.

1 X 25ml spirit 37.5% or over = 28p duty + 6p VAT. so your single shot costs 34p more than it should!

1 X 75cl bottle of wine at 13% vol = £2.05p duty + 41p VAT. that bottle of wine cost you £2.46p more than it should.

1 X 70cl bottle of spirit at 40% vol = £8.05p duty + £1.68p VAT. one bottle of spirits costs £10.18p more than it should.

Be honest, did you know just how much hidden tax we pay to enjoy ourselves, to toast a bride or run a Jager-train of 50 shots?

Just think how much tax revenue the government gets from every alcoholic sale in the UK! The numbers are mind bending, it's fucked up, and we haven't even added the VAT added when you buy a drink.

Let's go back to our pint of Lager.

It costs £5.00 at the trendy city centre bar.

The government have already had your trousers down for 62p on that one pint, but now it wants the purchase VAT on top.

£5.00 purchase price means, to keep it simple, a VAT charge of £1.00 that goes to HMRC.

Your pants have also now been whipped down and a total of £1.62 is making you squeal little piggy!

You have just been royally fucked over big time just because you want a pint after work, and you need a pint because you have just been paid and the tax man has just taken 20% Income Tax and 14% National Insurance Tax.

Be pedantic if you want and correct the numbers into exact figures, but you get the point.

In 2020 773 million litres of whisky were purchased in the UK, yes you read that right **773,000.000** litres.

This is over a **million bottles** of whisky, and whiskey with a "e", knocked back by the UK population, and this is just Whisky, think about adding vodka, gin and rum to the total.

Try to imagine the amount of alcohol duty paid into the HMRC on 773,000,000 bottles of whisky?

Moving up a gear let's think about all the alcohol produced, sold, bought and consumed in the UK as a whole.

The alcohol duty tax raises a few quid to say the least.

£13,001,000.000 (13 BILLION) IN ALCOHOL DUTY TAX

To put this into context, vehicle duty, or road tax as it is better known, raises just £7,002,000,000 (7 BILLION).

Alcohol revenue for HMRC is a vast amount and far more than I ever expected when I started thinking about this subject.

But for this case, I will stick with just the Scotch Whisky.

But here is the kick in the nuts, every penny of the duty tax is paid for by you because the cost is passed onto the customers, as it is in every business model, but with alcohol you are about to robbed yet again.

You now have to pay another 20% VAT on the purchase price.

VAT has already been paid on the duty tax, the tax is taxed and then you are taxed again…

What this boils down to is the fact the us poor saps in the UK pay tax 3 times on our happiness, our celebrations, commiseration, and reward after working out skin to the bone.

We are taxed approximately 54p from every £1.00 by the HMRC when we buy alcohol.

Why?

Because alcohol is a soft target and the excuse about protecting health can be used every time the levels are questioned.

If duty tax and 20% VAT was removed from the making and purchasing of alcoholic drinks they would cost over 50% less.

Germany, a country with proud beer making traditions taxes its alcohol by around half the UK amount, the USA only charge $1.07 cents on a gallon of wine.

We really are shafted by Westminster and it's just not fair to tax goods times so highly compared to other countries.

The journey through pubs over the last 40 years mirrors what has happened to society, everything is fucking expensive these days and normally a disappointment once it arrives.

But this should be no surprise to anyone if you think about it, we demand cheapness is available 24/7 365 and in doing so we unintentionally inflate the quality alternative.

Every time we buy a cheap branded meal in a plc owned pub chain the private restaurant owner is pushed a little bit further out of business because their cost goes up to compensate for the discounts demanded by the huge plc's ruthless CEO's in the never-ending drive for higher share prices and profits.

It is not humanly possible to deliver great, genuine, friendly customer focused service offering quality products in a PLC owned pub company. In a world of cost reduction, wage cuts, margin growth and bigger bosses bonus culture, no one can convince me that a teenager taking food to a table for under £5.00 per hour is happy to do it.

They are not, and who the fuck would be?

Why do our politicians and civil servants allow our hospitality workers to be cheated out of National Insurance payments that could even reduce the underpaid staff members pension long into the future?

The tossers in Westminster and Whitehall set minimum wages that a Victorian workhouse owner would be ashamed of.

Why do they value someone who is under 20 years old so poorly by paying them less than a 21-year-old, and even less than someone who is 23?

Would you be able to tell if someone serving you is 20, 21 or 23?

No neither can I, but we value each one less than the other?

Our heartless leaders, the cunts that we vote in, red or blue, treat all young workers as no more that cheap workhouse labour feeding the taxation machine.

A pub company employs a prick as a useless BDM and an Op's wanker who cut staffs wages to remove the cost of NI saving the pub company a fucking fortune while pushing up their own bonuses. This is all ok in HMRC eyes, and so is paying young hospitality workers slave labour wages, it's just plain wrong.

No one in Westminster or Whitehall says a fucking word to protect these vulnerable young people from these modern-day cruel pay rate conditions that are robbing young people of their own financial futures.

I have thought long and hard about this pension reducing trick that plc pub companies use to reduced labour costs.

Let me try to explain how I understand it:

If a hospitality worker has their hours reduced to remove any NI contribution, they are being robbed of 12-13% from their overall pay package and that will no longer contribute to their state pension pot.

A civil servant receives a very different kind of pension to the public they rule over.

Their pension scheme is called a defined benefit that is based on their salary throughout their career.

The public get an average of 3-5% pension contribution paid by their employer, topping up the employee's contribution, but only if they earn enough to pass the minimum threshold.

What is wrong with this pension level of contribution you may ask?

Here is the problem.

The wankers in charge who allow the plc pub companies to treat their teams so badly and rob them of their future pensions are themselves paid around a 29% pension contribution funded directly by YOU from your tax burden.

It's just not fucking right is it, private workers 3%, government cock-wombles 29%.

As you can see after reading this, the people in power, who allow plc pub companies to rob blind their employees, rip the hard-working pub using public off with menu trickery, treating hospitality employees as "less than human" money making machines built to build shareholder and bonus payment schemes, are very comfortable with how the system works.

Nothing in this book will affect any of them in their private clubs, discounted Westminster bars and secret societies, why should they give a toss, Guilford to Barnsley, every single one of them is the fucking same, lining their own pockets while pretending to care to keep their jobs, waiting for their multi-million-pound pensions.

I don't want to come across as political because I'm not really, but I do like the truth.

Let me mention one more thing about why I don't believe those in power give a toss about poorly treated and paid hospitality workers.

Much earlier I explained how plc pub companies reduce a team members hour to reduce their pay below the National Insurance Contribution (NIC) threshold.

Let me show you a few numbers that were correct at the time of writing.

Using Class 1 NIC, which is the NIC level the vast majority of us pay when paid through a company's payroll system, I can show you exactly how much of your pay is deducted every week in NIC contributions.

Let's use a set amount of £1,000, now I want to explain how and why the £1,000 is spilt into three sections:

For example, if you earn £1,000 a week, you pay NIC contributions:

21. nothing on the first £190
22. 13.25% (£102.95) on the next £777
23. 3.25% (£1.07) on the next £33.

Yes, you read that right, the more you earn the less as a percentage you contribute in NIC deductions.

Let's put this really simply:

If you earn £750.00 per week you will contribute £74 in NIC.

This is 13.2% from your total pay taken away in NI.

If you earn £1,500.00 per week you will contribute £99 in NIC.

This is just 6.6% from your total pay taken away in NI.

If you earn £2,000.00 per week you will contribute £115 in NIC.

This is just 5.7% from your total pay taken away in NI.

As you can see from the numbers above the more you earn the smaller the percentage is taken from your pay packet in NIC.

The big earners could easily afford to pay more, but don't have to.

Why?

Yes, they are paying a higher total of money into the NIC bucket held out and rattled by the HMRC, but that does not change the fact that the poorer paid are actually contributing a much higher percentage of their hard-earned pay packets into the NIC coffers.

This means that anyone paid over £190 but under £967.00 pay more to funds the NHS and social care than the wealthy.

If the highly paid, by this I mean anything over £1,000 per week, paid the full 13.25% NIC instead of just 3.25% on anything over £1,000 the NI pot would be spilling over.

This would probably pay for the NHS and social care funding gaps and allow the working class to pay a little less…

Just a thought…

This book is about pubs and their teams of incredibly hard workers.

I want all the people working in hospitality to keep more money in their pockets by paying less tax in all forms and I want the powers to clamp down on plc pub companies using the loophole allowing the no NI contribution to save on labour costs.

Chapter 12

What Is the Future and Conclusion?

So, what have you learned by reading about the inner workings of venture capitalists share-holder owned pub companies?

Well, by now you should understand much of their financial trickery and thoughtless manoeuvrings are effectively damaging their own employees and the quality of work life in their cash cow pubs brands.

The leadership of some of the biggest plc owned pub companies are pushing down pay rates of their employees, and it's just not right, almost all on paid minimum wage rates that only serve to line the pockets of the privileged few at the top of the plc pyramid.

Until I sat back and started to go over my own crazy pub-life history, hanging on by my fingertips through employment peaks and troughs that have relentlessly thrown me in the air with no safety net, then crushed my spirit under the weight of poor-quality top-down management, I didn't understand just how crazy it has been to spend almost my whole working life in the hospitality industry.

Working for over 30 years in pubs, only now have I realised how my own career, every working moment, and my own personal life has been intertwined, twisted, manipulated, and broken by the changes made to pubs we have all been forced to endure over the last 30 to 40 years.

The endless restructuring, rolling out and re-branding cheaper and cheaper "family food" pub chains that became an obsession for the new pub company owners, the financial city players, in their endless pursuit of bigger profits by making food the priority over drink.

The money grabbers stripped away the old-fashioned value of putting people, community, and friends first. Instead over the following decades the process of watering down every aspect of customer service and turning personality filled boozers into clinical soulless food factories became the mission, to create a system to deliver higher and higher sales from anybody with a spare £1 in their pocket. The gloves were off, families, drunks, mentally unstable, underage, and unemployed were all targeted by different brands, the pubs with morals were packed off into history.

I cannot tell you is why it has taken me so long to admit to myself that I have known for over a decade, tried to ignore, lie to myself and others and just make the best of it.

But now I can finally admit that working for a financial institutionally owned pub company is like treading water with a fucking great big anchor tied to your ankles.

You will survive as long as you franticly thrash with your arms and kick with your legs and feet as much as humanly possible. You will be panic stricken, always on the edge of drowning, but with a must survive will of steel and never give up attitude that will keep your head above the water delivering for the people who tied the anchor around your ankles. You will work like a slave for much longer than them at the top deserve, but they are counting on your loyalty while hiding their own contempt for the business end of the money-making machinery.

Sooner or later, you will tire, arms and legs become heavy with the burden of compliance, impossible targets, and poor leadership from the multiple management layers above, I don't know anyone at the sharp end who is not fatigued from the endless pressure and demands made of people working in a plc pub life.

Your energy will fade, all hope of reaching the bright future you were once promised all those years ago will be drained away by the greedy forces controlling every minute of your life, yes, I do mean outside working hours also, through a fast internet connection attached to LED screens pulling on invisible strings attached to your wrists and feet. Someone else is deciding everything you do, controlled in real time by the puppet masters as they follow every sale, every penny spent on wages, every pint pulled or lasagne microwaved, the bigger bosses are pulling all the strings all the time.

But the strings will one day tangle, fray and break, your arms will no longer be able to hold the heavy burden on the water's surface, you will slowly slip below the waves…

As the company directors' cash in their share options, they are also stealthily stealing your quality of life, your pride, dignity, resilience and faith in what was once a people centric dedicated business making everyone involved, customers and workers alike, happy, as simple as that, just happy, but no more.

Our pub teams delivered great quality service because they wanted to, in amazing atmospheres created by genuine people, but not now, it feels as if what atmosphere exists has been artificially pumped in.

Big pub companies are not there to serve you, or reward you for working so hard for them, where on earth did you get that idea?

They operate only to reward themselves handsomely at many levels, such as directors, board members and shareholders.

The only purpose is to stay alive and grow by generating income and profits and that is where you and I come in, we are the tools of the machine. Their business modal is the exact opposite of Robin Hoods good intentions, these pub companies exist to relieve you of the contents of a wallet or purse, and re-distribute it to others, the shareholders.

To be honest, that is the business model of almost every company in the world apart from a few charities, money is the life blood that maintains the corridors of power and executive corner offices high up in gleaming glass head offices around the world.

But spending money on a sandwich from a supermarket is not the same a buying a pint from a person stood 3 feet away, separated by solid wood or marble, buying drinks and food in real pubs is a personal connection, a human-to-human transaction that goes far beyond one person handing cash to another, the smile, the chat, the eye contact, this is what makes buying food and drink in a pub eye to eye with another human being so special.

Or at least, that was what it was all about years ago, do you ever receive that level of personal "non-scripted" service these days? Rarely is the answer…

I have tried to explain how the system is broken, there is a huge disconnect between the head office gods and the worker ants, the little people who take the income over the bar in poor staffing conditions for the goods and service that they provide.

I really hope that from now on you can see beyond the nice uniforms and name badges next time you visit a branded pub.

Almost every company, especially breweries, began as a small family enterprise, growing through generations of family members taking their turn in guiding the business through the next 50 years, helping it develop upwards and onwards until it was time to hand it over to a younger member of the family who take custardy of the family brand, a family duty, an honour, remaining in the name of the family that have gone before.

It was also expected that the family business would continue to benefit their town, the local community, their workers and continue their shared history together.

But there appears to be nothing that can stop mountainous money piles tempting a family member into selling their hard-earned heritage of brewing, hospitality, history, and the family name to the highest bidder?

Electronic money arrived, small to start with, but after a few years the plastic card began to change the way we pay for our treats in a licensed building.

Next, we saw the biggest change to our pubs since licensing laws were first introduced in 1872, longer pub opening hours were on the way.

Most of you have heard of, and even witnessed for yourselves, some dramatic changes to pubs over the years.

Enormous improvements to the licensing hours that allowed families to socialise together, properly in the local pub for the first time without a designated family room.

And along came some really stupid changes that allowed every pub to become a nightclub and opening until 1am, 2am, 3am as long as they wanted if they could prove the need to the local council.

Who can remember when pubs closed their doors on a Sunday afternoon?

Really, they did, I'm Gen X so I was there to see it with my own two eyes, NO booze between 3pm and 7pm, that was the rule of law.

In the drive to generate more sales and drive higher profits pub companies will always seek out, and manipulate, loopholes in the laws set out to control them, the new licensing laws had flaws.

A solution had to be found that allowed the pub to stay open on a Sunday afternoon, surely an area not yet exploited can be found?

That solution was FOOD

If you sold food in the form of a main meal to a customer, they were allowed to have an alcoholic drink to consume with their food.

FUCKING GENIUS, the tills could continue to ring ring ring.

I remember those days so well, we dreaded every Sunday afternoon, bollocks to Friday and Saturday nights being a pain in the arse, 3pm till 7pm on a Sunday was by far the worst time to be working of the whole week.

Managing the rule of law on a Sunday afternoon was a bastard of a job, a nightmare for all pub staff, but mainly managers because we were seen as the wankers stopping people having a full day out on the lash.

No one wants to be called the fun police.

The rules around alcohol sales on a Sunday afternoon between 3pm and 7pm were along these lines:

"A person being 18 years or over is allowed to buy and enjoy an alcoholic beverage while they are consuming a table meal."

Put simply, you could have a pint, or a cheeky glass of wine, between 3pm and 7pm with your Sunday roast if you wanted to.

Great, everyone is happy…

Or was it really that simple?

Pub teams and managers followed the rules and applied the Sunday licensing laws. We didn't like the stupid rules because they were not simple enough, or explained clearly, for many of the public to understand. On the other hand, the rules were just ambiguous enough for certain types of the public to try to twist them to their own advantage.

And so, the games had started, how many illegal drinks with the pub served today?

So many people intentionally misinterpreted the rules on purpose to get booze on a Sunday afternoon, and it worked if the buyer could outsmart new or easily fooled bar staff and managers.

But at the same time as we were fighting off every trick in the book to get a cheeky pint at 4:30pm on a Sunday, so many of the public just didn't understand, or couldn't comprehend the rules.

Most of these uneducated tossers were from in-bread council estates and just unable to see how a rule that was in place to distinguished diners and non-diners could apply to them, after all, they just want a drink, like him over there with a pint of Stella eating a gammon steak and chips.

I was working on the outskirts of Retford in a family food pub that was allowed to open on a Sunday afternoon between 3pm and 7pm as long as we had a full range of main meals available.

Now, here is where it got very confusing between 3pm and 7pm:

24. A customer can only purchase an alcoholic drink to consume with a main meal that is purchased at more or less, the same time.

25. A customer can purchase a soft drink without having any food between 3pm and 7pm.
26. If only 1 main meal is ordered only 1 alcoholic drink can be purchased with the main meal.
27. Sandwiches are NOT a main meal.
28. Sandwiches sold WITH chips on the same plate and NOT as an extra IS can be classed as a main meal.
29. A child's sized meal sold to an adult does not enable the adult to purchase an alcoholic drink with that meal as the child's meal is designated for a person under 18 years old.
30. It is not specified how many alcoholic drinks can be bought by one person to drink while they are consuming their meal. The dinner can only purchase alcohol for consumption by themselves.
31. It is down to the licensee's judgement how long a person can drink for, or how many drinks a person can consume once the main meal is finished. Rough guidelines say drinking alcohol is permitted while consumming a main meal.

Can you imagine trying to enforce these rules to people who did not care about the law and thought it was you as an employee just being an arse, I was a fucking nightmare!

And the worse thing, the same wankers would try the same con every couple of weeks like fucking clockwork. Sometimes they won in our pub, but not often, I really was the law enforcer.

Let me take you through a conversion I had with a twat in the summer of 1986, yeah 1986 sounds about, I remember it well because I was working with a young lady called Andrea Sullivan who had amazing long hair.

This is how the conversation sort of went:

"Can I have a bag of salt n vinegar and 4 pints of Stella" I'm sorry sir, after *3pm and you can only drink with a main meal.*

"I had my dinner earlier, 4 pints of Stella"

What time did you eat sir?

"About 1pm."

Where did you eat sir? "At home."

sorry sir, you can only buy alcohol while ordering and consuming a main meal.

"Alright, I'll have a prawn cocktail and 4 pints of Stella."

really sorry, that is a starter, the law says it has to be a main meal and you can only purchase one alcoholic drink per main meal you order and pay for.

"What about if I order one Sunday lunch and 4 Stella's?"

sorry, doesn't work like that.

"So, if it was a Saturday, I could have 4 pints of Stella?"

Yes sir.

"that's stupid, it's a nice day, we just want a beer sat outside."

I am very sorry sir; I suggest you take it up with your MP and get the law changed.

"Fuck off you prick; fuck your pub we will go somewhere else you fucking tosser."

sorry about that sir, we have to obey the law.

He kicked over a table, pushed a bin over and a flower tub as he left our premises.

If you worked in a pub that sold food on a Sunday between 3pm and 7pm you would have probably received similar abuse, it was really common for staff to be slapped, spat-at, screamed at, we all dreaded a warm sunny Sunday afternoon in a family pub, it really was a fucking nightmare.

One of the biggest improvements to licensing laws was when drinking all day Sunday 11am till 11pm became law in 1988, how we cheered and rejoiced the end of ANGRY Sunday's…

All the changes in licensing allowing longer drinking hours and family food revenue rolling in was really exciting the city.

Drinking and eating much more often in pubs became the next big thing for the city arses to set their sights on.

The brokers around the globe had woken up, eventually beer had become digitalised, the finance powerhouses started to lobby political parties and MP's, many of which are greedy little fuckers and will take the "donations", the free bee's that buys their allegiance to a cause that they don't really give a fuck about, but it will pay for a villa in the South of France.

Over the years we have watched changes to leisure rules and licensing laws under the disguise of alcohol being controlled and increasing consumer safety.

What utter Bullshit…

How the fuck does a law that allows idiots to drink alcohol 24 hours a day help control a known poisons consumption?

We all know someone that just cannot control themselves, they will drink every minute they can while any bar will still serve them booze in any form.

Opening up around the clock doesn't control the amount of alcohol being pour down someone's neck in the way it was meant too.

Funny fact, the government at the time actually told the media that opening for longer, even 24 hours a day, would reduce the binge drinking.

No, seriously, that was the reason, and it was passed into law.

Many sceptics, such as myself, thought it may be a way of adding into the HMRC taxation bucket with a huge bonus and un-budgeted increase in alcohol duty and VAT for purchase, but what do I know.

What In do know is, binge drinking did not fall, I was managing pubs and I know for a fact that it increased, massively.

Increasing drinking hours, all that was ever going to happen was this:

Speed drinkers no longer had to beat the closing bell at 11pm, oh no, now they could drink at a slower pace for much longer, 1, 2, 3 even 4 hours longer and they still binged the booze in the final 30 minutes before the new later closing times kicked in.

Someone clearly had not thought this through, it was always going to lead to a tsunami of alcohol fuelled boozing frenzy, fucked up livers, basic tossers becoming ultra cunts to each other and innocents, and even worse working conditions for the staff who were not only earning their wages in modern day workhouse conditions, but they were also now doing it even later into the fucking night while still being paid minimum wage.

On the 24th of November 2005 the law was changed allowing the purchase and drinking of alcohol 24 hours a day!

What the government had done was allow every licensed premises to become a fucking nightclub!

Party Party Party…

No need to pay for taxi into town anymore.

No need to visit a wank, shit quality nightclub and pay for overpriced drinks all night long.

Fuck the nightclub that charges £10 to get in, we can just stay in our local pub until 6am if they are licensed to open until daybreak. From now on we can spend the taxi and entrance money on even more shots and getting absolutely fucked-up.

And finally, we can make loads of annoying noise and piss into private gardens while staggering home at 2.30am because the bar will no longer serve you because you can no longer speak without drooling.

The new licensing laws are really going to cheers up the local residents. Just imagine waking up on Sunday morning and finding their garden has been used as a toilet, their car bonnet is dinted because it was used to shag a pissed-up slapper laid on her back, or being woken up in the early hours by singing lads who have failed to pull, but have still made the best of the night by drinking so many Jäger-bombs their stomach contents is now dripping down someone's front door and into their letter box.

Suddenly, out of nowhere, pubs in every corner of England and Wales were opening late, long into the night, but they would still be opening at 11am selling grog to anyone old enough from the moment the doors opened through until 1am, 2am, or even 4am in the fucking morning.

This was never going to control and reduce alcohol consumption of pub loving and binge drinking brits regardless of their age.

In modern UK we have moved away from the laws requiring alcoholics to wait until at least 11am to get their lips around a refreshing pint of 5% strength lager ensuring the achieve their first beer buzz of the day well before lunch time.

Most of us have had a drink at stupid o'clock, it is normally in the airport at 7am waiting for a flight to Spain. Nothing beats a cheeky pint followed by a vodka chaser as the sun is just beginning to rise above the runway tarmac.

A Bloody Mary at 6:15am is breakfast food in an airport, well, that's what I tell myself every time I have one, we all like to start our holidays as early as possible and as we mean to go on, basically, slightly pissed for the next 14 days.

I said a few paragraphs ago the plan to open later was not thought through and chaos could become the normal late-night activity in towns and villages across England and Wales, but, just maybe, if I put my cynical head on, just maybe it is not really "under" thought through after all?

Going back to the amount of taxation on alcohol, could this have been a way to stealthily increase alcohol tax revenue by a government that was quickly running out of other people's money to spend?

The licensing changes also allowed 24 hour off-licenses to sell booze to a mentally unstable suicide risks at 4am while they are alone also spelled the death of many nightclubs in towns and outer areas of our cities.

Why would the government not care about the demise of the old giant nightclubs that had entertained people for decades?

This was defiantly about tax revenue, and I will now explain the difference between a nightclub opening until 4am and a pub opening until just 2am.

The amount of alcohol consumed in Annabel's, Roxy, The Ritz, and venues like Ministry Of Sound dancing clubs was minuscule compared to late night drinking by locals in late night pubs, tax revenue was rolling in better than ever.

Nightclub culture had changed beyond recognition between early 90's and 2005, before the 90's people went to nightclubs to continue mainly drinking and, just maybe, have a 5-minute waddle and sway on the dance floor, or a smooch at closing time.

Low admission cost and high drink prices was how it was done.

But something was changing in fields, warehouses, abandoned building, the rave culture was an epidemic sweeping across the UK.

Dancing to a pulsating fast beat while under the effects of ecstasy become everything to the rave enthusiast, no alcohol was needed to have a magical time.

Hypnotic lights, a new breed of dance focused DJs, and drugs all came together in an exciting "un-licensed" and illegal 12-hour party, rebels from 18 to 60 years old were hooked and this caught out nightclubs big-time, they needed to get a piece of the new scene.

The police and local authorities were clamping down on illegal raves and prosecuting the organisers hard, and this was the opportunity the nightclubs needed. The word "night" was dropped, and they started to re-invent themselves into dance clubs very quickly, trying to copy the Ibiza club scene.

This also meant a very different business model.

High admission cost to make up for the lack of bar takings.

There is no duty tax revenue handed to HMRC from the sale of billions of bottles of water.

The dance and drug revolution created a hole in the treasury budget.

Have a quick think back to the chapter where I talked about tax raised on the purchase and creation of alcohol. Billions of litres of alcohol were no longer needed and as we know, tax revenue numbers involving alcohol are biblical.

Something had to change, and it did, licensing laws allowed potentially 24 hours drinking in pubs, ravers may not drink alcohol while dancing but pub users will down the booze every minute the bar is open for business.

What came next is truly astonishing.

We had moved pub closing times to the early hours, people wobbling through empty streets at 3am on their way home with nothing to accompany them except the odd prowling cat and neighbourhood burglar.

Now the plc pub companies want to open their pubs from 8am!

Why the hell would any pub brand want to open every day at 8am to sell beer, wine and spirits to accompany a Great British Fried breakfast?

Turns out that all the beer connoisseurs who frequent certain plc branded pubs from 8am onwards like to get in early because the beer tastes even better at 8am than it does at 11am. True story.

Breakfast Menu:
Full English with Toast includes pint of lager.
Scrambled Eggs on Toast includes double shot of Smirnoff.
Bacon Butty smothered in our own unique sauce created by mixing 50% whisky and HP classic.
Morning Coffee: with a 25ml shot of rum added.
Smashed Avocado on Sour Bread Crostini: served with Prosecco.

Breakfast in pubs is an actual thing, now almost all the plc pub companies have at least one of their branded chains open for breakfast and offer a full range from their bars for the early drinker in need of hair-of-the-dog because they were still drinking in the very same pub at 2am last night.

35 years ago, pubs had to close on a Sunday afternoon and piss everyone off.

Now pubs are trying to attract people in for breakfast with an alcoholic drink.

The pub industry really has gone bat-shit-fucking-crazy, it will serve anyone legally allowed to purchase alcohol at any time if it means more profit, and it is allowed by the powers in Westminster because it creates tax revenue.

Some of you who are well versed on licensing rules will still be wanting to argue that the laws are set out as they are to protect the public health.

Yeah right…

I was working in Derby when a new very large pub opened in the city centre, directly across the road from my pub.

It was huge, in an old bank and it was plc owned and branded.

New pubs opening never bothered me, I just saw it as an opportunity to attract more customers from that pub into mine.

Anyway, as most of us know, certain pub brands always put the general toilets so far away from the drinking area the number of steps you take to just take a piss and return to your seat would earn you an Apple Watch from health App Vitality!

It was the middle of the summer, a scorching hot day for a change and we had all the doors open in our entrance, an entrance that was arched, deep and rounded, it acted like a giant radar receiver, every sound amplified.

On this day we suddenly heard a really loud cheer by a collection of many different voices.

I was stood with Adin, a young manager who was learning from me at the time, and we just looked at each other?

We had no idea what had just happened.

Over the next week or so the weather remained bright, sunny and Balearic Island hot and we heard the sheering a few more times as the current week rolled by.

We did share a few customers with the big, branded pub opposite so one of our team asked a customer what the cheering was all about?

It turns out that when an "all-day-sipper" tries to hold on too long, because the shithouse is so far away, sometimes they miscalculate their own capacity, lose muscle control, and have had a bit too much happy juice, then they simply:

PISS THEMSELVES right there is the bar…

This is what is being cheered for fucks sake, an old man who has been drinking since early morning has now gushed like a hosepipe inside his trousers.

But the personal accident is not the real tragedy behind this story, the real astonishing fact is:

They would serve him again after passing him some tissue.

I have no idea if that was a one-off manager allowing this to happen, of if it has since been addressed and stopped, but that was really what happened in Derby City in early 2000's.

Allowing up to 24 drinking is to protect people did you say?

Get fucked you naive twat and wake the fuck up, since the 90's it has always been about money, extra taxes, financial institution lobbyist pushing ministers by giving them "donations" that help make decisions that will also push up share prices, it's always about the dollars and it probably always will be.

Have the plc pub companies pushed too far?

Do the plc pub companies drive their teams too hard?

What makes plc pub companies care so little about their employees?

Is there anything left to squeeze, sweat more or trim any further?

And what exactly is too far anyway?

Well, let take a look at that shall we.

I don't think there is anything left in the tank to be sucked out, trimmed off, or ripped away from the team members or managers of branded pubs chains?

They have been squeezed so hard over the last 20 years I cannot think of a single team member working the front line of a financial market owned pub company who is not exhausted, knacked, broken, sick of it, and running on an empty unguided auto pilot.

Wages reduced by swapping out expensive managers for wet behind the ear's cheap newbie puppet caretakers.

Bigger Bosses and modern BDM's lying to tempt these easily fooled newbies into taking on a new pub, then making them remove the full-time staff and replace them with part timers to save on NI payments is a fact you now know happens year on year.

Paying the most vulnerable and youngest staff members under £5.00 per hour and forcing kitchen teams to make double the amount of food for the cost of a single item has destroyed the soul, heart, care, welfare and teamwork out of the pub chains in the UK.

Employees working in the plc owned pubs stick together as a team and support each other while doing their best for the customers under terrible conditions.

But you also now definitely know that the teamwork does not go beyond the front-line pub team, there is NO team work between head office, the BDM, Op's manager and pubs they control.

To the uninterested hierarchy lording over pub employees, you know, the ones serving the drinks and cooking the food, staff are just a tool of the business, a worthless cost that dilutes profits and luckily, are easily replaceable cogs in the wheels that delivers the bonuses to a mid-level manager, share options to the CEO and the dividends to the tax dodging shareholders.

Have the pub chains shot themselves in their own foot, kicked an own goal straight into a pair of exposed red raw tender goolies?

I really hope so, they deserve a back-lash, customers and staff all deserve justice for the last 40 years, 4 decades where a great industry has been highjacked by the city slicker greedy cunts who will never give a toss about any of the plebs, also known as the working class, who earn their mountains of dosh.

What I would like to see is plc owned branded pub chains failing, slipping over on the un-branded ketchup they chose to buy because it's cheap, fuck the taste the plebs won't know the difference.

Let's take a nasty CEO of a plc pub company, one of those appointed by the venture capitalist bankers, on a sky diving trip above their beloved London City financial district and encourage them to jump. With any luck they will land right on the pointed peak that tops the Shard Building asshole first.

There you go Mr CEO, enjoy your stimulating peak in the city!

One day soon, if it hasn't already started, plc pub companies will reach a critical point where there is absolutely no fatter to trim, sweating the fucking asset will no longer be possible because the asset is drier than a 185-year-old fanny with chapped lips.

Even the marketing wankers with their tricky bollocks will have no where left to go, every ingredient is already the cheapest, every portion size looks like a kid's meal and the prices for these tiny dishes are about as unappetising as a Glasgow prostitute with two missing front teeth and facial boils offering you a 5-minute nosh in a storm drain for just £5.00.

The journey has nearly ended for real, the public have become wise, and everyone knows that the English pub landscape will soon be an enormous branded, take a flight to the bogs, pub on every high street in not too distant a future, all the other branded pub chains will eventually fade away and die.

Let's imagine it is 2030, where did it all go wrong?

Earlier I explained how pubs needed to complete with restaurants to take a fatter slice from the eating out trough, using microwave versions of chef cooked food to undercut fresh food restaurants on price and drive their own profits.

I just want to go back to this for a moment and add a bit of flesh to the bones.

Oh, it all started out so well, restaurant food in pubs, but the public knew the food wasn't quite as good, but for the price, it all seemed so worth it.

Look at the scampi, not being whole tail is not acceptable in a quality eatery, but in a pub, it can be forgiven if the price is right. (If you know, you know).

An ever-decreasing circle is not possible, it cannot go for ever.

Reducing size, quality, ingredients, supplier, measure, and weight can only be done to any dish so many times, the regular customer, your core bread, and butter spender, will notice, shit will eventually hit the fan.

What changes can be made to a simple plate that can reduce the costs involved, but also ruin a reputation earned slowly and surely over many years?

Gammon steak started out at 10oz, 3 years on it's now down to just 7oz.

13 pieces of scampi is now just 9 lonely pieces rolling around in the gaps the missing 4 pieces once occupied.

Steak and Kidney pie is now steak, kidney, and potato pie.

Cod is out, now it's called battered white fish (pollock in the small print).

Whole onion rings are now the scrapped-up waste that makes the reformed crap versions.

Homemade Yorkshire puds are now made by Aunt Bessie's.

Hellman's mayonnaise is now Bookers own.

The roast silverside has become vac-packed reconstituted sliced bits of beef.

The fish pie no longer contains prawns or salmon. and finally, The coffee is no longer Lavazza, it is Break Bros own brand.

When the customer starts to notice a slip in quality but no change in price, the rot has started to set in.

The regular customer will begin to question the food they are eating, it no longer looks as good as it used to look.

The problems being notices with the changing food now becomes something I call customer quality perception.

Food quality consists of 3 different factors, and all 3 have a huge bearing on the overall rating a customer will award a dish:

- The look of the food, if it does not look right or as expected, you are already readying yourself for a disappointing meal.
- Portion size is it what you expected, or even worse, is it not the same size portion as the last time you ate this meal.
- The food may taste perfect, the best you have ever had, but without the first 2, it will still be a disappointment, that is how the triangle of taste works, it all has to fit together to form a strong structure, a complete winning unit without weakness.

If your background is not in catering, you may think marketing is the be-all and end-all of hospitality. If you do think in this way you are so far out of step with what real people appreciate about food and the care taken to prepare, you may already be lost so far in bright and shiny delusion with believe pineapple belongs on a pizza.

The branded pub chain that once offered restaurant type food, at fairly high prices for a pub, has become just a bog standard, but expensive, pub to eat in churning out naff ping-ding cheap ready meals.

Hungry and busy people will still use the pub for a pit stop on the way home from the gym, lunch hour when working, feeding the kids after school, but it is no longer a big treat on date night or a family celebration venue it once was.

The actions of the pub company PLC have snatched defeat from the jaws of success with bonkers promotions, a complete failure to understand their customer base, and an attitude of superiority that makes them think customers are there to fund their next gimmick, fad, or theme.

This is where I think we are as a consumer society, right now following a global pandemic and rising inflation:

"Let go the Pasta Grill for your birthday."

"Fuck that, it my birthday, I want to go out for something to eat, not garbage pub food, if I am paying good money, I want good food."

This attitude is the result of plc pub companies own greedy actions and policies. By constantly focusing on returning profit for shareholders the customer has been largely ignored, not listened too, ripped off and now they will vote with their feet.

The quality restaurant has become the food treat of choice once again because they never dropped their standards, found cheaper ingredients or staff and they still employ real trained chefs who take pride in what the plate and serve to every guest.

Paying customers want to be served the best quality food prepared by people proud that know what they are doing.

This cycle of pub chains plunging themselves headfirst into hospitality history is not something that is new. Oblivion is the only destination if branded pub chain owners obey their paymasters desire for more and more profit converted from every £1.00.

It is the pressure from shareholders to increase the profit from, let's say 25p in every £1.00 to 35p in every £1.00 that drives the outcome of failure as I have talked about in previous pages.

PLC owned branded pubs, bars and value restaurants chains have destroyed themselves, committed commercial suicide for decades.

We will see a new name pop up on the high street on a name change on loads of local pubs, big, bold, brash, and giving it the fancy bollocks branding that excites the public and tempts them in.

But what follows after the first couple of glory years and rapid expansion across every city and town in the country is the same story over and over again, the brand in forced to return more and more money year on year to the investors, the cuts begin, and end game is now in sight, another brand will vanish and be forgotten as quickly as it started.

Some of these plc brands were household names, they were everywhere, in almost every town, on every retail park and in every mammoth sized food court. Now you know how a famous trading name with limitless potential can just vanish without a trace.

Here are a few names you will remember, but are no longer trading under that name, or under the same ownership that fucked them over the first time.

Happy Eater.

Pizzaland.

Little Chef.

Fatty Arbuckle's.

Berni Inn.

Yates (bought for pennies by Laurel Pub Co, now Stonegate).

Spirit Pub and all their brands (almost worthless and snatched up Greene King, surprise surprise, for a tiny handful of cash).

Hogshead.

O'Neil's.

Berlin's.

Henry's.

CASA.

Hard Rock Cafe (when Rank owned the brand).

Barracuda Bar.

John Barras.

Q's.

Chicago Rock Café.

I could go on and on with this list, so many great places to drink, eat, and have real fun have vanished without a trace.

Millions of us will have some really wild and great memories that we even today enjoy talking about with great fondness.

Teasing our mates about the mad, bad, and stupid things we watched them do in the fun and party pubs and bars where we shared those crazy crazy nights of laughter, dancing, flirting and loving. Great times.

After our favourite pubs and bars have been ruined again and again by knob-head BDM's and fucking idiots running plc demanding marketing departments, we are left with a past history that could, and should, be used as a RED FLAG WARNING template to avoid making the same mistakes in the future by the next set of young graduates who will be joining the plc pub companies with their BAs in flower arranging and surfing science.

I don't want to get caught up moaning about the next generation of useless graduates entering pub companies in mid management and senior positions, but what you now know is that they will deliver to a despondent and shrinking customer base an even worse experience than before because they will repeat the same cycle of failing customers and staff as they double down with the same heartless policies, the same tired and outdated ideas, but these tossers will still be allowed to line their own fucking pockets, just like the last lot did, but next time the damage could be so bad, so deep, the pubs they use as a personal cash machine may never recover and be lost forever.

Do you know that since 2001 25% of all the UK's pubs have closed, PERMANENTLY?

The PLC's controlling the branded chains drive the independents out of business in ways I have already eluded.

It's been a long and complicated journey from the humble local pub to the present plc stock market funded licensed retail supersized food factories. The past is consigned to history and currently a handful of CEO pricks and chair-wankers are driving investor-owned pub companies into a personality and character abyss by effectively turning the hospitality industry into licensed retail shops, quickly in and out after buying a quick tasteless microwaved meal and a single small diet cola.

And if an independent trader is doing well by delivering unique quality, great service and a genuinely welcoming experience, the plc pub company cancels the lease if they own the building, or they buy the building from the owner. The plc pub company forcibly takes the successful landlord's business off the independent and appoints a robotic cheap GM to manage the place down to their company standards. This is how they control a local market, the vast majority of the public who live in the area don't know that there is far better drink quality, far better fresh food available and a friendly atmosphere to be found away from the branded chain.

So, the public just accept that their local branded pub or bar is as good as it gets.

Will the city and financial institutions ever control and manipulate the whole of the UK's pubs, restaurants, hotels and public entertainment?

I don't think they can take over everything, I think the public, the pub user, the family diners, the pint while I watch the game drinker, are all becoming wise to the cons, the tricks, the greed and the manipulation, the people of the UK will fight back using their feet to go elsewhere.

Currently we are feed a huge amount of marketing that tries to convince us, implant into our sub-conscious, branded names using tiny hooks that attach themselves to the influencers within our brains. You will know what I'm talking about, certain words, sounds, people, voices, and images auto-train our memory reflection to always go for what we know.

The involuntary and relentless training of the spongy organ in our head's influencers our choice.

Let's take a slightly closer look at this with a few examples.

One company runs a really heavy campaign on local and regional radio station that always end with a short whistle, can you name it?

Another company uses a national treasure comedian. For many years the actual person featured in the TV adds, but know it is the very well-known voice that keep that brand at the for-front of your mind. What are they selling?

If I mentioned a TV advert where someone slapped their own arse to make the change in their back pocket jingle, could you name the brand?

If you hear a tune called "The chain" by Fleetwood Mac, what sport would you think of first?

Which lager says it is probably the best lager in the world?

If an arrow plungers into the ground, what are they advertising?

PLCs are very clever, and they use a lot of secondary marketing to create a compelling reason to visit.

The main one used in the UK is all about sport.

Can you guess the name splattered across the outside of the pub?

Your decisions are not always just your own, the autopilot in your bonce will always take you where you know, you understand, you feel at home regardless of how shit the offer is.

It takes imagination to break free from the pre-plotted route engaging with your feet, rebels seek out new, better, and different, the intelligent don't settle for ok, they find satisfaction at a new destination.

Future

Regardless of all my bitter and nasty talk about PLC controlled pub companies, there is only a couple I refuse to use because I don't agree with how I perceive the unethical treatment of their own teams and undervalued customers.

The other thing I dislike, in fact it boils my piss, is when an internationally owned pub company that is controlled by some of the biggest venture capitalist fund managers who are based in city's with stock markets anywhere around the world pretend they are the local, kind and friendly family-owned pub.

Just bollocks and be honest…

I also know through my investigations that some pub companies, even a few local breweries who own their own pubs, treat their teams really well. I have spoken to Hyde's and JW Lees teams and they, as no doubt do many others, treat their teams really well and consider their employees as valued, almost family, team members.

I think there could be a very bright future for the Great British Pub, our whole hospitality industry can bounce back, reclaim the high streets, the villagers and the food courts where fantastic quality items are delivered. Great drinks, quality food, brilliant personal service, and a quality working environment where team members feel valued and rewarded.

Independent hospitality has to be the future.

Any business that targets people must have a vision, and a mission to deliver it in a way that no one has to suffer to make it happen.

We are seeing a resurgence of independent traders popping up with just one pub, minding their own business while preparing quality food, serving perfect drinks, and it's all done with a genuine smile from someone who loves their job and where they work.

I seek out independents, even the big ones like one off garden centres, and why not, sometimes their food is superb quality and so obviously home cooked by really talented people.

There are so many small one-off traders in farm shops, tiny restaurants, cute wine bars, micro ale bars pubs, just plain old pubs with a landlord, the owner or lease holder who is modern in business practice, but old fashioned in hospitality and customer service.

That is where I want to spend my money.

It is these independent pubs where you can still find a great pint served by someone who cares fiercely about the quality of the drink they are dispensing, proud that the steak and kidney pie is full to brim with lean steak, quality kidney and beer lashed luxury gravy that delights everyone who tries the home-made star pie on the one off and unique menu.

What tops these quality one-off private businesses is that owner is making a good living, earning a very healthy profit and able to pay themselves and their staff well.

Instead of the business owner keeping every penny for themselves, the staff are being paid, £2, £3, or even £5 per hour above minimum wage rates because the owner is not a greedy wanker with no connection or empathy for their customers or staff, the owner sees the employees as family and friends, everyone wins.

There will always be two kinds of pubs, even in the distance future when most branded shit-holes are boarded up or turned into a Tesco Metro, you will find the privately owned independent traders delivering an excellent range of products for a fair price, and that gives to a choice, eat and drink great quality items in safe and charming surroundings or scoff down microwave food and guzzle alcohol is a plc owned super-sized pub with nowhere near enough staff on duty and the potential of violence between a rough married couple at any minute.

Personally, I don't want to sit on a chair that someone may have pissed over earlier in the day, just a personal preference.

How can anyone with even half a brain not prefer a quality and independent pub to a plc owned monster sized boozer where you can probably get drunk by pleasuring the imitation shag-pile carpet with your tongue?

I am going to try to explain the difference and why you should always choose the independent by comparing a world-wide fast food burger shop versus Gordon Ramsey as the independent.

Burger shop chains are vast in numbers, they are anywhere and everywhere. It is difficult to go to any destination without brightly lit fast food signage spoiling the view. Many years ago, I visited the Great Pyramids Of Giza and was shocked to see world-wide branded fast-food take-outs with brightly lit facades and plastic colourful signage within a few hundred meters of the Great Sphinx.

What made it even more silly to me was that the Great Sphinx was facing directly towards to pizza and fried chicken joints as if it actually wants a bite.

You always know there is a fast-food joint nearby because there will be fast food boxes, bags, napkins and grease paper, sauce pots and half eaten burgers, or chicken bones, strewn around nearby, discarded by ignorant twats whose ego is far too inflated to find a fucking bin, lazy bastards of all ages.

I have come to the conclusion that the vast amount of fast-food packaging ignorantly chucked into flower beds, doorways, left on statues and is spoiling our streets, parks, playgrounds transport hubs and even the country side, about is nothing to do with the age or gender and these pathetic fast-food munchers, it's much more to do with the type of person they actually are and the more than obvious intellectual deficit they are blighted with. Anyone with two brain cells can find a fucking bin, but then again, if you are addicted to eating fast food you may not have a second brain cell to rub against the first one…

Wouldn't it be great if all fast-food outlets had to print the purchasers house number and postcode onto all packaging?

A team of people could collect it, identify the buyers' home, return the dumped shit to their house and fine their selfish ass.

I bet this could be done with the tech we have these days, just an App on a phone waved over a reader with the food is ordered.

Hmmmmmmm I hope someone way smarter than me finds a way to make it happen.

So exactly why do people eat branded fast food?

Because they know exactly what they are getting.

It really is that simple, they have no imagination or fear everything they don't currently know.

We all know some dickhead who goes to Ibiza and only eats the same branded burger for two fucking weeks, or maybe that is you, WHY?

There will always be stupid people with no taste, you know the ones I'm talking about, those who follow like brain-dead sheep a marketing campaign that makes them believe that a product is good because there is a whistle on the end of the advert.

I'm not sure exactly when a whistle became synonymous with low expectations in your diet, I must have missed that episode of product placement bilge TV know as ITV's reality shows.

Most fast food is cooked by underpaid kids, many of which will have little to no conscience about how they handle the food you will be placing in your mouth.

Have we all heard of the 5 second rule?

There is a reason why a fast-food meal can be bought so cheap, it is probably made from cheap ingredients and prepared by line-cooks, not chefs, who are paid the bare minimum wage.

Would you do your best, be focused, undergo hours and hours of on-line hygiene training for £6.83 per hour, not a fucking chance.

Now let's take a brain washed branded burger chain fan who has been convinced by his new "posh" and educated girlfriend to try the food in the Gordon Ramsey inspired food pub.

He has never fancied one of those quality burgers that are grilled across the road from his normal fast food hang out, but now he finds myself in the unique one-off pub owned by an independent trader, a college trained chef who also spent 5 years working for a Michelin stared restaurant starting as a commie and working up to become head chef in that time.

She may well regret swiping right because she thought his tattoos looked cool.

He walks in and is greeted, not by a giant screen telling him to order by pressing the buttons, but by a human being who simply says "Hi."

He picks up a menu, has quick read and says, "what the fuck it all this shit, veal and artichoke?"

He has not the foggiest what to order because he has no clue what type of vegetable a scallop is, so ordering food is making him slightly nervous because he may not like it and look like a twat in front of the totty across from him.

Then he sees it, the word that that brings a smile to his face, gives him confidence in his food choice, and puts his stomach on standby to receive something it knows, it understands, and soon will satisfy the hunger pangs.

Reading the menu again ordering and he sees it comes with something called Emmental, but he can always pick it off.

The BURGER has been ordered, it has cost 50% more that the fast-food burger and he is already convinced it will not be worth the price when it arrives, but eating here gives him a chance and going balls deep into the poshest and no doubt best trimmer snatch he has ever had the chance to poke, and he may even get to shag her inside a house, not on the wet grass like Karen last week.

The burger arrives, thicker, juicer, the best looking perfectly grilled patty between two lightly toasted caramelised onion and red Leicester cheese topped bread bap halves, fresh and crispy salad on the base of the bun, home-made red onion battered onion rings and seasoned French fries cooked in garlic infused oil.

Biting into the handmade burger, perfectly seasoned, expertly grilled and carefully matched with the Emmental cheese topping, our fast-food fan is mesmerised with the taste, the juice running down his chin, taste buds in a state of excitement they have never known, now this is real food and his mind is blown…

That is what good food can do when compared to fast food.

Is it a fear of the unknown that stops weak and easily manipulated prats from discovering, eating, and enjoying great food every day?

I don't understand anyone's unwillingness to try something they don't understand and have never heard of, are they really too afraid to ask about a food dish in case they look a fucking idiot?

What a total waste of tastebuds they are…

The ones who are brave, intrigued, question, seek out and want new, better, and healthier alternatives will try what they have never had, seen or tasted before.

It can be a genuine thrill, awaking, and mind-blowing experience.

Who cares if you don't like it, it's just food, spit it out, and try something else, life is too short for eating the same food over and over again when the world is a smorgasbord of tastes, flavour and texture?

How many of you have tried an Oyster from the shell?

The reward for trying the alternative to fast food branded burgers.

- A burger made from 100% Aberdeen Angus beef mixed with a perfect blend of herbs and spices.
- Just the right amount of marbled fats to keep the burger juicy and dripping with taste.
- A fresh, never frozen burger because it was made the day before in the same kitchen by a trained chef with their own two hands, and then left to rest for 24 hours allowing perfect herb infusion.

- A perfect beef patty grilled by a chef with the same expertise needed to grill a chateaubriand.
- A quality bun made with organic red tractor sauced flour and baked by hand, topped with the greatest additional and yet welcomed flavours.
- Fresh lettuce leaves such as Rocket, Romaine Heart, Butterhead and Radicchio topped with Vidalia Onion rings, sliced Brandywine Pink Heirloom Tomatoes, and fresh Basil.
- Cheeseburger is it, how about vintage Cheddar, Monterey Jack, Swiss cheese with caramelised onions, Heirloom Tomato and Pimiento Peppers.
- Skin-on seasoned Maris Piper French fries.
- Trader-Joe's Organic award-winning ketchup.

Can you imagine being served a burger this good, this would rock your burger world, why the fuck would you want a machine produced circle of pressed cheap mince over this beauty, plus you will never need to discard a slice of gherkin again.

I hope many of you out there are now thinking differently, and hopefully, now you have read my words you now intend to change your ways, think differently about where you spend your money and what you are slipping beyond your lips without any thought to how the product was created, prepared, and made ready for you to consume in a fake and empty atmosphere.

Not all the bigger boys are as bad as the others, some pub companies have made huge mistakes because they were led by a long-term old-fashioned CEO who pulled the purse strings tighter every year. It was easy to go down the "cheap as possible" and "pile that shit high" for years and years.

But some plc companies are starting to change their ways, one has a new boss at the top and the shoots of change are emerging, employees are actually being considered, a real investment into quality has begun and genuine smiles are coming back to whole work force. I talked to a really nice BDM and Op's manager in the spring of 2022 and their positivity about the company thinking in new and improved ways was a joy to hear, I wish that company well, just ditch the brands.

The mission of delivering utter crap products on a plate, or in a glass, at impossibly cheap prices has run its cause, time to move on and make amends to the customers that have been treated as a money tree to fund stupid brands, crazy schemes and bonuses for wankers who certainly do not deserve a single bean.

Some of the mid-sized pub companies are moving away from the endless "on offer" tactic as they now realise that the general public have finally seen it for what it is, and what I have unravelled throughout these pages to those who still have the wool pulled over their eyes:

IT'S ONE FUCKING MASSIVE RIP OFF AND ARSE FUCKING!

The bastards have had your pants down for a long, long time, it's time to squeeze those cheeks as hard as you can and rip the robbing twats dick clean off, you don't want to be shafted any more, you know the tricks and what to avoid from now on.

The mid-sized companies may have seen the light, had an epiphany and wanted to change their relationship with what guests they have left, and that for customers is great news, but it will take time, so hope they stay on the journey of recovery.

If plc pub companies really want to change their repulsive ways the first step in redemption would be to stop torturing your knacked and broken teams with never achievable targets and cruel wage budgets, that would be a very positive step forward.

Some changes have started, you may have noticed for yourself that a number of branded pubs and become un-branded.

A number of pub companies have started to phase out hideous cheap branded chains serving abysmal food and replace them with business models that follow more ethical treatment of their guests by charging realistic prices for better quality food and drink.

When people understand that paying a little more change everything they don't mind.

Who is going to complain about better ingredients?

Who is going to complaint about better pay for the workers?

Who going to complain about wider choice and variety?

But what about the gigantic stock market controlled super-sized plc pub companies, what are they doing?

The huge internationally money market owned share holder driven property portfolio monsters that sell food and drink as a biproduct of owning the buildings, will not change for years to come.

Why should they because for them it is not about the quality of food or the treatment of the staff, for the biggest companies it is only about creating a revenue stream to take offshore and bank in another continent. Using their properties for hospitality use is only about increasing the property and brand value by showing that every year even more profit can be accumulated, hence increase value on the stock markets of the world.

Changing a business model means spending money, de-branding could mean losing value, and spending money means can risk short turn returns and scaring away major shareholders and that can damage a PLC overnight causing a share price crash.

Institutional investors own over 50% of the UK's largest pub company and its brewery, so they do have an enormous influence on the company's executive board decisions, risking loss is not in the interest of shareholders so they a say on when and how money spent, and only if it will make more money.

Don't expect the big boys to change anytime soon, you are stuck with 1'000's of Pasta Grill Kitchen cheap branded pubs selling you poor quality items and being served by staff who little more than modern day financial slaves.

What is interesting though, if not slightly funny, is when you realise just how successful old fashioned and traditional pubs have become once again. Their popularity is growing all the time as more and more customers turn their noses up at cheaper than chips branded pub chains that never deliver what they promise, when was the last time you were not, even slightly, disappointed with a branded food and drink out-let.

So many examples to choose from, but for now I'll mention a few: Salad bars that look like half a dozen children have been playing with in as they would a sand box, pre-mixed cocktails, ready meals nuked in a microwave, red wine from a chilled head on the bar and meats cut against the fibre grain making them tough when grilled.

Guests discovering the experience of genuine hospitality is rare today, and if it is combined with the quality of an independent pub, not branded, food menu that is delivering chef prepared dishes, it is driving a successful, but not huge, niche market across the UK. Most old-world towns, historic villagers and medieval city blocks have its own independent pub waiting for you to discover with a host who wants to make your day with their quality drinks and culinary skills.

If you seek out the independents, even if you drive past 5 branded pubs to get to it, it is worth it, you are helping them survive and they are treating you to something special, a product created from their heart will skill that have taken a long time to learn.

So where have we learned?

- I don't like branded pub; er you don't say...

(Except Hooters and Hard Rock, I like both of those for very different reasons and enjoy visiting them in many cites)

- I not very keen on the new breed of leadership who are fucking up pub companies.
- I don't rate branded food and now you know why
- I hate the way plc owners treat their employees
- I have shown you why pubs in the 80's was not that good
- I have explained how city banker greed has changed UK pubs
- I have revelled way too much about myself when I was young
- I have explained how money is made at the cost of people.
- I have also made lots of people say, "was he talking about me?"

What I have done is explain, through my own journey for almost 40 years, the evolvement of UK pubs and breweries, the destruction of UK owned brewing and foreign ownership of a nation's heritage, namely the Great British Pub.

What do I want?

Stop giving your hard-earned cash to international robbing bastards that own your local pub.

Ignore it, walk past it is giving it the finger.

Spend your money, yes probably a little bit extra cash, with the privately owned, tenanted and independent pubs, restaurants and businesses throughout the UK's length and breadth.

Only we can breathe new life into the UK hospitality marketplace by no longer being marketing zombies.

There is a better future for UK pubs, and we can create it by rejecting those who don't care about UK tradition, our lowest paid workers, and put so simply…

You Pint

My last little bit of the book is this:

It's a job for you…

Go through the list below and answer each question yes or no.

This little test applies, not only to the brilliant people working in all areas of hospitality, but it will also ring true for almost everyone working in non-licensed retail, such as shops and any type of, big or small, customer facing environments.

At the end count your yes's vs your no's?

Are the book contents all in the imagination of the author?

YES / NO

Are any of the characters based on real people?

YES / NO

Are some of the mid-level managers in these huge pub companies as bad as the author says they are?

YES / NO

Do you, as an employee, ever really feel valued by head office?

YES / NO

Your area/regional manager, are they a cunt and acts above you all?

YES / NO

Are you fairly paid for the work you do and the skills you possess?

YES / NO

Should weekend and late-night work be paid extra?

YES / NO

Does head-office know who you are?

YES / NO

Are you paid double time on bank holidays?

YES / NO

If you are offered a similar job for much better money, will you go?

YES / NO

Do you feel valued by the company you work for?

YES / NO

Are you intending on remaining in the hospitality industry?

YES / NO

Do you recognise anything in this book from your workplace?

YES / NO

How many "No" marks have you counted in total?

If you got just 1 NO, this is what to do.

- Join a union and encourage everyone else to do the same.
- Sit down with your boss to discuss pay rates and why you are being held on the very base rate of minimum wage?
- I there any chance of all the under paid staff going on strike.
- Look for a new, better paid, and respected job.

They only way to improve working conditions and pay rates in the big players of the pub industry is to bring them to their knees through staff shortage.

Can you imagine a pub company with 3,000 pubs and 45,000 employees grinding to a halt?

Every single front line worker going on strike on a Bank Holiday Weekend or FA Cup Final Day, the impact would be devastating on the greedy pub co and maybe they would finally take notice.

It's down to the individual reader to decide if this book is all make believe or the full beans truth, if you have worked in the industry, put the hours in, then you will actually know if my words are true fact or a work of fiction.

I have really enjoyed writing this angry rant and daft commentary on the pub industry since 1982.

Did you ever go to the offy for your dad?

Have you ever had your knicker elastic stretched by someone else while learning against the bar?

Have you ever woken up and thought "who the fuck are you?"

UK pubs have been and continue to make a unique and wonderful contribution to our wonderful Isle, everyone has a memory from a night out, good, or bad, reading these pages has definitely raised the odd smile on your face.

I ask just one thing, be very picky about where you spend…